THE FAITH
of the
COUNSELLORS

❋

Paul Halmos

LATE PROFESSOR OF SOCIOLOGY
THE OPEN UNIVERSITY

Constable
LONDON

Published by
Constable & Company Limited
10 Orange Street London WC2H 7EG
© 1965 Paul Halmos
First Published 1965
Reprinted 1966
Reprinted 1969
Reprinted 1973
Reprinted 1976
Second Revised Edition 1978
Reprinted 1979
Reprinted 1981

ISBN 0 09 462110 1 paper

Printed in Great Britain by
Redwood Burn Limited, Trowbridge, Wiltshire.

THE FAITH OF THE COUNSELLORS

By the same author

SOLITUDE AND PRIVACY
TOWARDS A MEASURE OF MAN
PERSONAL SERVICE SOCIETY
THE PERSONAL AND THE POLITICAL
(forthcoming)

For my son
Anthony Michael Halmos

ACKNOWLEDGEMENTS

In preparing this volume for publication, I have received valuable help from Mr. R. F. Atkinson, and Mrs. Elisabeth Irvine, who drew my attention to many points of weakness in an earlier version of the text, some of which I could subsequently strengthen. I should like to thank them for their interest as well as Lord Simey, Professors E. J. Shoben Jr., T. H. Marshall, D. M. Mackay, Mr. John Wren Lewis, and Mr. Brian Farrell for reading some parts of my first manuscript and commenting on them.

My appreciation is due to Mrs. N. Davies for subjecting the first draft of my manuscript to a close scrutiny for mistakes of style, grammar, and punctuation. I hope that not too many of these crept back into the final version.

I should like to thank the Editor of *New Society* for allowing me to include in this book some passages from an article of mine which he has published. P.H.

Keele, May 1965

My warmest thanks to Ena Halmos for helping me to prepare this second edition. P.H.

Milton Keynes, 1977

CONTENTS

Men have brought their powers of subduing the forces of nature to such a pitch that by using them they could now very easily exterminate one another to the last man. They know this—hence arises a great part of their current unrest, their dejection, their mood of apprehension. And now it may be expected that the other of the two 'heavenly forces', eternal Eros, will put forth his strength so as to maintain himself alongside of his equally immortal adversary.

Sigmund Freud, *Civilisation and Its Discontents*

Preface to the 1970 Edition[*]

Since the first publication of this book, I have had occasion to discuss its principal tenets with clinical and social workers, as well as with sociologists, and others. The clinical and social workers sometimes wondered what the book would do to the various regimens of professional training. After all, 'training' in skill and knowledge is a recognised and legitimate enterprise, but is there a training in 'faith'? And, above all, what place, if any, are we to allow to unverifiable hunches, beliefs, and arbitrary sentiments as distinct from knowledge and skill? Yet even those who asked these questions could see the paedagogical sense of putting the student-trainee through the intellectual questions and exercises of this book. They have also been willing to regard the student's exposure to this book as a contribution to his preparation in clinical or social work.

No matter what they thought about the conclusions of the book, the tutors and trainers, in social work especially, have accepted its paedagogical usefulness. The book deals with problems of personal functioning in a professional service, problems which are of fundamental importance to those who are being trained. These problems are oddly ignored in most training courses and the book may now change this to some extent.

Inescapably, I should like to regard this work as somewhat more than an addition to existing training manuals. The sociologists with whom I have been able to talk about *The Faith of the Counsellors* have shared with me the view that the growth of the counselling professions constitutes a characteristic strain in current social change. Cultural-moral change in contemporary industrial societies would make much less sense without considering the implications of the following pages. Even though I had to write another book to discuss these implications, at a greater length (*The Personal Service Society*, London and

[*] This Preface appeared in the Second American edition

New York, 1970), some social implications of what I am studying in the present book are already briefly considered in its fourth chapter. These will be more fully elaborated in *The Personal Service Society*.

In addition to sociological interest, I have encountered an especially wide and varied response from theologians of several kinds. Somehow, it is inevitable that the enquiry, which I undertook to disclose unconfessed metaphysical premises in scientific-professional formulae, would interest theologians, that is to say, those who have always maintained that behind conscientious and fervent professional-moral concerns, there always lurk premises of this kind. And, of course, no-one would deny that professional personal helping is charged with much moral concern. Yet in training for knowledge and skill, this concern is not often illuminated for fear that its spontaneity and vividness will pale in the light of day.

Naturally, there have been some few disputations and arguments about the theses of this book. To deal with these disputations and arguments I could often draw attention to appropriate passages in the book without having to supplement these with new illustrations or new arguments. As a consequence, I find no necessity as yet to change the text for this new edition. It is, however, true that certain queries have been conspicuously more frequent than others, and so I thought that the Preface to this new edition ought to reflect briefly on those few points which readers have tended to raise most frequently.

This book is about professional workers engaged in the field of intimate personal helping. These professional workers are formally trained in techniques and taught the concepts as well as theories of their practice. The book asks, how much of their practice is based on logically evolved theories, concepts, and proved techniques, and how much on categorical beliefs, affirmations, or loyalties? The answer to these questions is sought through a careful examination of the literature on this intimate personal-professional helping. The counsellors—psychotherapists, psychiatrists, case-workers, and others—often communicate through the normal channels of academic and clinical journals, books, and so on. They are, in fact, a highly articulate, literate, and communicative group of professionals. In their books and papers, they searchingly present the first principles as well as their inferences, conclusions, and regimens of practice: *they* tell us what *they* believe to be the case and the author of this book, a sociologist interested in contemporary cultural and moral change, need only marshal the testimony of the counsellors themselves to identify certain underlying agreements which, strangely enough, the counsellors have not credited with much importance yet. It is necessary to remember that the citations in the book represent the counsellors' own views and not mine. As a sociologist, my own 'faith', if such there is and whatever it is, is not the subject matter I am engaged in studying. Of course, one's sympathies may not be entirely concealed, but I am sure that on those occasions when they come into view in the distance, they can be easily discerned to be extraneous to the subject matter.

In citing the testimonies of the counsellors, I endeavour to show that there is an almost ubiquitous 'backsliding' into a theological-mystical frame of reference and an almost compulsive repetitive refrain of pastoral-moral first principles in the writings and pronouncements of the leading theoreticians and practitioners of counselling. Naturally, when this practice is highlighted for them, the counsellors, embarrassed by the remainders of the 'spiritual' ancestry of their thinking, attempt to disown the compromising notions as mere literary metaphors, or slips of the tongue or pen. A remarkable line of defence coming, as it does, from those who are professionally committed to attribute significance to slips of the tongue or pen. Some psychoanalysts, for example, try to dismiss my puzzlement about their habit of using terms such as 'spiritual factors,' 'communion between therapist and patient', 'I-and-Thou relationships in clinical or social work settings', 'loving a patient', and so on, for they think that these are mere figures of speech. On other occasions the line of defence is that modern psychoanalysis has penetrated to the pre-oedipal depths of the mother-child relationship, which is constantly being brought back into therapy, bringing with it the reliving of a total and absolute relationship that the erstwhile child, now an adult, has had, and can now re-experience. This is done so that anamnesia, recall, or insight be secured. It is this total and global relationship to which 'communion', 'I-and-Thou', and the rest relate: 'no mythical, mystical or quasi-religious notions are involved', writes S. H.

Foulkes.[1] There are usually three points I offer in reply to this line of defence: *first*, the ultimate categories of a total and global mother-child relationship as presented by Freud or later by Melanie Klein are manifestly metaphysical and indistinguishable from 'mythical, mystical, and quasi-religious notions', Eros and Thanatos are no less metaphysical or mystical than Agape. *Second*, it is remarkable that psychotherapists and psychoanalysts should adopt and widely use a theological and mystical terminology and imagery, and that they should borrow from Martin Buber or existentialists of a metaphysical and often mystical orientation, in order to express rigorously scientific notions and formulate scientific hypotheses. This practice certainly suggests that they do not wish to do without certain advantages of a poetical-pastoral air and posture.

The *third* point needs to be developed step by step.

All sustenance of human effort must be motivated or it comes to an end. Mere inertia of activity would not sustain a road sweeper's eight-hour work day: to complete the day he must have at least the carrot of his wages. However, all perseverance of any complexity must be supported by the satisfactions of mastery, and wages alone would not secure accuracy, or reliability, or perseverance. Professional work in the medium of human relationships will go even beyond this. This sort of work cannot thrive on mastery or craftsmanship or manipulative virtuosity alone. The non-professional personal self of the worker will have to enter the relationship between worker and client. The worker will have to let this happen, for without it the work would become vacuous, lifeless, and paradoxically not very professional! And indeed all counsellors use their personalities as much as craftsmen and artists use both their imagination and their hands. But the 'use of one's personality' is a mere circumlocution for the 'personal involvement' of the counsellor; and 'personal involvement' or 'countertransference' is a love-hating or ambivalently working bond between worker and client. The positive concern with which the counsellor controls and guides this ambivalence for the benefit of the client proves that the ambivalence is not a fifty-fifty matter and that there is more 'love' than 'hate', if the process is to continue with any hope

[1] *Psychiatry in a Changing Society*, Ed. by S. H. Foulkes & G. Stewart Prince, London and New York, 1969, p. 207.

of success, that is. So there we are: the counsellor has incorpo-
rated in his 'technique' a category, the scientific status of which
is, to say the least, dubious. The analysts tell us that their
concern, protectiveness, solicitousness, or even love is the outcome to their 'introjected parent-imagos'. Here the hoary genetic
fallacy comes into view once again. Who cares what the infantile
antecedents of this positive, adult, and professional concern
are, when it is clearly left unexplained what factor, what ad-
mixture, what conditions convert the infantile antecedents into
the highly refined and sensitive adult-professional performance!
Chickens do not equal eggs and tulips are not equivalent to
bulbs: the counsellor's care for his clients is not the same thing
as his erstwhile infantile defences. The point of this book is to
show that the counsellors themselves confess to believing this
to be the case. It is emphatically not my purpose to convince
the reader that *in my opinion* this is the case. I should like to
impress on the reader that my belief is of no consequence here:
I am engaged in a documented study of the faith of the counsellors, the ideological climate of the counselling profession
itself, a profession of which I am not a member.

The next query I should like to anticipate is usually prompted
by the reader's willingness to come to the assistance of those
whom I quote and who, in their view, seem to need this assistance. Perhaps my source did not mean what I think it meant
and if only I cited the full context to which the quote belongs,
we would get an entirely different picture?

The lapses from a language of science, indeed of applied science,
which I quote, are no arbitrary excisions from context. The
matter I quote *is already out of context* where it appears, and constitutes an admission that the counsellor tries to have the advantages of the seriousness and evocativeness of these extraneous
notions and then insists that they are either no more than trivial
literary digressions, or that mystical language is used merely
to show the total and undifferentiated infantile dependence on
the mother, and later on the counsellor.

The writing of this book was not prompted by a need to
enter into polemics with the counsellors. In fact, those who
read on will become aware of my marked respect for this new
professional speciality. It is so much the stranger that a kind of
lack of comprehension—much like a defensive 'denial'—dis-

closed itself in some very subsidiary and sometimes carping criticisms which can be shown, without any difficulty at all, to be pointless. For example: why does Halmos 'lump together' psychiatrists, psychoanalysts, psychotherapists of various brands, social caseworkers, and some others? But, then, why does a contemporary sociologist 'lump together' doctors, lawyers, architects, and so on, and call them 'professionals'? Or, for example, why does a zoologist 'lump together' orang-utans and chimpanzees and call them 'primates'? So long as there is evidence that there are generic qualities shared by several *species*, their 'lumping togther' into one *genus* is not only legitimate but also illuminating and creative. I claim that my documentation makes it, at least, strongly plausible, that there is a body of principles about psychology, about the nature of human growth and development, and about the scope of professional intervention in this growth and development, which entirely warrant that the *genus* 'counsellor' be given the same sociological legitimacy as, for example, 'class', 'status', 'competition', or many of the other sociological categories possess.

Another objection raised by some practitioners was levelled against the implications of the name itself: 'we don't counsel', we merely elicit from our clients and patients that they counsel themselves. But deliberate 'eliciting' itself is an intervention, and an influencing of another to respond in a way different from the way in which he would have responded without the intervention. To my mind the difference between the notions of 'influencing' and 'advising' or 'counselling' is of no great moment if indeed there is a difference at all. All professional personal helping is, by definition, afforded to achieve something through personal influence. An idiosyncratic rejection of my label 'counsellors' may well suggest that there is some anxiety and even guilt felt by practitioners about their unconfessed directiveness. I think that my elaboration of their directiveness ought to be therapeutic for them and certainly guilt-allaying, for I argue that they have no reason to feel guilty or even self-conscious: there is no personal helping in professional work without personal influencing. What one cannot avoid for that one cannot be blamed!

This book is a study of a contemporary belief-system, indeed of a contemporary ideology. It is not a tract of advocacy or a testimony to the author's own commitments, let alone to his faith. I stress this again to counter the obstinate refrain about the 'author's faith'. Of course, the author's sympathies show, because he refuses to put on a mask of indifference in order to preserve an air of impartiality. And yet, I feel, that I should not be made part of the social scene which I describe. Alas, this aim is not always achieved. When, for example, I describe the process in which the contemporary intellectual deserts political solutions, I am often taken to have subscribed to this view myself. I am certainly not a political nihilist who believes that political solutions are discredited. I merely undertake the task of portraying many contemporary socially concerned yet idiosyncratic intellectuals who, while withdrawing from political interest, involvement, and activity, do not wish to abandon society altogether and continue to care for their fellowmen in the several one-to-one relationships of therapeutic and case-work care. As a sociologist, all that I was putting forward was that the species of apolitical intellectuals exists, that their numbers are large enough to affect the cultural-moral climate of our times. The reader, out of sheer economy of effort, may have been enticed into thinking that this was not only a diagnostic observation but also an advocacy. I should like him to note that this is not so.

The same hasty reading and economy of effort may make the reader think that when I present my analysis of the elements of the counsellors' faith I am not only stating what these elements seem to me to be, but also that I approve of these elements or that I advocate their inclusion in cases where they may be overlooked. Once again, this is certainly not intended. An analytic-descriptive account of a belief system is an empirical exercise followed by the formulation of general propositions. There is no place in this sort of exercise for declarations of belief and preference. Yet, of course, I would be less than human and certainly less than sensitive to the concerns of my own scientific curiosities if my sympathies or antipathies could not be inferred from what I am saying. I strongly believe, however, that this does not get in the way of a matter-of-fact task of investigation and reporting.

On the other hand, the author of this book has also been regarded as the upholder of a not always flattering magnifying mirror for some counsellors. Even ordinary mirrors are sometimes resented when they reflect not only attractions and visible virtues, but also the residues of indulgence, excess, and unwisdom in general. The desire to smash the mirror suggests some hazards of flying splinters for its upholder. These are occupational hazards and I have no desire to beg for sympathy.

Cardiff

April, 1970   P.H.

Preface to the 1978 Edition

The Preface to the 1970 American Edition has not yet been seen outside the USA and I hope that its inclusion here will be helpful to a wider readership now. Also, this second British edition is a welcome opportunity for the author to bring the statistical material of the second chapter up to date and to correct some minor errors of phrasing.

During the last 13 years much has been changed in the world of social care and control. Many now teach that care is a mere function of control and certainly deny that it may be the other way round. They say that there can be no caring institutions with caring workers employed in them unless political control has voted the money for them. Others hold that without the faith of the counsellors caring institutions could not find caring workers to staff them. In a way both of these kinds of people are saying that there is no genuine dilemma here, only a single social concern or involvement, a 'hybrid' of care and control. They both try to avoid the error of choosing between the faith of the counsellors and the creed of the revolutionaries by offering their ecumenical solution in a hybridised social concern and social action. In my book, *The Personal and the Political* (Hutchinson, London, 1978), I argue that there cannot be an ecumenical solution. My caution to those who have not yet read this latest book of mine is this: the political critic of personal care overlooks the fact that even in his utopia everybody will have to be a counsellor to his fellow citizen if that utopia is to have any worthwhile moral meaning at all. Whether we believe that such a utopian society is possible—or desirable—we must assume that in it solidaristic practice will depend on a universally professed faith of the counsellors.

By the time utopia is upon us the political ideology of control will have achieved what it has aimed at: the state will have withered away and control will have disappeared or changed into care.

The 'withering away of the state' was, in fact, the first 'end-of-ideology' theory. The wielding of political controls have been so successful that they have abolished the wielding of political control. In utopia care has the stage all to itself. Hence, we are obliged to conclude that according to the Marxist theory care will continue, for ever whereas control will end.

So much for the parity of care and control, so much for the fifty-fifty merger in a hybrid of the personal and political.

Milton Keynes   P.H.
September 1977

Introduction

✳

To advise people about their personal affairs has always been regarded as a thankless and futile task. The principal professions which have been known to meddle with other people's private business, such as the clergy, medicine, and the law, can afford to go on undaunted by the ingratitude and obstinacy of the advice-seekers, for they each have their main professional expertise to keep them feeling worthwhile. There are special skills for the procurement of salvation, health, and justice and, at least, these established professions can be sustained by the knowledge of possessing these important skills and using them for the advantage of others. The clergy, medicine, and the law do not entirely disbelieve in their competence to advise and in their clients' good sense of complying with their advice. It was only in this century, after the Freudian explorations began to be understood, that 'advice-giving' by the responsible and learned, or even pious professional has become suspect. From the psychoanalytical clinical explorations, a new method of helping others in some personal and private predicament has developed, which prescribes that the person in need of help should be assisted to discover more about the history of his preferences and aversions than he normally contrives to know and understand, and that he should be assisted to make his decisions in the light of new insight, more or less spontaneously gained, and not in the light of directives or advice received.

Clearly, this eliciting the 'true' selves of help-seekers is a lengthy and laborious process. The clergy tended to regard it as a corrupting self-indulgence; the doctors did not believe in it for a start, and, at any rate, their relationship with patients was of a more authoritarian kind; nor could the lawyers be bothered with it. Meanwhile the psychological and clinical 'accountants' went on with their explorations of the personality and continued recording, reporting, and theorising. They have pleaded with us to make us see that *helping* not only depended on *exploration*, but largely consistéd of it.

At first, the clinical auditors and reporters successfully maintained an air of neutrality. The psychoanalysts enforced a discipline of non-intervention and non-involvement : they were supposed to keep out of the moral decisions of their patients and conceal their own personal predilections and dislikes whilst performing professionally. Later, however, as their numbers increased and their method was transcribed into the idiom of social welfare work, of the sociology of human relations, of general medical practice, and so on, the principle of non-intervention underwent some changes and the outlines of an ideological system became visible. This century has seen the development of a new professional activity practised by people of widely varying training and expertise. Psychiatrists, lay and medical psychotherapists, clinical psychologists, social caseworkers of several kinds, and some others, have all learnt to share the assumptions and values of the new philanthropic expertise of helping through caring-listening-prompting. In this book, I call the practitioners of this expertise 'counsellors', and explain why, as a sociologist and social psychologist, I regard them as a new social factor of considerable influence on the cultural and moral changes in twentieth-century western society.

The term 'counseling' (spelt with one 'l') has been used in a narrower sense in the clinical and welfare literature, especially in the United States. In this narrower sense it has usually been taken to mean a comparatively brief period of meetings—possibly only one meeting—during which a professional worker tries to help a client to sort out his educational, vocational, and adjustment problems by discussion, clarification, advice, and possibly also by referral to agencies which may give material or administrative help of some kind. It seems to me that, at its best, 'counseling' will also include an attempt at the clarification of motives and will, therefore, shade into a kind of 'brief psychotherapy'. And so, in this book the distinctions commonly claimed to obtain between counseling and psychotherapy will not be stressed. Basically and essentially all the practitioners of counselling (with two 'l's' and in my sense), have a common origin and a common aim : their common ancestor is the giver of spiritual solace and their common aim is health, sanity, a state of unspecified virtue, even a state of grace, or merely a return to the virtues of the community, adjustment. Although the multiplicity of these terms and notions does not make the goal any more sharply delineated—for each notion is nebulous, undefined or even indefinable—the associated images and therapeutic fantasies show that there is a reasonably large measure of consensus among the counsellors about the aims of their ministrations.[1] To some extent, all counselling procedures share a method: they are all 'talking cures', semantic exercises, they all attempt treatment through clarification of subjective experiences and meanings. Admittedly, in calling them all by the name that is already expropriated by one of the special groups, namely 'counsellors' in the narrower American sense,[2] I might cause confusion among those readers who have missed this page. Yet in choosing this term to stand for the whole genus of personal helping I was especially attracted by the 'advice-giving' element in the meaning of the term. It is an openly interventionist and directive element which more truthfully reflects what I believe is going on, whilst the terms 'psychotherapy' and 'social casework' tend to conceal it.

There are two ways in which one could justify using the term 'counselling' in this comprehensive sense, two ways in which the lumping together of a multiplicity of procedures including psychotherapy and social casework could be explained. One could either say that the highest common factor in all these helping procedures is not only large enough but happens to be *the decisive part* of these procedures; or one could say, somewhat less radically, that the highest common factor in all these activities, though not always decisive, is *important and characteristic enough* to justify the grouping together of all these different helping procedures under one concept.[3] I think that those who will find some of the central

---

[1] Cf. *Towards a Measure of Man*, by P. Halmos, London, 1957, pp. 60–79.

[2] It seems to me that, in the United States, 'counselors' (apart from the legal variety) are mainly advisors attached to educational institutions. Their principal function is educational and vocational guidance though they also engage in a brief and simple form of psychotherapy. Cf. *The Work of the Counselor*, by L. E. Tyler, New York, 1961. Cf. 'Counseling and Psychotherapy: Split Personality or Siamese Twins?', by F. L. Vance and T. C. Volsky, *American Psychologist*, Vol. 17, 1962, pp. 565–570. These writers observe that ' "counselors" engage in psychotherapy and "psychotherapists" counsel', and find it hard 'to justify totally divergent training or treatment programs' for these two professions.

[3] Cf. 'Historical Survey of the Evolution of Casework', by Annette Garret, *Journal of Social Casework*, June 1949, Vol. XXX, No. 6, pp. 219–229. Also: 'Distinguishing between Psychotherapy and Social Casework', by Jules V. Coleman, *Journal of Social Casework*, June 1949, Vol. XXX, No. 6, pp. 244–251.

ideas in this book reasonable will agree at least with the less radical of these two views : I am attracted by the more radical one.

I intend to present the social role 'counsellor' as a sociological category, as a role comprising a set of functions in the social division of functions. I do not wish to imply that this set of functions has now been explicitly institutionalised : only the specialist groups have been institutionalised in various degrees of definiteness, for example, the professional specialisms in social work, in psychoanalysis, in psychiatry, and so on. The generic identity of 'counsellor' is no more institutionalised than the generic identity of 'whitecollar worker'. In fact, whilst the latter is recognised as a widely known sociological category, the former, 'counsellors', is not yet so recognised. One of the purposes of this book is to make the reader aware of the sharply contoured sociological reality of this set of social functions and of the deep impact which the discharge of these functions makes on the moral-cultural structure of our societies, especially in the west. This purpose is even more in my mind when I think that the reader too might be a counsellor. For I very much wish to draw him into an argument and hope that the argument will be no less fruitful to him than it may be to the beneficiaries and observers of the counselling activities.

The counsellor's influence on his society is in a process of rapid growth; the fourth chapter of this book contains some relevant material on this influence. This is what mainly explains my sociological interest in the contemporary counselling philosophy. In studying this philosophy one observes that the counsellor is reticent about his first principles. He is wont to deny that he asserts anything non-deterministic and non-mechanical about the nature of his help or indeed that he asserts these qualities about the nature of man. As a rule, he wants us to believe that a psychological theory is all that is needed to explain, account for, and justify his practice. A shy and desultory mention will be made of a few metapsychological premises as prime movers but no elaborate claims will be allowed for any kind of 'mystery' in his own vocational loyalties. He will firmly disown these or impatiently change the subject if it is broached. Yet while he unprepossessedly labours to help his clients he cannot but communicate to us some fairly definite propositions about his work and about the nature of man, and these propositions do not seem to follow from his scientific assumptions. In my reading of his literary confidences I find that he willy-nilly betrays a tender-mindedness of which he is consistently ashamed or, at least, self-conscious.

When a counsellor concernedly and sympathetically intervenes he knows—though he does not in fact, and need not, remind himself of this while working—that this concern and sympathy is essential to the good functioning of his intuitive understanding and, therefore, of his technical skill. When the counsellor is challenged to locate the origin of this sympathy in the map of his universe he will invariably find it in some low corner. The talk is usually about 'sublimated voyeuristic tendencies', 'a need for restitution', and the like. We are not told of how the low order metapsychological sources of energy generate their high order destinies, how rationality is chosen irrationally, and how his painstaking care for others and his tough-minded objectivity become wedded.

The following is a typical illustration of the way the counsellor's motives are treated :

'Sexual curiosity is as much a motive drive in the work of a psychoanalyst as it is in the work of doctors, nurses, scientific investigators, historians, novelists, and artists. Through personal analysis, sexual curiosity is purged of its infantile characteristics, it is no longer of the "peeping Tom" variety. *Curiosity becomes adult and benevolent*, because the psychoanalyst is not engaged upon a surreptitious gratification of his own immature sexuality.' (Italics added.)[4]

But what is it that makes curiosity 'adult and benevolent'? What is the agent of transformation? If the sexual source contains the agent of elevation, of emergence, of 'sublimation' then perhaps it is not merely such a source after all? And those who are outside the counselling professions cannot help observing that the counsellors too are aware of this.

In spite of the many humanistic disclaimers the counsellors often admit their doubt about humanistic protestations and perspectives. 'A therapist cannot avoid trying to formulate a conception of human beatitude which rises above individual and cultural conditioning . . . "Human Nature" which he is concerned to see expressed more fully can be defined only in terms of an *ideal* which he

[4] *Collected Papers on Psychoanalysis*, by Ella Freeman Sharpe, London, 1950, p. 121.

believes can be realised or worked towards effectively.'[5] In his labours the counsellor seems to be guided by an aspiration, by a high-minded conception of what his client might become and should become. By persevering in his efforts to help, the counsellor seems to make a point, take a stand, and declare for hope. At a time when, according to all commonsense standards, the client appears incorrigibly useless the counsellor is, in fact, saying 'You are worthwhile!' and 'I am not put off by your illness!' This moral stance of not admitting defeat is possible for those only who have faith or a kind of stubborn confidence in the rightness of what they are doing. Yet all that the counsellors freely confess to is a mere technique, an elaborate professional etiquette, or a sheer casuistry of professionalised neighbourliness. Just the same, their obvious dedication, persistence, and unthinking affection confess to much more. I will try to show that the literature of counselling is an inspired literature as much as it is a scientific one, and that even in their ascetic disowning of inspiration the counsellors testify to an inspired dedication. Above all, I hope to show that this apparently paradoxical stance is actually prescribed for the practitioners of counselling, no matter whether they are psychoanalysts or social caseworkers, clinical psychologists or psychiatrists.

On the whole, the counsellors are frankly and humbly agnostic, and for this reason, their much-restrained piety is plausible and acceptable in the sceptical age in which they have to work. Yet they use a language of reverence, and even a theological language and imagery, as if they could not do their job effectively without their evocative power.

It would be easy to ridicule the indecision and ambiguity implied in so much of what they say but it is certainly not my intention to make fun of a predicament which we all share. Nor am I at all impelled to do so by the dispassionate study of the facts : too often when I come in contact with the counsellors' indecision and inconclusiveness, I become aware of a nobility and moral discipline, which are sufficiently marked to protect the counsellors against the theorist and his intellectual scruples. Out of indolence, at least, the counsellor could take short-cuts, and his moral resolve to make a greater effort, to look again—even when it is disheartening to look again—is a kind of moral tenacity which the counsellor's psycho-

[5] *Psychotherapy and a Christian View of Man*, by David E. Roberts, New York, 1950, p. 115.

6

logical assumptions have left largely unexplained. The counsellor applies himself in a way which suggests a set of convictions, a powerful mood, a moral stance, a *faith*. To call this exercise an outcome of faith is, I believe, well warranted for it has many of the characteristics of human experience and behaviour with which we associate the notion of faith.

Usually, the counsellor's momentous professions of faith appear embedded in lengthy discourses on technicalities or on scientific theory, and consequently their presence and importance are overlooked. If they are quoted, as I will do in this book, the counsellors tend to complain that the quoted matter is 'taken out of context'. Certainly, the context is as a rule technical or theoretical, and entirely positivistic, whilst the mystical or 'existential' matter quoted, appears in this context as a *lacuna* of foreign material : it *is* already out of context! The practice constitutes an admission on the part of the scientific-technical-positivistic writer that he cannot keep up the positivistic-scientific discipline. Almost as if a long-sustained pretence lapsed and the underlying reality were disclosed for a short while. But if so, what is 'out of context'? The professions of faith or the technicalities? 'The social worker is not dealing with a social illness (whatever that is),' writes Noel Timms, 'and her "treatment" is a matter of broad moral behaviour towards others rather than a type of scientific treatment.'[6] So long as such things are said with full awareness of the departure from positivistic thinking one can complain only because literally nothing is said about the implications and consequences of such departure. But to highlight what is *already* out of context is not the same thing as quoting out of context! I am especially anxious to make the reader see that the plea of 'out of context' against my method of documentation cannot be allowed.

As a sociologist, I have been interested in tracing the emergence of the stream of social and moral innovations in our times, and have found it necessary to attach some importance to the oddly silent renaissance of social responsibility and concern with which the counselling philosophy may have to be credited. I will try to show that, at least to some extent, the counsellors have been responsible for a revival of interest in the rehabilitation of the individual, and a loss of interest in the rehabilitation of society. Through their modern advocacy of fellowship, understanding, and compassion,

[6] *New Society*, 3 September 1964.

they have weakened the mid 20th-century intellectual's political involvements. I will consider this decline in political orientation, which is both an outcome of the spread of counselling activities, and a favourable social context for their further spreading.

In perusing these pages the reader will soon note that I am very much on the counsellor's side. In fact, he may think that I give the counsellor more credit for noble professional motives than the counsellor would care to claim. Whilst I am content to leave this to the reader's decision, there is another matter which I will not leave to him : this is the response to some of my ideas, that they are much more a testimony to the faith of the person who expounds them, than to the faith of the counsellors. I should like to get this point out of the way at this early stage. The documentation of my thesis is carried out with the help of carefully collected citations from the literature of counselling. In this way I have done an entirely pedestrian job to disclose and highlight an influential mode of thought in our times. The following chapters are intended to be interpretations of socio-cultural change, and not oracular statements. The interpretations are *based* on what the counsellors themselves are saying, and my critical review of what they are saying has one purpose only : to show that the counsellor's practice and theory depend upon assumptions and value judgments, which have a potent influence not only on his work, but also on the culture of the society in which the counsellor works. These value judgments are almost inextricably involved in the technicalities of counselling work, as if the techniques of loving were inseparable from the loving use of techniques.

This book is addressed to a great many people. First of all, it is for the general reader whose qualification is that he is interested in the moral and psychological credentials of those who give him help with intimate personal problems, who give him advice of a psychological nature, who 'counsel' him or do social casework on him, who treat him in psychotherapy, psychoanalysis, and so on. Secondly, I offer the book to the counsellors themselves whose importance and whose responsibilities have grown in this unevenly prosperous age. Most of all, I should like to stir up a new kind of constructive self-criticism among the counsellors, the kind that no longer specialises in the self-mortifying exercise of unearthing foibles and defects only, but objectively locates and defines the essential virtues of their professional service. It is possible that

8

pastoral counsellors and, indeed, theologians might consider this book of some use to them, for it is certainly not irrelevant to their concerns. Above all, I hope that students of social work, both the so-called pre-professional and professional kind, will be encouraged to regard this book as a textbook for a course in 'the philosophy of personal assistance', or as *one* of their textbooks for the course in 'the theory of social casework'. And finally, I hope that sociologists, especially those interested in social change, will examine this study of the counsellor's personal service ideology and of its influence on the actual and probable future course of social change.

CHAPTER ONE

The Discrediting of Political Solutions

In the past, if there was something wrong with the society in which a man had to live he would turn to the political and moral reformer; if a man's body was ailing he would consult a doctor; and if he had a sickness of the spirit he would seek help from the priest. Those who had the vocation or mission to better their fellow-men's life chose practice in one of these three fields. The last two have already yielded some of their functions to the counsellor—of this I will say more in the next chapter; the first vocation, the political, is the burden of this chapter. In what follows I am endeavouring to present a historical account of changes in certain attitudes to the political methods of 'bettering' man's condition. This historical account was written in 1965, for the first edition of this book, and the same account would have to be given today for the second edition if we were to describe what had happened to the faith in political initiatives during the middle decades of this century. Since the end of the 'Sixties there has been a strong political revival in the west and a corresponding disillusionment with personalist or personal counselling solutions. And now, by the end of the 'Seventies it would be appropriate to study the 'discrediting of personalist solutions' by political radicalism. Whether such a thing has happened, or is possible, I examine in *The Personal and the Political*. In the coming pages, I am concerned mainly with the mood of the west in the mid-century.

To plant my construction firmly in the ground, I have brought together some of the main factors which, it would seem to me, have caused the political solution of man's problems to lose much of its trustworthiness and dignity. I listed these factors under seven headings but there is nothing magical in the number seven, for almost all of them are complex and composite factors and capable of being broken down to more elementary parts. The order in which these factors are to be listed reflects the way they have come to mind and not their relative significance.

In the twentieth century, medicine has made the premature death of the individual all but unnecessary, and physics the premature death of the human species almost probable or, at least, almost certainly possible. We live longer and more healthily, and we threaten ourselves with extermination. We have the means of securing welfare for all, and also the means of sending us all to kingdom come. It is all in our hands. This is what is so terrifyingly new in our predicament. Clearly, the apocalyptic problems of today are more apparently of our own making than human problems have ever been in the whole history of mankind. Our extensive knowledge of the universe is matched only by our vast ignorance of the proper use to which this knowledge could be put. Standing at the centre of this stupendous predicament is the small, lonely man who is, after all, responsible for it. Yet, he pauses, as if the imminence and size of the danger had paralysed him. As if the ultimate emergencies had made him politically tongue-tied. One of the most disturbing aspects of his ignorance and indecision is that, even with the best will in the world, he could not hope to assimilate and master all the knowledge and relevant expertise that would be necessary for making really well-informed decisions of a far-reaching political nature. At a juncture in the history of man when TIME towers above us in the shape of a huge venomous toadstool cloud, this insufficiency, this helplessness in the face of such a great variety of esoteric expertise, assumes great importance. Certainly, even in much simpler times no one could hope to take into account *all* the ramifications and consequences of his acts; one might claim that there is no entirely novel factor present in our political decisions and that we are no more hampered in resolute actions of a political nature by ignorance of the consequences than were our forefathers. But the point is that since those less difficult times the complexity of the human situation has increased in almost the same measure as the gravity of the hazards entailed by the actions in the political arena. One might go so far as to say that in these circumstances few sensitive and imaginative individuals can help being paralysed into inaction. It is not for me to judge this timidity morally but to point to an actual psychological factor operating against a political stand and a political interest. Perhaps because of its dramatic thermo-nuclear context, this seems to me to be the *first* factor in the decline of political certainties during the mid-century.

The mid-century western intellectual felt obliged to be dispassionate and objective. He developed an ideological cramp and could not make an energetic or determined move in any direction, even in the right one. In those sordidly romantic years when destitution, hunger and disease were conspicuous and abundantly present in the ordinary Anglo-Saxon and Scandinavian neighbourhood, it was easy to come by passionate certainties. One emphatically and combatively disapproved. When the opulent nations had all but swept away the more scandalous forms of material inequities and iniquities, their citizen-intellectuals did themselves out of political catharsis altogether. Of course, men have not always used political opposition and contest as the principal forms in which to register discontent with their vulnerable, painful, and mortal lot. From Christ to Wesley and from Copernicus to Freud, much rebellion against the *status quo* was waged with little, if any, reference to politics. After some centuries, during which the political intellectual flourished side by side with others, administration and technology began to edge him out of the centre of the picture. Naturally, it was too early to think that politics in the west had already been supplanted by administration and technology. Yet the aspiration of the mid-century intellectual was that this state of affairs should at least be approximated. One might say that ideology demanded that ideology be replaced by social science and that politics be made all but unnecessary by scientific and technological planning.

The scientific and technological age is the age of reason, and in the age of reason honesty tends to equal intellectual honesty. Intellectual honesty seems to require even today that what science in its mathematical purity does not license should not be acted on. The honestly truthful man will be expected to see that to strike the pose of political certainty is fraudulent. In an age in which to be unscientific is almost to be immoral, the ideal of truth-seeking becomes the *second* factor of the process which leads to political apathy. This is not to say that the 'truthful age' is obsessed with objectivity, verification and numbers; the age is generously pleased with and playfully indulgent of unthinking spontaneities in art and in harmless living. But for categorical propositions, and also for respectable action, it demands that one should really have science at one's elbow. Objectivity about facts is morally superior to acting on them in almost any manner. The moral principles of the age prescribe even for the warmhearted and compassionate counsellors in personal matters that their psychology should be thought of as a science and that their psychotherapeutic mission should be persued with credentials authorised by science. In this climate of opinion even charity and kindness must be planned, ordered, and scientifically controlled. It seems to be of little effect on the counsellors that this *imprimatur* of science in respect of human conduct has been discredited by philosophers who have shown that the facts of science do not make precepts of conduct irresistible.

The enormousness of the mass society, the inhuman clumsiness of procedural routines, the monolithic blundering in so much that is planned and decided 'on high levels', are commonplace objects of contempt. The sensitive intellectual of the west today cannot relate himself to these things at all without violating his deeply-felt need to discriminate and dissent. It has become axiomatic that he would only abuse himself and corrupt his better nature by taking part in ideological-political action. He would merely waste his substance on some kind of public address in which he would have to oversimplify his meaning to enable him to reach all his listeners. Thereafter he would only learn to hate himself on account of the hypocritical blurring of honest distinctions.

The critical westerner has reached the conclusion that political statements are merely *ex post facto* justifications for political resolve and action, and not accurate propositions about facts, let alone reliable predictions. In politics deliberate streamlining of truth is essential if it is to be advanced with any determination and speed. By now, all large-scale prescriptions irritate us and we tend to believe—not altogether unreasonably—that all ideological formulae are made up to deceive. At a time when political advocacy is suspect, when which all forms of persuasion, let alone propaganda, are discredited, no self-respecting would-be betterer of the human lot would seek to associate himself with a politically didactic or politically persuasive position. The betterer can more easily conceive of himself as an 'educator', but only when this role prescribes a personal relationship between himself and the taught. Personal tutorship and guidance, yes! But no platforms, no proselytising! With some exceptions—mainly in education—to advocate, to demand, to protest publicly and to appeal over the heads of one's friends and acquaintances in order to address oneself to audiences and publics of strangers, is tainted with insincerity and reeks with egotistical dominance. The hankering for the platform is taken as evidence that one has no friends to address, and that if one has to choose between loneliness and the impersonal togetherness of the public meeting one should choose loneliness, for the public meeting is a mere counterfeit of communion, a mirage of it. For the critically alert intellectual, it is almost as if impersonality of address were inseparable from dishonesty of purpose. The culture of the age almost prescribes an obsessive censorship of one's motives, and thus, with the widely publicised correlations between psychopathology and politics, many an energetic and discontented intellectual is effectively discouraged from seeking a political expression for his discontent. For the western intellectual, logico-discursive honesty is superior and cleaner than the moral-doctrinal consistency and firmness of the ideologist; for him, keeping faith with reason is nobler than the embracing even of a reasonable faith. And if faithfulness to reason commands inaction then inaction will be morally superior to intervention of any kind. Everett Knight's *The Objective Society* quotes Dostojewski to sum up this predicament : 'So at length, gentlemen, we have reached the conclusion that the best thing for us to do is to do nothing at all, but to sink into a state of contemplative inertia.'[1] To those who feel that action is messy, always slapdash and arbitrary, contemplative inertia may present superior attractions.[2]

It is worth recording how and why intellectuals of the mid-century grew weary of political panacea. The expediencies and dishonesties perpetrated by various ideological 'managements' had discredited almost all reform movements, or at any rate had generated a mood of derisory suspicion about them. The educated man of the west could no longer don the uniform of a political allegiance without feeling a little ashamed and a little apologetic about the masquerade, and so he now seems to prefer to go naked politically. The changes in the history of political ideas this mid-century could be described as changes from the politics of social philosophy to those of social psychology. As if the plotting of social

[1] London, 1959.
[2] A similar point is made by F. Riessman and S. M. Miller in 'Social Change Versus the "Psychiatric World View"', *American Journal of Orthopsychiatry*, January 1964, Vol. XXXIV, No. 1, pp. 29–38.

action were now less and less by the simple co-ordinates of economics and power, and more and more by the biopsychological co-ordinates of human learning and unlearning. The intellectual of this era naturally suspects all systematic political theorising, because it normally proves that the theoriser is either ignorant of the complications of reality or he underestimates their importance, or worse still, he pretends that they don't exist. 'Berlin and Weldon and Popper agree with T. S. Eliot and Michael Oakeshott that systematic political theorising is a bad thing,' writes Iris Murdoch, adding, 'The former think it so because it is "metaphysical" and opinionated and obscures the scientific business of altering society for the better.'[3] And the latter, I suppose, think it so because the sweeping and undiscriminating theory is gross, unjust, and neglectful of the uniqueness and 'spirituality' of the human genius. Rather similarly, the counselling man who repudiates politics or feels indifferent to politics would do so because of either the former or the latter reason.

Yet a simple alternative such as this would hide other important distinctions we must make. The professional counsellor's political interests atrophy in a lifetime of professional ministration to the individual instances, to individual needs. It is not much use for us to bewail his tendency to be oblivious of the larger social issues when he has to earn his living as well as his self-respect in resolving problems of the single case. The large tasks, the issues of the great society, are not within his professional scope, and it is quite natural that both in training and in subsequent practice he will inadvertently transfer his curiosities, his excitements, and his sense of usefulness from the impersonal world of social reform to the initmate world of social therapy. The many ways in which man's condition could be improved have differentiated planned helpfulness into an incredibly large number of specialities and kinds of professional expertise. The man with a 'full-time social conscience' generally seems to render some service to his fellowmen. In the mid-century in the North Atlantic culture area, this service tended to be a personal service more often than a political one. With all its hazards and doubts a personal service rendered to individuals and their families affords to the personal service worker direct access to the whole sequence of the helping operation. No substantial relegation of part of this service to others need go outside the worker's

[3] *Conviction*, N. Mackenzie (Ed.), London, 1958, pp. 225–226.

own area of direct experience. The overriding reality of man's concern for his fellow man is the *third* factor in the list of factors, discussed in this chapter, which has, paradoxically, contributed to the mid-century evisceration of western politics. Certainly, even the counsellor admits to an expertise, consisting of general rules, having to be learnt irrespective of the uniqueness of concrete cases; but whatever generalities and rules there may be in this expertise, they are guiding principles of approaching the individual client and not signposts to a political utopia.

The expansion of counselling activities and interests in the mid-20th century is now part of our recent social history. The political reform movements of the past, whether Marxist or not, aimed at 'betterment' which they primarily defined, firstly, in terms of an increase in political freedom and, secondly, in terms of an increase in material welfare. It was expected that the resulting political and economic equities would automatically create the conditions necessary for cultural refinement and robust sanity. At any rate, if there were any doubts, the reformers would say that they would cross those bridges when they got there. It was in the second half of the nineteenth century and in the twentieth century that a politically and economically emancipated middle class, both more populous and influential than ever before, began to ask questions about welfare to which there seemed to be no political or economic answers. The answers offered by Sigmund Freud and his followers had the attraction that they were in keeping with the deterministic principles of science; also, amidst the cult of middle-class privacy, they temptingly offered to elevate concerns with private serenity to the rank held by concerns for public justice. As an outcome, psychotherapy and social casework have become avenues of betterment attracting ever larger numbers of socially concerned intellectuals to professional careers, in which their principles were applied with various degrees of explicitness and depth. The range of the so-called helping professions which demonstrably derive at least some of their working principles from the psychotherapeutic theories of healing is remarkably wide. Whether they work in a clinical or non-clinical setting, they have ingeniously contrived to professionalise their love for their fellow men and have cleverly invented institutions, in which they can conceal the fact that they 'prescribe themselves' by prescribing techniques.

Governments, so far hostile to the suggestion that they might mingle more and more charitable, as well as personal, procedures with those scrupulously formal and impersonal ones prescribed in their statutes, are now thrown on the defensive. This has been markedly in evidence in that area of social service in which crime-prevention and the treatment of offenders fall. The statutes which provide for probation, for psychiatric treatment, for rehabilitation, and so on, assign more and more significance to unspecified and as yet unspecifiable personal services of professional workers, and less and less to fixed and definable material and institutional provisions and sanctions. Even in the treatment of the workshy in Britain, to determine whether 'his idleness be subsidised' through National Assistance, the officers of the National Assistance Board, or, more recently, of the Supplementary Benefits Commission, will be guided by considerations which the statutes are unable to specify. In the secularised revival of care and concern for persons these considerations must be kept clinical, and moralistic views must not be allowed to obtrude very much. Of course, this process is resisted by those who regard the psychotherapeutic ideology as subversive. From time to time, both the makers of statutes and their executors point out that the counselling ideology depletes our resources, because we are enjoined by it to pander to all kinds of idiosyncrasies which do not deserve to be protected. They warn us that too much indulgence of the weak, the impudent, and the clamorous will only make them weaker, more impudent, and more clamorous. Against these appeals, to go back to the general moral-political principles, the counsellors' point of view increasingly prevails : the new statutes continue to give a growing scope and discretionary initiative to the clinically trained samaritans.

The *fourth* factor in the antipolitical trend is closely associated with the factor of compassion for persons. This consists in the attitude that methods other than personal are wasteful, ineffectual, and therefore pointless. Literate man has become exasperated by the superficiality of regimented and centrally controlled life, and technological man has become exasperated by the wastefulness and inefficiency caused when bureaucratic agents classify creativeness and initiative. Even if there was no deep personal concern for the welfare of others, there might be concern for the wasted efforts exerted by gross and large-scale measures. Dean Inge's views on preaching—as compared with personal pastoral counselling—well illustrate this concern : 'If we were set to fill a number of narrow-

necked vessels—and we are all narrow-necked vessels—should we
set them up in rows and dash a bucket of water over them? That
is the method of the pulpit. A few drops may get in here and there,
but most of the water is wasted . . .'[4] The counsellor will add that
the therapeutic potential of large-scale, and mainly impersonal
action is small for the same reason.

At any rate the counsellor will argue that there is an absolute
incompatibility between sympathy with the one and sympathy with
the many, and this because the former is personal and the latter
is inevitably administrative, organisational, institutional, political,
and therefore, impersonal. Cultivation of the latter would blight
the chances of the former. The counsellor has a strenuously argued
defence for his desertion of political interests : '. . . some analysts
say half-jokingly that in order to do the finest analytic work that is
humanly possible, the analyst would have to live in a monastery on
top of a mountain !'[5] Here the counsellor himself offers a testimony
to the effect that the counselling role and function is ideally a first
cousin of the pastoral role and function instead of being a blood
relation of the political role and function at all.

Reforming zeal often comes to be regarded as an unlikeable
passion. The advocates of betterment weary us, for they appear
to us obviously out for their own salvation. Yet even people of
sensitivity may be observed trying to live with the notion that
to right the wrongs of the world one must be prepared to be uncritical, conceited, opinionated, and obstinate. Not surprisingly, the
discovery of this requisite of political behaviour produces its reaction : sobered, people turn to the task of righting the wrongs of
single human beings. People dimly feel that to do this for the single
one, they must be prepared to care for him, and, sated with the
bullying zeal of reformers, this is both a nobler and easier thing to
do. We may say, of course, that caring for the one and moving the
many are not sharply separable alternatives. After all, even the
crowd-compellers are not always devoid of compassion : their greed
for justice is often generated by pity and sympathy. One may argue
that they are only wholesalers of human betterment who are in a
hurry to reach out with their warmth to many people at the same

[4] Quoted by J. Sutherland Bonnel in *Psychology for Pastor and People*,
New York, 1948, p. 12.
[5] *Practical and Theoretical Aspects of Psychoanalysis*, by L. S. Kubie,
New York, 1951, p. 177.

time. Yet it is by now generally maintained that those who love mankind are too often not very fond of people, and that those who serve causes are singularly inept at bandaging a wound or holding the head of a sick person. It seems to me that the contemporary disillusionment with politics has, at least, something in it of the nature of a fear of this sort of alienation. The *fifth* element in our moral-cultural climate which is prejudicial to a political interest is the realisation that one must be estranged from warmth and immediate human contact to be so ardently interested in the abstract logistics of society. This is the realisation that the counsellor's role of personal involvement is incompatible with an actuarial thinking about people. I think that the political sociologist Lipset talks about 'alienation' in politics rather confusingly : he suggests that politics were made into an alienated activity only when the critical and detached intellectuals assumed political roles of importance.[6] The crux of the matter is, as I see it, not that the critical intellectuals have alienated politics but that political functioning is selectively preferred by more or less alienated people, whether intellectuals or not. To put it bluntly, the formalised and exploitive human contacts of political manoeuvre are more congenial to the alienated individual than to the one who is intimately related to his fellow men. Naturally, excessive alienation would disable even the politically oriented intellectual, for his schizoid detachment would eventually isolate him in the caucus and lose him the loyalties of his supporters. In these cases, unless he is an exceptionally accomplished cynic, he could not manage his political affairs consistently, for he would not be able to conceal his callous selfishness and lack of genuine concern. This *fifth* factor, working against political interest, follows from the psychology of the so-called 'betterers' of society. Taken in the extreme, there are two kinds of betterers, two kinds of righters of wrongs : those who would first rectify the anomalies of society before giving a personal helping hand to the individual, and those who would consider the personal assistance of the individual as more urgent and potent than the bettering of society. It would, no doubt, be wiser to try to do both at once; but human beings find such double duties too strenuous and sooner or later most 'betterers' concentrate on a single-minded service or allegiance. Sooner or later most 'betterers'

6 *Political Man*, by S. M. Lipset, London, 1960, p. 311.

find refuge from the strain of equilibration by reaching a solid platform of single-mindedness about their mission in the world. Of course, the psychological limitation to be two things at once could have ended in everybody being intensely politically oriented, and it needn't have caused a decline of political interests only. Yet I should like to list this as a factor, for without it the influence of the other factors would have been far less sweeping.

Scrutinising these factors responsible for the growth of apathy about political matters, we find that they form a spectrum and not a group of discrete items. The next factor, for example, shades imperceptibly into the former ones. This, the *sixth*, is the aesthetic objection to the political life. Intellectual dishonesty of the slogan is not only reprehensible as an untruth but it is also vulgar and boring. The utopias are either trashy daydreams of adolescents or they are monstrous nightmares of mechanised humanity. The fulfilment itself is either dreariness and pointless finality for the more sensitive or, indeed, the liquidation of sensitivity altogether. The potency of the aesthetic objection can be seen, already in our times, when first contacts are made with the world of a material utopia : paradoxically, even when the grand reform scheme and the ideological plan manage to accomplish some real material improvement in the life of society, as Labour did in Britain in 1945–1951, disillusionment can ensue, caused by the ever-receding goal of security, equity and comfort. When social reform, inspired and informed by moral vision, succeeds in removing the grossest forms of social abuse, and indeed succeeds in supplying some of the ingredients of comfort, the beneficiaries cling to the material rewards and by-products of their former moral and spiritual aspirations, and now rather deliberately forget, thus abandoning, these aspirations, for it seems to them that to continue their former restless idealism would risk the material advantages they have gained. The beneficiaries do not wish to be reminded that, no matter how much material security and material welfare we build around us, we remain vulnerable and mortal 'from the cradle to the grave', and that without the moral vision of an ideal scheme of things, indeed, without an ideological design, we may continue to remain confused, aimless, and dangerously quarrelsome. Opposing this sort of continued restlessness with the idea that a bird in hand is worth two in the bush, merely encourages aesthetic objections; for the aesthetically fastidious, the bird in hand is not obviously worth two in the bush. At any rate it is a narrow-minded, dull and unimaginative thing to go on mouthing unrefined laments about the material wrongs of a human condition in the centuries of the Industrial Revolution. Starvation, disease, degradation through destitution, overwork, child labour, and many other gross iniquities, were surely no longer characteristic experiences of the citizens of the welfare state, In fact, catering for the basic needs called forth 'council architecture', 'council culture', 'school and canteen cuisine', 'mass culture' (spelt out in brief and simplified paragraphs of the less scrupulous organs, the press), and so on, have effectively disposed of the starker miseries of the Industrial Revolution and replaced them—in the eyes of the aesthetically fastidious—with drabness. There is even a renewed scepticism which questions the very sense of frantically improving things materially, and generates a squeamish dissatisfaction with the vulgar amenities and with the superficial literacy of an ever-growing *petit bourgeois* society. Lipset quotes the editor of a Swedish newspaper, 'Politics is now boring. The only issues are whether the metal workers should get a nickel more an hour, the price of milk should be raised or old age pensions extended.'[7] This is a characteristic reaction of the replete intellectual, who kept up his interest in politics while there was a fight and a righteous battle in it, but preferred to retire from it when the disputation ceased to be diverting. Certainly, there is a moral disapproval of so much concern with trivialities, yet the edge of the complaint is one of distaste, of aesthetic criticism. Coming from another welfare state, the British, Professor Titmuss' plaint is almost identical,[8] '. . . there is little to divide the nation on home affairs except the dreary *minutiae* of social reform, the patronage of arts, the parking of cars, and the effectiveness of corporal punishment.' According to some writers, the mood of satiated torpor, of complacent and comfortable dullness, is already upon us, and therefore, now, when the need for *panem et circenses* has been fully and regularly met, there is no cause for dynamic initiative of any kind. H. Tingsten, another Swedish writer, explains: '. . . the importance of general ideas has been so greatly reduced, that . . . one can speak of a movement from politics to administration, from principle to technique . . . the margin for dis-

[7] *Op. cit.*, p. 406.
[8] *The Irresponsible Society*, by R. M. Titmuss, London, 1960, Fabian Tract 323, p. 3.

cussion on principles is exceedingly narrow, and debates become as dry as vague negotiations ... In place of conflicting ideas we are faced with competing bureaucracies ... It is obvious that the vitality nurtured on impassioned battles of ideas cannot be maintained in the successful democracy's atmosphere of levelling and compromise. We cannot have it both ways ... we cannot wish for vitality at the expense of stability.'[9] It is, of course, an open question whether we are fair in describing this state as 'apathetic' and lacking 'vitality'. The nostalgia for the old fervour and for noble causes is understandable enough, but it is far from obvious that their superannuation has made our life duller. Naturally, if it could be proved that our comforts have made us less supple and that we are more likely to bungle, to be amateurish, and repeat stereotypes endlessly because our good fortune has made us lazy and even blind, then there would be a cause for aesthetic discontent with welfare. Nonetheless, this is the way some contemporary fastidiousness would express itself, and exert its moral-cultural influence on society.

Yet another factor fostering antipolitical sentiment is inherent in the contemporary social reality: the anonymity and *anomie*[10] of the individual and his loss of contact with the community. So long as political action is aimed at organisational and institutional changes it will not catch up with the personal miseries of the lonely individual. Since the time of Marx, and his immediate successors, till the fourth decade of this century, sociologists, such as, for example, Max Weber, Pareto, Karl Mannheim, and scores of others, were preoccupied with issues of political and administrative control of society, with issues of power and of freedom. The social scientists of those decades, sociologists, political and social philosophers, economists, and historians, were primarily if not exclusively macro-sociological in their interests and ideas. They were interested in structural totalities—social classes, orders, leadership changes, *élites*, and in the general social edifice of the social whole. That the dominant social realities were political, or economic, or bureaucratic, or were pivoted on power and on

---

[9] 'Stability and Vitality in Swedish Democracy', *The Political Quarterly*, April-June 1955, Vol. XXVI, No. 2, pp. 140–151.
[10] The 'normlessness' and social disorganisation especially in evidence during periods of rapid social change.

coercive groups, was understandably a good enough reason for social scientists to study these things. In those times social class, property, military organisation and priestly *charisma* were still supreme and decisive, even in the Anglo-Saxon and Scandinavian democracies. As the life of western communities began to supply the individual with a measure of private security and freedom, regardless of his special social privilege and sectional power, the individual became aware of social realities much nearer home : the neighbourhood unit, the family, the primary group. Significantly, the origins of micro-sociology are more closely associated with thinkers who lived in prosperous industrial democracies than with others. Charles Horton Cooley's 'primary group', and Ferdinand Toennies' *'Gemeinschaft'* are the earliest representatives of this trend of social thought, and group dynamics, sociometry, and so on, are the current vehicles of it. In the wake of psycho-analysis, systematic experimental studies of 'Human Relations' in industry, and elsewhere, have expropriated a great deal of sociological time and attention. Since the mid-century, the micro-sociological realities have not only gained in importance, but have, at times, overshadowed the longstanding concerns with the problems of the Great Society. This outcome has been precipitated by the more efficient sheltering of the large majorities of individual citizens from gross economic insecurities, at any rate in the more prosperous societies of the west. When wars and economic slump do not threaten too fiercely, the individual citizen's main social worry is how to adjust to his suburb, his housing estate, or his peer-group; his main anxiety is about his acceptability in his work group or neighbourhood or reference group, and about the parental, marital, or filial mismanagements of his emotional needs. The crucial difference between being a sociologist of the 'great canvas', and being a miniaturist, cannot be understood in terms of a Marxian analysis alone. There are personality differences which may have a bearing on why one chooses one thing or the other to study, and the increasing social desolation in the mass society may have encouraged the recruitment of intellectuals to micro-sociological study, who would have been temperamentally unsuited for macro-sociological theorising and polemics. The systematisers and theorisers of the grand sweep of the social process as a whole are, in a way, safely protected against the microscopic analysis of person-in-society which would inevitably involve them personally.

Macro-sociology, rather like history, can be studied at a distance, from the outside, as it were; micro-sociology, on the other hand, must be studied at close quarters, from the inside, through participation. Micro-sociology imperceptibly introduced certain fundamental changes into the methods of social science. Nowadays, an analysis of what happens in a foreman-worker relationship, or in any other face-to-face group, would not be thorough and frank enough without references to deep-psychological processes inevitably involving the so-called participant observer. We have reached a stage in social science when, at least in some sectors of it, to be a 'student' or 'scholar' entails being an analysand, a therapist, a group member, and so on. In the early 'Forties an increasing number of prominent sociologists openly listed their personal psychotherapeutic experience as a valuable and even essential qualification of their expertise in sociology. Indeed, those who managed institutions such as the National Training Laboratories in Bethel, Maine, or the Tavistock Institute of Human Relations in London had to insist that their social scientists had these qualifications. The element of change I am trying to highlight is this: since the early 'Forties there has been a change in the 'key' of social science thinking, a shift towards a great deal more micro-sociology and an accompanying shift in the social scientist's role. For the earlier social scientist, 'participation in the observed' smacked of bias: for the modern social scientist, it is becoming a necessary condition of achieving a deep enough penetration into the recesses of social reality. The social science of the 'political era' was a predominantly political social science, and one that much helped to stress political priorities; contemporary social science is frequently small-group oriented and stresses therapeutic action.

I have listed seven complex factors which I considered as conspicuously working in the creation of a 'non-political man'. To make his profile sharper, here they are again in brief.

Firstly, the complexity of the social issues is alarming and the moral obligation to find out about everything relevant would be too onerous, were it at all possible. Knowing that it is not possible, and scared by the catastrophic consequences of an error, one is driven to escape to the familiar, concrete, and warmly human case.

Secondly, having been repelled by the mendacity of grand generalisations, by the deceptions of ideological doctrines, by the lures of utopias, and by the political expediencies, scientific man tried to impose his rigour of truthfulness on his thinking about society and hoped to derive some satisfaction from thereby retrieving his intellectual integrity and honesty.

Thirdly, he discovered that he could express compassion for his fellow man by tending to his personal problems in the newly invented role of secular counsellor. In the agnostic age, this was a scientifically and technologically respectable way of being pious or, at least, socially responsible. The professional role has made tenderness sensible and unsentimental and, correspondingly, one could stop being socially overconcerned about political matters and express compassion politically.

Fourthly, political action is wasteful of human sympathy; it either fails to reach those one wants to help or it hardens and depersonalises the character of one's care at its source as well as in its results by the time it is distributed among the many.

Fifthly, people feel they must be either one thing or another: it would seem that they can't care for persons and impersonal causes at the same time sufficiently to make a difference to both. To be political one must be impersonal and to be impersonal one must be hard. As the antipolitical man has already expressed a preference, so this now amounts to a decision to do one thing *personally*, one-pointedly and exclusively and *not* the other.

Sixthly, politics are stereotyped; tactical considerations dictate that they should be addressed to the lowest common denominator; it is for this and other reasons that the political act or the political interest is regarded by the idiosyncratic intellectual as dull and debasing.

Seventhly, the loneliness of man in mass society and his increasing concern with personal relationships has encouraged the emergence of a micro-sociology, a sociology of friendships, acquaintanceships, and face-to-face co-operation. In turn, this micro-sociology has begun to make the withdrawal of political orientation scientifically respectable. The change in the preoccupations of mid-century social science has been self-fulfilling; the development of micro-sociology encouraged the politically indifferent individuals to seek the social rehabilitation of the alienated and of the lonely in the small face-to-face group. Whereas in the past the principal prompting for an interest in social science was the belief that a knowledge of the society at large and of its structure would help to change society, to restore man to a communion of men, now it seemed that this communion of the alienated, the excluded and the lonely could be more promptly accomplished through the knowledge of the small group and through the use of this knowledge in finding acceptance and a more intimate personal role in that small group. During the period of political scepticism the sociology of the face-to-face group, of the small group, and of the personal interactions of individuals in these primary group situations further delayed the reappearance of a strong political involvement of man.

CHAPTER TWO

The Coming of the Counsellors

Man's scepticism about the effectiveness of political solutions is a perennial phenomenon. It comes and goes: its season is when the overall rules are intolerable and political action must be taken to change them. The season passes when the action—having been taken—still leaves people lonely, unloved, alienated or confused. The action taken to create a truly solidaristic society always accomplishes less than it has aimed at. There comes a pause or an interval in the one-pointed political fervour in which individuals turn their attention to their own private composure whatever the political system in which they are obliged to live. It is not that the personal and the political cannot operate side-by-side: it is just that periodically one or the other seems to attract more speculation and a greater profusion of ideological schemes (see my book, *The Personal and the Political*).

The last strong personalist pause of the mid-century reached a high degree of sophistication and saw the preeminence of the personal over the political as a lasting one. It even announced the end of political ideologies and this 'post-political man' fancied himself emancipated from regimenting political doctrines and loyalties. But, 'post-political man' has not rid himself of his humanistic heritage and concern. He still cares, but now he prefers to express his compassion as a free-lancer, or at most as a conscientious objector to indiscriminate solutions. He has not abandoned his Christian moral tradition, and he is ready to attend to his fellow-man's problems personally. He would wave aside suggestions that by legislative acts or by changes in social institutions one could dispense with personal ministrations, but he has not altogether abandoned the idea that these ministrations could be made more readily available to people, and their effectiveness possibly also increased by large-scale measures and provisions. Therefore, he does not entirely acquit society of the responsibility for society's plight, yet, at the same time, he distrusts gross administrative or overall organisational panacea for man's miseries. Notwithstanding the plaint about the agnostic and faithless humanity of our age, a good many people seem to revert to a self-conscious Christian posture. The reflective man of the west is either a former material-ist who has become disillusioned with materialism or a Christian who has acquired a scientific conscience. No matter which, he is not likely to be content with either an exclusively 'apothecary-surgical' or 'salvationist-mystical' or 'political-legislative' solution of man's problems. His intellectual training puts him ever on his guard against 'nothing-but' solutions, and thus he is much attracted by what K. R. Popper has dubbed 'piece-meal social engineering'. All that is expected of him, he believes, is a cautious, 'empirical', and trial-and-error stance, as well as a ready-to-learn and ready-to-be-proved-wrong humility attitude to guide it. One must also remember that 'the Freudian utopia is to be found in the sanctum of the psyche', as Martin Birnbach put it,[1] and that mental health is much more important than milk and honey in the *Walden Two's*[2] of contemporary sociological day-dreaming. Yet there is always an unconfessed hope, a secret conviction even, that all this cultivating of little personal salvations, this gentle tending to circumscribed and limited anomalies, will somehow in the end add up to a comprehensive moral purpose, a kind of humanistic Kingdom of God.

And so, man's sensibility to his fellow man's needs continues and seeks expression in the professionalised concerns and ministrations of the counsellors. In view of the leaden weight of scepticism, and of the disbelief in man's spirituality, coupled with the scepticism about political man's mission, there was nothing surprising in the proliferation of professional workers, whose basic principles of work are, that human happiness and unhappiness are more or less autonomous conditions of the single individual, and that their personal access to the single individual, seeking help, is the only method that could possibly make any marked and lasting differ-ence to him. At the beginnings of the welfare state, it seemed that governmental policies would take care of the stereotyped and

---

[1] *Neo-Freudian Social Philosophy*, London, 1962, p. 42.
[2] By B. F. Skinner, New York, 1948.

classifiable material ills, and that the counsellor could throw himself fully into the study of personal and intimate miseries. Of course, even when large-scale measures are implemented they may miscarry by the time they reach the peripheries of the public community and affect the private individual. The political reformist, impressed and perhaps sobered by this, would now advocate that more of the community's resources be devoted to services which could be rendered by professional workers to private persons. 'Out of the truth of quietism there stems a new rebellious humanism, the politics of antipolitics',[3] is the kind of scintillating paradox which would bring out the quality of this politician's predicament, though, of course, in this case, it is the truth of modern personality psychology which inspired 'the politics of antipolitics'. Quietism or psychology are unlikely to sire rebellions. Yet, what emerges is clear enough: when community resources have already been devoted to the basic material needs, and welfare legislators are obliged to observe that the individual and his family all too often fail to turn these material improvements to their advantage, the welfare legislators were persuaded to stress the importance of the personal, incalculably human, and private elements of the situation. Though retreating from a reformistic to a therapeutic position they were now fighting a rearguard action trying to vindicate the validity of the general ideological and political principles even in the area of their private concerns. In the course of this action, the conservative politician appeals to the traditional Christian conscience and patriotic duty of the citizen who, with a little goodwill, ought to be able to solve his private problems if only he responded to this appeal; and the Soviet politician presumably makes a similar appeal to the socialist conscience of the citizen, expecting, of course, a somewhat prompter response. The democratic-liberal politician attempts to blend the traditional Christian tones with the overtones of scientific scrupulousness and intellectual honesty and makes an appeal to rationality and good sense. Today, radical political appeals to the clients of counselling services are being made to arouse them to see that these services are redundant or, at best, of secondary importance in an egalitarian society. On the whole, democratic-liberal and conservative politicians have continued to sympathise with the extension of personal counselling activities as an essential part of the furthering of welfare in society.

[3] *Out of Apathy*, by E. P. Thompson, London, 1960, p. 188.

Thus subsidised by state and local government, more and more of these counselling positions have been created for professionally specialised practitioners mainly in social work, social casework, clinical psychology and psychiatry. The professionalisation of personal helping which followed has proceeded along sectional lines but it soon became apparent that there were important generic elements in all forms of counselling whether clinical or non-clinical.

'The Faith of the Counsellors' is a central feature of what is generic in all forms of counselling : all counsellors seem to be imbued by sentiments of worthwhileness in giving personal service to others. Surely, this attitude is not entirely novel : there are some continuous and notable precedents of this in the history of the last two thousand years. To confess to this continuity would seem to many a counsellor as insincerely pious. Alongside with the 'depoliticising' of social concerns there has been a constant and deliberate attempt to discard all vestiges of sentimentalism about social solidarities. The contemporary socially conscious individual is ashamed of postures of charity and to detect styles of the 'lady bountiful' in a social caseworker would amount to an insult to her professional sincerity and seriousness. Professionalisation has proved an excellent camouflage for the counsellor's 'agape' and the formal-technological jargon, the impersonal clinical manners, the social science collaterals, and so on, have all helped to reassure the counsellor that he was doing a job of work and no more.

Yet in tracing the social-cultural conditions which helped along the development of this new vocation we need not be hampered by the counsellor's self-consciousness about the ancestry of his vocation. In the civilisation of the west the Christian interpretation of social and individual betterment has been the ultimate guide both in the dark credulity of the past and in the bogus clarities of more recent times. It is a commonplace observation that the force of this interpretation and the authority of this guide have considerably declined in the age of modern science. Indeed, it is a tired theme and a wearying business to speak of the shepherdless millions of our times pinning their hopes on laboratories and logic. Nonetheless, the emergence of the professions of secular counselling could not be adequately explained without reference to contemporary man's banishment from the fold of an ancient faith, from the bond of companionship, counsel, and inspiration, that faith has meant to man throughout the centuries.

No detailed documentation of this decline is necessary for the facts are all too well known. Merely to set off the forthcoming diagnosis with sharper contours, I should like to cite at least two sufficiently revealing pieces of stocktaking:

'The *British Weekly* (March 10th and 17th, 1955) published articles on the Decline of Non-conformity, and showed that though the membership of the major Free Churches of England and Wales had continued to increase from 1900 to 1910, from that time, before the commencement of the First World War, a gradual fall in total membership has taken place; in 1935 membership was almost equal to that of 1901. But the decline of the Free Churches is more serious than the loss of membership suggests ... (On the other hand) ... the decline in the strength of the Established Church is harder to measure since there are no "membership" figures. Technically its numbers are always increasing with the population advance, but clearly this gives no indication of real strength. But we have some comparative figures from Sheffield that demonstrate the losses since the "Eighties". Thus the 1881 census of worship gave total attendances at adult services of the Church of England on an average Sunday as 33,835 at a time when the population of the city was 284,410. In 1956 with the population slightly over half a million, the comparable figure of total attendances is between 12,000 and 13,000. It should be noted that the 1881 figure does not represent the high watermark, but a point of comparison.'[4]

Matching this earlier British example with a later American one we find that the process of change is still continuing in much the same direction. Based mainly on Gallup Poll data R. L. Johnstone reports that in the USA, weekly church attendance has declined slowly but consistently from 1958 to 1971.[4a]

In presenting these testimonies about the decline of formal devotional behaviour in two western communities during this century, far be it from me to make out that those Victorian years were an era of serenity, mental health, and adequate personal care for all,

[4] *Church and People in an Industrial City*, by E. R. Wickham, London, 1957, pp. 167–168.
[4a] R. L. Johnstone: *Religion and Society in Interaction*, New York, 1975, p. 293.

and that with the decline of formal worship there has been a decline in all these good things, a decline attributable to the passing of pious practices. In spite of the many and frequent present-day reports about the shocking incidence of mental illness in our communities, and in spite of the comparative absence of such reports in Victorian times, it is well understood nowadays that we cannot claim to know of a progressive deterioration in mental health during the last hundred years or so. Even if we could agree on what we meant by 'mental health' or by 'mental illness' we could not hope to obtain reliable information on these in respect of the past. The testimony about the decline of religious practices is quoted to show that, even if we take the incidence of mental illness as unchanging today, these practices discharge their function of alleviating, and even of therapy, less and less. Thus the breach presented to the contemporary secular counsellors was conspicuously and invitingly there to be occupied.

Nor is the decline of religious practices the only important change which bears on this matter. We cannot help being impressed by the promptness and thoroughness with which the various secular personal services have put themselves forward to act *in lieu* of the spiritual consultants and guides of former times. If one recalls the crude failing and gross hypocrisies of some rude religiosity in the past, one cannot but consider the secularisation of personal care a major step ahead. But whether it is that or not is not my concern here; the observation has been made only to stress that the present account is not given to add yet one more plaint to the jeremiads about the loss of faith in our times but rather to point to a possibility of its strange recrudescence.

Let us then look at the recorded changes which have taken place before, and side by side with, the arrival of the psychotherapeutic and counselling professions. A comparison of the statistics of twentieth-century Church and medicine in England and Wales suggests that at least some succession in the allotting of duties and responsibilities must have been taking place.

The following figures have been extracted mainly from the 1901, 1951 and 1971 Censuses:

Clerical Personnel in England and Wales

	1901	1951	1971
Clergymen (Church of England)	25,235	16,751	
Roman Catholic Priests	2,849		
Roman Catholic Priests, Monks, Nuns, etc.		17,154	
Ministers, Priests, of other religious bodies	11,572		
Ministers of other religious bodies		9,986	
Missionaries, Scripture Readers, Itinerant Preachers	10,096		
Itinerant Preachers, Scripture Readers, Mission Workers, etc.		7,307	
Monks, Nuns, Sisters of Charity	6,458		
Clerical Personnel			41,140
Total :	56,210	51,198	41,140
Population :	32,527,843	43,757,888	48,894,500
Population per one 'clerical professional' :	579	843	1,188

The number of people per one clerical professional has more than doubled in seventy years.

It would be tempting to simplify matters and conclude that these two tables give an outline of the 'take-over' of personal services by medicine and its ancillaries. That this is not, in fact, an accurate account of what has happened will, I hope, become somewhat clearer as we go along.

The rapid expansion of medical services was, after all, not brought about by the increasing demand for new spiritual counsellors in lieu of the old. The growth in the life sciences, and with it the progress in physical medicine are chiefly responsible for this expansion. Yet the doctors have assumed the functions of secular counsellors, for it seemed easier for them to do this than for others. The doctor has '... very important associations with the realm of

Medical and Paramedical Personnel in England and Wales

	1901	*1951*	*1971*
Physicians, Surgeons, General Practitioners	22,698	42,839	
Midwives	3,055		
Sick Nurses and Invalid Attendants	65,306		
Subordinate Medical Services	4,718		
Trained Nurses and Midwives, Assistant Nurses, and Student Probationers		235,397	
Qualified Medical Practitioners			65,710
Nurses			415,130
Total :	95,777	278,236	480,840
Population per one 'medical and paramedical professional' :	*340*	*157*	*102*

In seventy years the number of people per one medical and paramedical professional has fallen to less than one third.

the sacred', writes Talcott Parsons[5] which would help him to inherit the functions of the clergy. His familiarity with death, his superhuman asexuality and virginity (as fantasied by the patients) when seeing and touching the naked bodies of patients of the opposite sex, his licence to take certain chances with human life, and some other features of his profession certainly contribute to professional *charisma* which will mark him out as a successor to the 'discredited' pastor of earlier times. As science and public health standards have greatly increased the number of medical workers, their relationship of trust with their patients has inevitably extended the opportunities of patients to use these technicians of the body as personal consultants and, indeed, through their dependence on these technicians in times of pain and mortal

---

[5] *The Social System*, London, 1952, p. 445.

anguish they have got used to exacting from them the personal attention which they so much needed. At the same time, the discerning medical man has always known that many an illness of the body is mainly a sickness of the soul, and, therefore, the take-over of counselling by medicine was a natural and spontaneous continuation of an ancient practice. 'An indeterminate number of America's 215,000 nonpsychiatric physicians', writes Jerome D. Frank, 'use psychotherapy with many of their patients, often without recognising it as such.'[6] And, no doubt, the same could be said of Britain's physicians or of physicians in other countries.[7]

But it would be a serious mistake to think that modern secular counselling is an integral part of modern medical practice. There have always been doctors who played well the roles of 'confidential personal adviser', 'moral counsellor', or just simply 'fatherly friend'. The trouble is that, busy as they were with fighting their ultimately losing battles with the frailties of the body, they tended to assume hastily that they could settle the less complicated personal problems by a 'pull yourself together' sort of exhortation and a friendly but firm demeanour.

In fact, doctors are untrained and, therefore, unqualified to render assistance through intimate personal consultation about moral or social problems. To the unreflecting lay person this would come as a surprise; the truth is that those who select young men and women to be trained as doctors neither know what personal qualities make for good counselling nor would they think these qualities to be decisively important in the selection of future workers, at any rate, in medicine.

In their training, medical students do not receive instruction in the principles and techniques of personal counselling : this kind of tuition does not form a normal part of their medical training. Those who are in charge of training doctors today don't seem to regard the skill of counselling as of especial value to medical or

---

[6] *Persuasion and Healing*, London, 1961, p. 11.

[7] In a paper read at a conference on psychotherapy in the Soviet Union (Moscow, 1956) K. I. Platonov said that 'the usual ways of reassurance, encouragement, persuasion, and explanation, so commonly used in medical practice, are, after all, among the essential elements of general psychotherapy. In this sense, *every physician must be a psychotherapist*', and he added that establishing 'a desirable rapport with the patient' and stimulating 'in him a trusting attitude towards the physician', were among the objectives of medical practice. (*Psychotherapy in the Soviet Union*, Ed. by R. Winn, London, 1962, p. 29.) Italics added.

surgical practice. It is easy to find confirmation for this. In a report published by the British Medical Students' Association, for example, we find some evidence that the prevailing attitude to psychological training is negative. Of the 17 medical schools covered by the report 6 indicated that no teaching of normal psychology was given. In the teaching of psychiatry, the number of lectures varied from 7 to 32 and compulsory ward rounds varied from 0 to 16. In 9 out of 17 schools no formal inpatient rounds were compulsory and, with the exception of Sheffield, in no school was attendance as a student in a mental hospital unit compulsory. Needless to say, even these odd lectures in 'normal psychology', a sprinkling of teaching in psychiatry, and some desultory 'ward rounds' do not amount to training in counselling or psychotherapy. By the end of the 1970s every medical school has included the 'behavioural sciences' in its teaching programme yet a training of the physician in counselling his patients has not been appreciably advanced by recent changes.

The plea of *ars longa vita brevis* may have some force here though it almost certainly works in the wrong direction : it would seem that the very practice of physical medicine is seriously impeded by these omissions. On the other hand, one must observe that an intensive study of physical medicine is not always favourable to the fostering of proficiency in the appraisal of human relationships. It is not necessarily an evil that there should be division of labour, and that some should have excellence of material, technical, and theoretical knowledge, and that side by side with them others should have distinguished aptitudes for counselling on personal matters. What is important to reiterate is that medicine is no automatic qualification for counselling and that training in medicine is not so designed as to contribute in any way to the personal, as distinct from the medical, helpfulness of the practitioner.[8]

Clearly, the medical profession, *qua* a profession of physician-technicians of the body, does not seem the obvious secular inheritor of the pastoral function. And I write this not because I am so simple-minded as to believe that the procedures of modern psychiatric

---

[8] 'The model of mutual participation ... is essentially foreign to medicine.' ('A Contribution to the Philosophy of Medicine', by T. S. Szász and M. H. Hollender, *A.M.A. Archives of Internal Medicine*, May 1956, Vol. 97, pp. 585–592.) This is one of several reasons why the role of physician and the role of counsellor may be incompatible.

counselling have ever been better understood by the clergy than by the materialistically oriented physician. The simple truth is that counselling skill does not presuppose medical training and that the emotional investment necessary for a good many specialisations of that training would hamper the development of a skill in counselling.

Both church and medicine are still here with us to contribute in the work of personal help. The doctor's clinical mentality, scientific training, and his dispassionate acceptance of all that is human compares favourably with the fervently judgmental attitudes of the pastoral counsellor; on the other hand, there are some momentous advantages on the side of the pastoral counsellor as well. Yet intellectuals of the sceptical age are unable to accept these advantages, and intellectuals of the psychoanalytical age are understandably unwilling to yield authority over behaviour to the practitioners of physical medicine. The contemporary intellectual, attracted by a vocation of counselling, will assume, rightly or wrongly, that whilst in the past the clergy and the doctors did all the counselling, today they have become laymen who occasionally dabble in a technique in which they have received no training and hold no qualification.

And so the conditions necessary for a new social function, a secular and professional expertise, to come into being have been given. Today, those who ardently care for the betterment of man's condition express themselves in sustained professional caring for others without much reference either to God or to the human body. Let us now see in more concrete terms who these people are.

In trying to list the professions of counselling I cannot hope to realise perfect fairness and accuracy. Some may be included unjustifiably, especially when the counselling function is not obviously their principal function. Then again others may be omitted because of my ignorance of their actual contribution to counselling. And so I do not claim that my enumeration is exhaustive; its purpose is not to present a definitive inventory but to illustrate a feature of a major social change.

The first of these counsellors is the modern *psychiatrist*. Though there used to be 'alienists' in the nineteenth century, they were mainly tied down with the institutional care of the functional and organic psychoses, and their treatment of the neuroses comprised an assortment of blind techniques, exhortations, and *placebos*, most of which have now been completely discredited. Modern psychiatrists are medically qualified people who, in Britain, have gone through a three years' postgraduate training in psychological medicine and hold a Diploma of Psychological Medicine or some equivalent qualification. It is not a required part of their training that they systematically master a skill of counselling or a technique of psychotherapy. It is certainly not required that they submit themselves to a personal psychotherapy or analysis, or even to a thorough personality examination *before* admission to training, so as to establish whether on personality grounds they would be suitable to be entrusted with prolonged, deep-probing, and self-involving psychotherapeutic relationships with patients. Many psychiatrists voluntarily seek some sort of special training in psychotherapy, having spontaneously realised the limitations of their formal qualifications, but the majority freely engage in all forms of counselling and psychotherapeutic procedures for which they have not received any systematic training, and for which they may not be very well suited on personality grounds.

It is difficult to obtain accurate information on the number of qualified psychiatrists in Britain, but membership figures of The Royal Medico-Psychological Association may be a helpful indicator of the probable size of this subgroup of counsellors :

Membership of The Royal Medico-Psychological Association (1910–1961) [9]
and of the Royal College of Psychiatrists (1977):

Year:	No. of Members:
1910	722
1920	661
1930	819
1940	1,053
1950	1,221
1960	1,789
1961	1,920 (approximately)
1977	4,600[9a]

There are a small number of qualified psychiatrists who do not choose to be members of the Association, and the above figures include some relatively junior-grade doctors, who are in training,

[9] These figures were kindly supplied to me by Dr. A. B. Monroe.
[9a] Discounting about 1,000 overseas members from the total of 5,600.

and have not yet obtained their qualifications. 'Although there is bound to be an element of guess work,' writes Dr. A. B. Monroe, General Secretary of the Association, 'you would not be far wrong if you took the membership of the Association during the various decades as constituting between 80 per cent and 90 per cent of the qualified psychiatrists in the country at a given time. This is likely to be an underestimate rather than an overestimate.'[10] It is well known that the clinical orientation of this group is extremely varied and that there are many among them who would certainly refuse to be described as 'psychotherapists'. A good many special-ise in physical methods of treatment, in administrative manage-ment of institutions, and many of those who engage in psychologi-cal therapy of one type or another will also combine psycho-therapy with physical treatment of several kinds. Only a minority will devote most of their professional time to psychotherapy proper without the use of physical aids. According to one very recent American study,[11] in which the incidence of psychotherapeutic orientation of psychiatrists was assessed, it was found that 70 per cent were in favour of psychotherapeutic methods and techniques, 23 per cent had a definite somatotherapeutic orientation, and 7 per cent were for sociotherapeutic techniques. Of course, these ideological orientations do not necessarily mean that the psychia-trists in this sample had the opportunity to practise the techniques and methods they preferred. In Britain, however, one's impression is that the somatotherapeutic orientation is predominant. Yet these complications do not invalidate the procedure I have adopted : the subgroup is not only licensed to practise counselling but is indeed the only counselling subgroup which enjoys con-siderable legal protection in its counselling practice, and is recog-nised by public opinion as so licensed.

Then there is the very slowly growing number of *psycho-analysts*, lay or medically trained, a number of whom are formally qualified in psychiatry as well. *The International Journal of Psychoanalysis*, in a roster published in 1962,[12] lists 103 'Members' and 155 'Associate Members' of the British Psycho-Analytical

[10] Private communication from Dr. A. B. Monroe.
[11] 'A Study of Sociotherapeutically Oriented Psychiatrists', by D. Ehrlich and M. Sabshin, *American Journal of Orthopsychiatry*, April 1964, Vol. XXXIV, No. 3, pp. 469–480.
[12] November-December 1962, Vol. XLIII, Part 6.

Society. One ought to qualify this by mentioning that no fewer than 14 of the members and 35 of the associate members lived outside Britain. There were also some 58 *child therapists* trained by the Anna Freud centre, The Hampstead Child-Therapy Course and Clinic,[13] as well as 28 trained by the Tavistock Clinic in London, and so in all there were approximately 295 psychoanalysts practising in Britain then. Some 14 years later, in 1976, the total membership of the British Psycho-Analytical Society was 353.[13a]

It would be a mistake to underestimate the psychoanalysts' importance for in spite of their comparatively small number, the influence on clinical thinking and on general counselling practice exerted by this highly trained group is considerable. The authority of this group is much enhanced by the stringent admission requirements for training, the intensive personal analysis required as part of the psychoanalytic training, the extensive literary activities and international links of the psychoanalytic profession, as well as by the professional services rendered to certain numbers of highly placed patients, to artistic, literary, and scientific leaders. The papers and books written by psychoanalysts are read by a large number of those who belong to other counselling professions, and fully qualified analysts are in constant demand as lecturers and tutors in schools of psychiatry, of social work, and in other academic and professional training institutions. These activities of the psychoanalytical *élite* spread their therapeutic ideology, even though much of what they teach is eclectically assimilated in all conceivable combinations of dynamic theory and behaviouristic conceptualisation. Yet the framework remains broadly Freudian, and the recent theoretical disagreements have not in fact produced an organisational schism, nor are the disagreements especially important in the context of the present book. The separateness of the practitioners applying rival theories will not complicate matters in a sociological study of their ideological influence.

Counsellors who regard themselves as C. G. Jung's followers are certainly to be included here. 'The Society of Analytical Psychology Ltd.', the association of *Jungian analysts* in Britain, has at

[13] Based on private communications from Miss Ruth Thomas, Course Tutor, and from Mrs. R. Szur, Honorary Secretary of the Association of Child Psychotherapists.
[13a] Cf. *Report* of the British Psycho-Analytical Society and the Institute of Psycho-Analysis, 30 June 1976.

present 67 members only[14] and its therapeutic and clinical philosophy is not sufficiently at variance with that of the dominant Freudian group to modify the moral and sociological opinion generally held by counsellors of all kinds on the betterment of man's condition. The therapeutic ideology which I will analyse at some length is, if anything, even more characteristic of Jungian thinking than it is of Freudian thinking.

I have not been able to discover more than five Adlerian 'Individual psychologists' in Britain, but I have been able to find another 19 *child psychotherapists* by 1965 and another 15 by 1977 trained and qualified by 'The Children's Centre, The Institute of Child Psychology Ltd.' (Founded by Dr. Margaret Lowenfeld).[15] Finally, according to the Bulletin of 'The Association of Psychotherapists', founded in 1951, a collection of partly Rogerian but mainly eclectic workers function as 'psychotherapists' with an assortment of qualifications, one of which is training analysis of a similarly eclectic and unspecified kind. According to this Bulletin,[16] there were approximately 30 full members recognised by this Association as 'psychotherapists' by 1961 and 165 by 1977. A small number of these were also members of older and more explicitly 'denominational' (e.g. Jungian) groups. These splinter subgroups do not affect the reasonably homogeneous ideology of the counsellors, and merely add further numbers to the better-known major subgroups.

The next subgroup of counsellors consists of those *psychologists* who in Britain are employed in the National Health Service; it is in this framework, as well as in the child guidance services of local authorities, that psychologists are more likely to engage in counselling practices than when they are otherwise employed. Of these the total number employed in the National Health Service in 1960 was 223[17] and in 1975, 690. During recent years the number of educational psychologists has grown considerably. Their association's membership has risen to 703, a figure which does not include

---

[14] Based on private communication from Dr. G. Stewart Prince of the Society of Analytical Psychology, London.
[15] Based on private communication from Mrs. K. E. Curling, Secretary of the Institute.
[16] Bulletin No. 3, London, 1961, and also private communication from the Secretary, Mrs. A. P. de Berker and her successor, Mrs. J. Lawrence.
[17] 'Interim List of Psychologists in The National Health Service as at 1.12.59.' Issued by the British Psychological Society. May 1960, and also information received from the Dept. of Health and Social Security in 1977.

all those who practise. A conservative estimate of the total in 1977 is nearer to 800.[17a] It is understood, of course, that the majority of these psychologists work most of their time as diagnosticians and assessors as well as research personnel, and are not intensively used as psychotherapists or counsellors.

Yet, employed in local authority departments, schools, hospitals and child guidance clinics, the psychologist is often used as a therapist, especially in the absence of a formally qualified psycho-therapist or child-therapist. With the connivance of the clinical director or consultant, who is usually a psychiatrist, the clinical psychologists often 'treat' or 'counsel', using techniques which are congenial to them, often eclectically adapting what they have read, heard of, or seen done in the clinical setting around them. In addition to clinical work, psychologists sometimes function as 'consultants' in industry, but this role contains elements of a much less personal and rather more administrative and technological nature.

Apart from the professional groups already listed there are some others, marginally placed between the mental health and education services, such as, for example, teachers in schools for maladjusted children, and others. In the work of these, however, the thera-peutic and paedagogical elements are too intimately mixed for us to regard them as 'counsellors', but they are important ancillaries to the counsellors in clinical and local authority employment. According to List 42 issued by the Ministry of Education in 1956 (and subsequently amended up to 1958) there were 37 boarding schools, 78 boarding schools and 16 non-maintained schools for maladjusted children.[17b] According to the June 1960 membership schools, 78[17b] boarding schools and 16 non-maintained schools for maladjusted children. According to the June 1960 membership list of the Association of Workers for Maladjusted Children, the Association had 344 members, heads of schools, teachers, and some others, most of whom had opportunities of engaging in counselling of some kind.[18] In 1975 there were 1,062 full-time

---

[17a] From information supplied by the Hon. Secretary of the Association, Mrs J. Currie.

[17b] *Statistics of Education*, HMSO, January 1975.

[18] The initial membership of this Association was 40 in 1951. (From information supplied to me by the Hon. Secretary of the Association, Mr. O. L. Shaw.)

teachers in these schools.[18a] Staffs of approved schools and of prisons may also be mentioned but in these cases, more often than not, counselling activity (if it can be called that) is brief, desultory, and largely inexpert. The situation is rather similar for the National Assistance Board officers and Ministry of Labour officers who, when dealing with the workshy, for example, may not be allowed to let themselves be guided by counselling conciliatoriness, but are expected to apply the statutes with some measure of disciplinary severity. Though there are some signs that staffs of penal institutions and welfare officials dispensing material aid are increasingly influenced by a counselling mentality, these workers are certainly not counsellors in the sense of this book.

By far the largest group of counsellors, with a constantly increasing trained membership, is that of *social workers*. These, through their many specialisations and divisions of function, somehow fragment their impression of size, power and ubiquity. After all, a probation officer is not normally called by his clients a 'social worker', nor is the almoner so addressed by the patients, in spite of the recently made energetic attempts at replacing the feudal term by 'medical social worker'. Because of their association with specific services, courts, general hospitals, local authority child care departments, and so on, lay public opinion tends to think of them as separate professional categories with fundamentally different theoretical and practical preoccupations. Also, the practical issues involved in dealing with problems in these various areas of work seem to have encouraged people to think less of their advising, guiding, and counselling functions, and more of their paramedical, statutory, or other administrative specialities. Naturally, almoners, probation officers, school attendance officers, and so on, have many duties other than personal guidance and counselling, and the public has been allowed to continue believing that their work in the main consists in some impersonal though good-natured service in some special field of health or welfare administration. Most people would have found it difficult to believe that personal consultation on motives and feelings must now be made available on such a vast scale to such a large number of people. To have to concede the universality of the need for this sort of service is to have to face the precariousness of one's own adjustment. Not unexpectedly, there is no

[18a] *Ibid.*

shortage of critical and impatient comment. The 'no-nonsense' objectors are often heard describing the counsellor's deep concerns with personality problems as morbid preoccupations, which—the objectors say—also happen to result in the pampering of generally inadequate people. According to the objectors, all that we owe people is a square meal and a square deal. Such a view conveniently objectifies the human problems, so that the problems may look both manageable and, therefore, less disturbing. Some of the public, and even the better informed, have been led to think of social workers as publicly provided friendly officials, who in some inexplicable way are qualified to dispense generous doses of often unsolicited common sense to people in some sort of trouble or difficulty. But however confused the public image of the social worker, workers continue to recognise what is generic in the counselling functions in different areas where varying specialist skills are also required.

The Census report of '51 and '71 state that there were 22,151 and 61,240 'Social Welfare Workers' in Britain, but it is impossible to say what categories of social workers were included, and what other occupations were also included which should have been differently classified. Approaching the matter from the other side, from the side of the professional associations of social work, the membership lists yield the following much smaller numbers:

SOCIAL WORKERS IN BRITAIN

Census totals:	*1951*	*1971*
	22,151	61,240

Membership of Professional Associations in Social Work in Britain

Name of Association	*approximate number of members*	
	1961	*1977 (March)*
Institute of Almoners	1,200	
National Association of Probation Officers	1,500	3,850
Association of Psychiatric Social Workers	846	
Association of Child Care Workers	1,000	
Association of General and Family Case Workers	120	
Association of L.C.C. Children's Care Organisers	120	
Association of Social Workers	600	10,035
Totals:	5,386	13,885

These totals are a great deal smaller than the figures reported in the Censuses, and they comprise a miscellaneous assortment of training levels and counselling expertise. In fact, probably no more than approximately half of the 1961 members could be described as having received systematic training in counselling or in what social workers call 'social casework'. However, a larger number of the 1977 members have received some training in counselling. Almost all of the others in the Census totals are known to engage in social casework from time to time, or even most of the time, without being especially trained and qualified to do so.

It appears then that in Britain and in the United States the total number of those who are professionally called upon and, indeed, are explicitly qualified to give personal service of a psychological nature to others, that is the number of *counsellors*—excluding members of the clergy and of medicine, other than psychiatrists— is approximately the following:

I. An Estimate of the Number of Professional Counsellors in Practice in Britain

	(around 1960)	(around 1976)
Psychiatrists	2,400 [19]	4,600
Psychotherapists	400 [20]	550
Psychologists	150 [21]	1,500
Counsellors		800
Social Caseworkers	2,700 [22]	13,900
Totals:	5,650	21,350

[19] Taking the 1961 membership of the Royal Medico-Psychological Association as 80 per cent of the total number of psychiatrists.

[20] Includes all psychotherapists with known affiliation to professional associations.

[21] An estimate of the number of psychologists engaged in some counselling practice.

[22] See above: approximately half the total of the previous list.

II. An Estimate of the Number of Professional Counsellors in Practice in the United States:

	(around 1960)[27a]	(around 1976)[27b]
Psychiatrists	11,637 [23]	22,700
Psychotherapists	1,540 [24]	3,000
Psychologists	2,412 [25]	16,472
'Counselors'	10,000 [26]	50,500[27c]
Social Workers	45,000 [27]	55,000
Totals:	70,589	147,672

[23] Based on private communication from R. F. Lockman, Director, Manpower Department, American Psychiatric Association.

[24] Based on the Roster of Members of American Psychoanalytical societies (*International Journal of Psychoanalysis*, November-December 1962, Vol. XLIII, Part 6) which lists 1,540 full members and associate members. No doubt several of these are also members of the American Psychiatric Association, and so, to avoid counting some counsellors twice this figure should be reduced. At the same time, according to private information from Professor H. L. Ansbacher, there are 113 Adlerian therapists and according to similar information from the Secretary of the New York Institute of the C. G. Jung Foundation for Analytical Psychology there are 75 Jungian therapists in the United States. In addition to these there must be others practising Rogerian, Rankian, Reichian, or other psychotherapy not yet included, and therefore, I have decided to leave the figure of 1,540 unchanged.

[25] Based on the National Science Foundation: *American Science Manpower Employment and Other Characteristics 1954/1955*, Washington, 1959. The total number of psychologists is given here as 10,163 of whom 2,412 are stated to be employed in counselling work.

[26] E. J. Shoben writes, 'In 1960, 30,000 persons were concerned with "scheduled guidance activities" in secondary schools across the nation, (U.S.) although only about one-third of them were functioning as full-time guidance personnel.' ('Guidance: Remedial Function or Social Reconstruction?' *Harvard Educational Review*, 1962, Vol. XXXII, No. 4.) Consequently I included only 10,000 of these in the above list.

[27] This estimate is based on Gordon Hamilton: 'Helping People—The Growth of a Profession' in *Social Work as Human Relations* (New York, 1949, p. 14), and being eleven years old 'around 1960' it is an underestimate. Gordon Hamilton wrote there: 'It is estimated that there are somewhere between one hundred thousand and one hundred and seventy-five thousand persons in social work positions in this country (U.S.); of these, about fifteen thousand have completed the appropriate graduate training, and about thirty thousand more have had only one year professional training.' Only these last two categories appear in the above list.

[27a] Based mainly on annual reports of professional associations.

[27b] Same as [27a] but in the case of U.S. Psychologists I have included only 'Fellows' and 'Members' of ten divisions (out of some 33).

[27c] This includes *all* counsellors not only those in secondary schools. Cf.: C. G. Wrenn, *The World of the Contemporary Counsellors*, Boston, 1973. p. 250.

This, in Britain and in the United States, is the moral-cultural *élite* whose far-reaching influence on the ideological trends of our times has made me enquire into the philosophical and moral premises of their theory and practice. These premises are constantly being reviewed by the more reflective and literate members of this multifarious collection of counselling subgroups. Their learned papers and case studies appear in their professional journals, and their longer discourses are frequently put out in book form. This is an understandably introspective professional *élite*, strongly assisted by self-criticism against surprise attacks. But self-searching does not weaken this subculture's cohesion or the intimateness of its internal communications. Most of this communication is predominantly psychoanalytical in its general principles and orientation, though most of it is not written by the qualified psychoanalysts themselves. The rank and file of the counsellors, those who are not in the vanguard of original writing or associational activity, readily respond to this leadership by the writers and communicators, and so both their practice, and their thinking about their practice, are permeated and guided by the notions and interpretations of their more articulate and communicative colleagues.

It is important for me to draw attention to the broad unanimity of opinion prevailing here—in spite of the wide variety of social statuses involved—in order to underline the wide applicability of the conclusions I may be able to reach about the character of the counsellor's creed and canons. I intend to document my portrait of the counselling ideology—shared by all, from the medically trained psychiatrist to the social caseworker—by citing admissions, whether inadvertent or not, from the literature of counselling of all kinds, and I justify this method of surveying this ideology by showing, as often as it is possible, the similarity of views held by counsellors working on different levels.

In view of their comparatively small total numbers, the 'coming of the counsellors' may not seem so momentous an event after all. I have already stressed that the influence of this professional group is far greater than their numbers. But there is another reason for regarding the emergence of the counselling function as an instance of major social change. The concluding paragraphs of this chapter will try to justify this belief.

Until recently, we have considered science, technology, and the race for more sophisticated material comforts as activities especially characteristic of the western world. The rockets which soared above Asiatic Russia sending one Vostok after another into orbit and the transistor sets marked 'Made in Japan' have all but put paid to this western pre-eminence. It seems to me that the remaining characteristic pursuit of the western cultural area in the mid-twentieth century, as yet unmatched by anything like it elsewhere, is its secularised and institutionalised philanthropy and personal care, which have managed to fuse in themselves its scientific and technological achievements with its unique tradition of Christian neighbourly service, and with its more recent secular morality of socialistic community responsibilities and community care. The social scientific philanthropism of the counsellor would seem to have the advantage that it could be accommodated by all reasonably consolidated ideological systems. One might predict that, with its increasing prosperity, even the Soviet Union would have to follow some western counselling practices by adapting them to her needs. So long as the faith of the counsellors remains implicit and inarticulate, there appear to be few obstacles to this.

As the material standards of civilisation continue to rise, so a higher standard of living will be expressed in terms of a more rapid increase in new *services* rather than goods. It is already exciting to watch the luxury trades trying to insinuate needs in people and finding that, at least with some of the more affluent, there is a saturation point beyond which a healthy covetousness will refuse to grow. There may well come a time, possibly sooner than we dare hope, when increments in our welfare will consist mostly, and eventually almost entirely, in services rather than goods, and especially in personal services of the counselling type rather than in material amenities. A comparison of tables I and II on pp. 46 and 47 may lend some weight to this prediction. Taking the 1960 U.K. population as 51 million and that of the U.S. as 179 million, the latter being almost exactly three and a half times the former, I multiplied the total number of British counsellors by three and a half so that the two totals should be comparable. Accordingly, the two totals would be:

U.K.	U.S.
19,775	70,789

And so even after this adjustment the United States still had approximately three and a half times as many professional counsellors in the field than Britain. Taking the population of the U.K.

'around 1976' as 56 million and that of the USA as 211 million, the latter being nearly three and three-quarters times the former, I multiplied the total number of British counsellors by this amount so that the two totals should be comparable. Accordingly, the two totals would be 16 years after the first:

U.K.	U.S.
80,063	147,672

And so, in a matter of 16 years the rapid development of counselling services in impoverished Britain reduced the gap between the two figures so that the U.S. number is less than twice the British figure. Even this is an overestimate of the gap because having included a much wider group of 'counselors' in the American figure in 1976 than in 1960 the convergence of the two numbers ought to be regarded as even more marked than my figures would show. Although this kind of comparison raises interesting issues we shall not pursue these here.

In a way, to provide the wherewithal of material comfort—from washing machines to television sets and from family cars to modern housing—we do not require a great deal more new technology. We require mainly good sense and some decades of peace to equip all the homes from China to Ghana, and to let people be persuaded by their new comforts and knowledge of their value to resist a strangulating procreative excess.

But to attend to those whose marital, parental, or filial relationships, or other human ties are harrowingly disturbed, and to those who are in fear or pain as a result, we do require a *new* knowhow, or, at least, a rapid refinement and expansion of existing techniques. In the long run our standards of physical amenities grow, more and more honour and prestige, more and more recognition and love, will go to those who will be able to supply the vital non-material amenities and comforts of existence. Consequently, more and more able and ambitious men and women will seek qualification and employment in the counselling services and more and more of the counselling morality and etiquette will be disseminated to become an essential part of society's morals and conventions. Leadership will go to those who think of new and more effective ways of reducing anguish without at the same time reducing alertness. There is every reason to believe that the scope and influence of the counselling professions will become progressively larger and larger as material needs are met. It is certainly not to be feared that in our opulence we shall be more callously self-indulgent and oblivious of others than we were when we used to be full of bitterness and righteous protest.

These preoccupations seem to focus on the cultivation of the social and clinical sciences as the main avenues towards future betterment. Yet preoccupations with the condition of our fellow men are also *concerns*, and indeed ardent moral involvements, no matter how apparently intellectualised and restrained they are. It is then perhaps premature to speak of the *End of Ideology*[28], and more to the point to examine the interesting process of transvaluation in our social concerns. It is now actually being understood— even in the U.S.S.R.—that there is no inevitable geographical proximity between the Kingdom of God and the Land of Milk and Honey, no inevitable negative correlation between the level of prosperity and the number and severity of psychoneurotic symptoms. One ought to add to this that the more scrupulously a society realises an equality of opportunity the more it deprives its failures of the excuse that 'the cards have been stacked against me', and its brilliant deviates of the opportunity to act in rebelliously creative ways.

Were it not for the 'coming of the counsellors' we might well complain of 'ideological sterility' in our times, as some of our young writers do.[29] As it is, we are now confronted with a new system of implicit and explicit doctrines exerting considerable influence on the mode of our social actions. The full meaning of these doctrines must now be further examined if the practice, which they guide and inspire, and if the moral climate of our culture, to which they substantially contribute, are to be better understood. In the following sections the analysis of these latent doctrines will be documented from the authoritative statements of the practitioners themselves. The sections are devoted to separate themes which closely interlink and cohere in a unified world view. The contours of this world-view have already been sketched; the following is hoped to provide a map of the interior of this world with, no doubt, a good many spots in between still marked 'unknown'.

[28] By Daniel Bell, Free Press, Glencoe, 1960.
[29] Cf. *The Glittering Coffin*, by Dennis Potter, London, 1960, pp. 86–89.

CHAPTER THREE

The Elements of the Counsellor's Faith

The Counsellor's Love as Therapeutic Skill

Even at the beginning of modern psychoanalysis Sandor Ferenczi, one of the most able of Freud's followers, and one of the earliest supporters, begán to advocate a more 'active' interventionist treatment of the patient than the classical Freudian method allowed.[1] He pleaded that more indulgence in the patient's need for love was essential to his successful treatment. It was Ferenczi who, towards the end of his career, began to teach that the 'indispensable healing power in the therapeutic gift is love'[2], and that 'psychoanalytic treatment... should take place as a natural, concerned, personal relationship, a part of life, not something removed from the experience of everyday living'.[3] Indeed he is quoted as saying that 'psychoanalytic "cure" is in direct proportion to the cherishing love given by the psychoanalyst to the patient.'[4] Freud regarded Ferenczi's deviation as wrong and dangerous. The complete break between the two was averted because of Ferenczi's gentle and pliable personality and, of course, because of his death in 1933. Since then the advocacy of the 'therapeutic gift of love' has never been entirely in abeyance. Yet it is only recently that the compelling notion is showing signs of absorbing more of the counsellor's naive and tender attention than scientific psychoanalysis could justify.

[1] 'Further Development of an Active Therapy in Psychoanalysis' (1920) in *Further Contributions to the Theory and Technique of Psychoanalysis*, by Sandor Ferenczi, London, 1950.
[2] *The Leaven of Love*, by Izette de Forest, London, 1956, p. 6.
[3] *Ibid.*, p. 8.
[4] *Ibid.*, p. 15. Also cf. several chapters in *Final Contributions to Problems and Methods of Psychoanalysis*, by Sandor Ferenczi, London, 1955.

I am referring to the comparatively new development in the counsellor's attitude towards some deeply disturbed cases, and also to the way this attitude is now being explicitly extended to all cases. We now hear, with increasing frequency, that very disturbed patients first need love and unqualified solicitousness *before* they can be approached analytically and interpretively. The premise is that these patients have suffered intense initial material deprivation and that before some restitution of this, administered by the deliberate offer of parental protectiveness and unconditional acceptance, they will not be able to respond to 'uncovering' psychotherapy at all. This kind of management of patients was not at first thought of as psychotherapy, but rather as a preamble or introduction to psychotherapy. But now, the provisional orientation is being extended beyond this and being 'supportive' has now become a normal part of psychotherapy.[5] The nature and significance of these changes can be better seen in the light of examples.

D. W. Winnicott holds that 'all those patients whose analyses must deal with the early stages of emotional development before and up to the establishment of the personality as an entity must be mainly 'managed' and not 'analysed'.[6] In Winnicott's view, this method is appropriate in dealing with regressed and psychotic patients whose problems are pre-Oedipal in origin and who crave *mothering* above all. Guntrip very rightly points out that, as the roots of the psychoneuroses always reach back to the pre-Oedipal history of the individual, so 'the line of demarcation Winnicott draws between the management for the psychotic and psychoanalysis for the psychoneurotic breaks down. The position that seems to be emerging is that, at all stages, psychotherapy has to be an appropriate mixture of mothering (management) and analysis (giving insight). The deeper the level on which treatment has to operate, the greater the patient's need for the mothering he failed to obtain'.[7]

The deprivation originally suffered by the patient is a deprivation of mothering, a deprivation of primal, absolute, and unconditional loving. Helene Deutsch explains, for example, that the unmarried mother's demand for a child is often a sign of deprivation

[5] Cf. *Psychotherapy of Chronic Schizophrenic Patients*, Ed. by C. Whitaker, London, 1956, p. 144.
[6] *Collected Papers: Through Paediatrics to Psychoanalysis*, London, 1958, p. 279.
[7] *Personality Structure and Human Interaction*, by H. Guntrip, London, 1961, p. 413.

in her own childhood, and observes, 'Every experienced psychiatrist and social worker knows in such a case of compulsory motherhood that she can often save the girl by being a substitute mother to her.'[8] The relative frequency of cases in which this interpretation may be valid is not at issue here, but rather that a prescription for treatment of this very characteristic kind is tried on along with other procedures even when, in a certain case, this interpretation is certainly not the dominant one. The decisiveness of this line of approach is vividly conveyed by S. G. Margolin who actually recommends 'literally infantilising the patient'.[9] A similar point is made by M. M. Gill who speaks of the psychoanalytic technique 'exerting a nonspecific, steady, unremitting regressive pressure';[10] or by I. Macalpine in whose opinion 'psychoanalytic technique creates an infantile setting', to which 'the analysand—if he is analysable—has to adapt, albeit by regression'.[11] A good many other counsellors, as we shall see, enjoin their colleagues to produce a facsimile of this primal and unconditional loving for the benefit of the patient. Naturally, the complexities of the ego-reinforcing love of the counsellor would be oversimplified if we were to understand that *all* that happens in counselling of this kind is the belated, deliberate, and studied mothering of a regressed patient. The crux of the matter is that love is expressed in all counselling; the counsellors now say, that it must be expressed, if counselling is to make a difference to the patient. This view is in keeping with Ferenczi's doctrine that 'the physician's love heals the patient', and with Ian D. Suttie's assessment of counselling as a 'cure by love'.[12] The new emphasis consists in the definition of this therapeutic love as *mothering* or *parental loving*.

The most vivid illustrations of this synthetic parental loving come from child-therapy. Writing about group work with children under the age of seven, and referring to one of her child-patients, Madge Hamilton, a psychiatric social worker, informs us casually, '... several times I lifted him over the threshold, kissing him as I

8 *The Psychology of Women*, London, 1947, Vol. II, p. 300.
9 *Psychoanalysis and Human Values*, Ed. by J. H. Masserman, New York, 1960, p. 67.
10 'Psychoanalysis and Exploratory Psychotherapy', *Journal of The American Psychoanalytical Association*, 1954, Vol. II, pp. 771–797.
11 'The Development of the Transference', *Psychoanalytic Quarterly*, 1950, Vol. XIX, pp. 501–539.
12 *The Origins of Love and Hate*, London, 1936, Chapter 14.

did so in order to temper the rejection'.[13] Episodes, such as this, are frequently reported in the literature. A child care officer's report about a ten-year-old girl, in serious difficulties in her foster-home, contains the following passage, 'I said that I expected she was feeling a bit sad. She nodded and did not protest when I put my arm around her and cuddled her.'[14] An entirely legitimate and probably appropriate method of approach but it is not the product of 'skill', of technical mastery, or of deliberate and calculating tactic, for were it either it would be unskilful, it would lack mastery, it would be bad tactic. But on this matter I shall write more later.

In another study, a relationship, not unlike this one, is described by a social caseworker. She reports her treatment of an eight-year-old girl who needed preparing for a surgical repair of her cleft lip and palate. The caseworker visited the child in hospital on many occasions, and obviously entered into a 'warm, giving, and purposeful' relationship with the child. In reading her account one cannot help noticing the frank mutuality which the two must have experienced. For example, 'in visits during Sue's first few days in the hospital, our time was spent having fun and doing things together so that we could get to know each other'.[15] Loving this child in her anxiety about the operation and in her separation from her family is the vital part of the therapy, without which the conversational gambits tried by this worker would have missed their mark.

But it is not only with children that love, as an essential requisite of therapy, is identified. Throughout the counselling professions the green light for a patient and loving parental care, as a psychotherapeutic *technical* device, has now been given.

At the time of writing this chapter I came across an article by M. L. Sheppard on 'Casework as Friendship: A Long Term Contact With a Paranoid Lady'[16] Long term indeed! Ten years of unsparing friendship between caseworker and client, floral tributes brought along personally to the funeral of client's husband, taking client out to lunches, gifts and presents, and every sign of warm

---

[13] *Sociological Review Monograph*, No. 6, 'The Canford Families', Keele, 1962.
[14] 'The Understanding Caseworker', by Olive Stevenson, *New Society*, 1 August, 1963.
[15] 'Helping a Child Adapt to Stress, the Use of Ego Psychology in Casework', by A. K. Lloyd, *The Social Service Review*, 1957, Vol. XXXI, No. 1, pp. 11–21.
[16] *The British Journal of Psychiatric Social Work*, 1964, Vol. VII, No. 4, pp. 173–182.

and sustained mutuality. 'At first she received my gifts to her with worry,' Sheppard writes, 'and ashamed looking away; but now she can take, and when I leave her nowadays she kisses me on the cheek, as if I was a younger relative, while I return her kiss.' Sheppard tells us that over a period of ten years, 'I did not probe into her history: in fact I still do not know her background history'. And all this total personal attention is given with the explicit renunciation of 'demanding' 'anything of the client' or 'feeling' that 'we have a "right" to return of affection or reciprocal behaviour which we might still expect from our friend'.

Mrs. E. E. Irvine, an experienced and thoughtful psychiatric social worker and theoretician, whose approach to her work is entirely psychoanalytical, writes that it is appropriate for the social caseworker to play a parental role and that 'the worker's own feeling response is an essential part of the help she gives to the client'.[17] This prescribing of parental love is no longer that special concession to some few intractable clinical cases Winnicott had in mind at first, but is now to be embodied in the work code of counselling as a vital part of the procedure. 'The worker will have to function as the "good parent" does,' T. A. Ratcliffe, a psychiatrist, tells caseworkers in his address to one of their meetings,[18] evidently advocating a precept to which he himself readily subscribes in his own practice. That the ideal of the counsellor's 'good parenthood' is not entirely new is so well brought out by Mrs. E. E. Irvine that I should like to cite it here in full :

'Octavia Hill, for instance, had the warmest maternal feelings for her clients, and never went to the country without bringing back innumerable bunches of flowers for her enormous family. She offered to a very deprived and rejected social group a relationship in which they could respond to her emotional warmth, learn to identify with her courage and self-confidence, and experience her genuine appreciation of their own capacity for response and self-help. Such attitudes seem to have worked remarkable changes in numbers of clients. They were not, however, easy to maintain; the early literature of social work

[17] 'Transference and Reality in the Casework Relationship', *The British Journal of Psychiatric Social Work*, 1956, Vol. III, No. 4, pp. 15–24.
[18] 'Relationship Therapy and Casework', *The British Journal of Psychiatric Social Work*, 1959, Vol. V, No. 1, pp. 4–9.

contains much evidence of the struggle to walk this way between the Scylla of over-indulgence (based on guilt towards the deprived and outcast) and the Charybdis of self-righteous contempt for the "undeserving" (based on paranoid anxieties about the danger of insatiable exploitation by these damaged clients).'[19]

The moral inspiration of this kind of writing is so much the greater as it is offered with self-denying modesty. There is no solemnity, pomp, or fuss about lofty moral purposes. Yet even if 'courage' and 'self-confidence' are also provided their unflattering psychoanalytical tabs, the writer herself could not want us to think that these tabs bear the full account of the substance of these virtues. Mrs. Irvine's obvious admiration for Octavia Hill's motherly compassion would simply collapse but for Mrs. Irvine's faith in values not analysable in terms of the theory which serves as a basis of her thinking. Moreover, sailing without a goal between Scylla and Charybdis would be pointless, for in Montaigne's words, 'no wind makes for him that had no intended port to sail unto'. The distant-looking aspiration of the counsellor and her fine equilibrating act has an avowed purpose, however mute the avowal and however unassuming the witness. Those of us who study reports such as Mrs. Irvine's—and there are countless other reports—are strongly inclined to think that *according to the counsellor* the avowal is the more potent factor of her helpfulness, and that it carries more therapeutic weight than her theory or technology. Also, the whole issue of training counsellors is deeply affected by the way we construe this issue, for the training of a counsellor in theory and technology may elicit this avowal or even enrich it, but training will not create it. The notions of kissing a child, or embracing him, or bringing people flowers, are simply not associated with the notion of training or skill. Certainly, kissing may be therapeutic, and this has not altogether escaped our attention; yet we might find it difficult, and perhaps not entirely wise, to include tuition, in its theory and practice, in the training of counsellors.

Writing about the psychotherapy of the schizophrenic, A. Burton declares that in the 'Therapeutic Encounter' only the young or the saints (*sic*) are capable of total commitment and warns that those who are weary should not try shamming it. 'In such an

[19] *Loc. cit.*

encounter...' Burton warns, 'all artifice is valueless and the playing of roles counterindicated.'[20] And yet, paradoxically, he does seem to prescribe what E. H. Erskine calls 'basic trust' and a kind of relationship which is like 'a marriage, with all the overtones which this implies but with the sexual aspects confined to fantasy. Female schizophrenics come to therapy wearing their wedding rings anew, or shift them from the right to the left hand and back, depending on the current status of the marriage.'[21] One ought to add that all this 'love of the most unvarnished order'[22] must not appear to be 'contrived', for especially the schizophrenic patients are quick to spot effortful role-playing behaviour on the part of the therapist. They are 'already specialists in the meaning of unreal and inappropriate behaviour'.[23]

On the other hand, the deliberately assumed and played role of parental caring is not entirely an insincere and artificial makeshift. Even on the stage, the Stanislavski school of actors has shown that acting can be a performance of personal dedication, an ongoing ('through action'), a 'a service of the soul', the sincerity of which is not in doubt to the method actor. For Stanislavski the actor's performance is a 'spiritual exercise'[24] in which the fabrications of the imagination are sanctified by some kind of a faith in the worth and dignity of the performance. Understandably, the proximity of 'dissembling' and 'acting' has put the creative actor at a disadvantage when claiming or striving for a sense of nobility of function. Yet this is an unjust disadvantage for, after all, we do not as a rule question the veracity of the musical instrumentalist who gets transported by his own contrivances and manages to take his audience with him. Just because the musical sentiments are deliberately invoked and staged we wouldn't dream of calling a performer a deceiver, who indulges in pretending and make-believe. The parallel with the counsellor's performance is close: 'I simulate anger, tenderness, sometimes shock, irritation, a lot of things,' writes T. P. Malone, a psychiatrist, 'and one of the things that to me has meant the most is the fact that in the simulation of these

---

[20] *Psychotherapy of the Psychoses* (Ed. Burton), New York, 1961, p. 186.
[21] *Ibid.*
[22] *Ibid.*, p. 185.
[23] Quoted by Burton from J. Arlow, 'Discussions of Dr. Fromm-Reichmann's paper' in E. B. Brody and F. C. Redlich (Eds.) *Psychotherapy with Schizophrenics*, New York, 1952, p. 117.
[24] Cf. C. Stanislavski: *Creating a Role*, London, 1963, pp. 48–50, and *An Actor Prepares*, London, 1959, pp. 271–280.

feelings, I often get the real feelings within a matter of minutes.'[25] This brings to mind Martial's remark that, 'Lawyers are men who hire out their words and anger'; if one wanted to be cynical about the counsellor one could say that the counsellors are men and women who hire out their care and indifference, their love and hatred. And at the other end, the patient's end, R. D. Laing says about the hysteric's bid to 'become mad' that 'the counterfeit can engulf the person's life as much as the "real thing" '.[26] In fact this is now a generally known and favoured hypothesis according to which the 'enactment of a role' changes the personality of the role-player.[27] The Stanislavski method of acting merely anticipates this social-psychological hypothesis when inviting actors to change their personalities temporarily into what the role portrays. In this sense, one might almost speak of the 'Stanislavski method of psychotherapy'. Of course, the actor is called upon to play many roles and the numberless provisional personality changes merge in very special ways in the actor's self but the counsellor plays mainly one role only—in the professional sector of his life at any rate—and the significance of this cannot be overestimated. The counsellor's identification with the role he constantly plays results in a rare and impressive accumulation of a sympathetic and caring attitude towards others.

During the training of counsellors this 'role enactment' appears to have an even more paradoxical quality than during later practice : during training, one must inevitably imply a cultivation in the candidate of a spontaneously caring attitude, and this in spite of the obvious incompatibility of the motions of deliberate 'cultivation' with 'spontaneity'. Yet, the dramatisation, the putting-on-an-act, is itself a product of an interest, a one-pointed orientation, and of a resolve to train and practise. And *these* are no more 'pretended' than our acts of satisfying hunger or thirst. It is not only that acting involves the total personality of the actor but, more importantly, the total personality must be surrendered to the role by an act of will, in the first instance, so that this total involvement should rapidly ensue. Even if one agreed to use the unflattering terms of

[25] In C. Whitaker (Ed.), *Psychotherapy of Chronic Schizophrenic Patients*, London, 1956, p. 165. An interesting paradox, analogous to the one discussed here, is implied in the title of W. Schofield's book : *Psychotherapy, the Purchase of Friendship*, New Jersey, 1964.
[26] *The Self and Others*, London, 1961, p. 37.
[27] Cf. a most recent review of this by T. R. Sarbin in *Personality Change*, Ed. by P. Worchel and D. Byrne, New York, 1964, pp. 176–219.

'pretence' or 'bluffing' one could say that there is no necessary pretence or bluffing in the resolution to pretend or bluff. The sincerity of the resolution is not impaired by what acts follow, on the contrary, the acts of 'role-playing' partake of the initial sincerity. And should the counsellor use these terms, though this would be in keeping with the self-abnegating modesty of his profession, he would be 'selling himself down the river' by denying himself the credit of his good intentions and his sincerity.[28] One should not lightly dismiss the possibility that the *need* to play the counsellor's role is an aspiration *to be* the kind of person defined by the role. Therefore, the 'behaving as if' is not an act of dissembling but a genuine movement towards an ideal. In life, even if not so much on the stage, the wanting and being able to play a role often betrays the presence of at least some qualities of the role in the person who is set on playing it.

The passages from the counselling literature so far cited to explain this demand for parental role playing also turn out to be illustrations of the unconditional and total absorption of the worker in the client-patient. The alibi of the worker, that he is only making himself instrumental to therapeutic success by assuming a parental role, playing the role as an actor would, becomes suspect when the literature explicitly demands that the worker should enter into *communion* with the patient, that there should be *empathy* between worker and patient, and that the worker should *love* the patient. One finds for example that W. R. D. Fairbairn's 'object-relations' theory and therapy often couches its tenets in the language of Martin Buber's writings. Fairbairn leaves little doubt about this when he says, '... what I understand by "the relationship between the patient and the analyst" is not just the relationship involved in the transference but *the total relationship existing between the patient and the analyst as persons*'.[29] The italics added, and rightly too, for this notion of 'total relationship' is not psychoanalytical and it does not follow at all from the metapsychology of psychoanalysis. The notion is an article of faith and not a scientific hypothesis. It is a notion which makes a mere 'role-playing' interpretation of love difficult to accept.

[28] T. N. Rosen, another psychiatrist, voices a similar view in C. Whitaker. (*Op. cit.*, p. 171.)
[29] 'On the Nature and Aims of Psychoanalytical Treatment', *The International Journal of Psychoanalysis*, September-October 1958, Vol. XXXIX, Part V, pp. 374–385.

There are, of course, attempts at taming the run-away mysticism of these ideas by introducing pedestrian terms such as 'supportiveness'. L. G. Selby, in a comprehensive survey of the literature of social casework, shows that writer after writer, on all kinds of counselling, includes 'supportiveness' as a part of counselling. Selby herself regards it probable '. . . that supportive treatment . . . is the major helping method currently employed in most social agencies and by most casework departments . . . It is an appropriate way of helping the clientele of most agencies . . .'[30] But soon enough this writer too reverts to the reverential language of the numinous and confesses that the achievement of psychotherapeutic results through supportive acts 'may sound relatively simple and not particularly demanding of subtle skill on the part of the therapist, *provided that he can empathise easily and enter into a positive and giving relationship with his patients'.* (My italics.) No matter how much critical knowledge and controlling skill he must simultaneously use both to be 'supportive' *and* to avoid the well-known pitfalls of supportiveness, he must also 'empathise' and be 'giving'.

It is interesting to see the canons of 'empathising' included in the most prominent textbooks of some counselling subgroups. For example, when Lois Meredith French wrote her textbook on *Psychiatric Social Work*[31] 'empathising with a client' was to her extraneous to the skills which the psychiatric social worker was to use. In her early study of psychiatric social work, treatment interviews were described as ranging 'from the provision of an opportunity to talk freely to a sympathetic listener to a highly technical process'. Yet she goes on to say, 'the catharsis derived from the former may be achieved by any worker, or, for that matter, by any person who has the capacity of establishing . . . "empathy" with another in trouble. *Every social worker uses it.* Yet such a process is not therapy', she adds, for psychiatric social work 'is a specialised process developed by skilled workers . . .' Thus every social worker uses empathy, but empathy is not skill, and skill is also necessary. It would seem from this that skill without empathy might fail while empathy without a vestige of conscious and deliberately applied skill might succeed. One might even hazard the conclusion that the social worker's professionalisation of this kind of helping is

[30] 'Supportive Treatment: The Development of a Concept and a Helping Method', *The Social Service Review*, December 1956, Vol. XXX, No. 4, pp. 400–414.
[31] London, 1940.

at least sometimes superfluous : any person who has the capacity for establishing empathy may be able to help. And so, it may not be easy to answer fully a critic who might say that, after six decades of sophistication, the counsellors have not discovered much more than that loving another in need of help may be the one thing decisively therapeutic to him.

The use of terms such as 'empathy' or 'rapport' or 'communion' suggests a mutuality and parity between counsellor and client. Mutual and reciprocated feelings, in this case realistic or not, include in the experience of both participants an awareness of this reciprocity and a sharing of this awareness. The claim for an 'I know, you know, I know... etc.' series appears to us grotesque only because of the implausible infinity of this series, yet surely, an implicit assumption of this infinity itself is part of the awareness of a profound mutuality? Of course, the infinite regress does not exist in articulated phases on both sides, as it would be in a game of tennis, but it merges into the blurred total serenity or ecstasy of a communion. Yet ego-minded as we are, we hasten back to the starting-point, the two coincidental selves, and resolve that there is no reality beyond these separate and narcissistic selves. Certainly, our scientific mode of thought would discourage us even from looking for such reality as this. Nonetheless when the counsellors write about this they give us the impression that there is more in this mutuality than their own scientific categories would let them hypothesise. As a fully accurate step-by-step analysis of the dual process seems hopeless, and as the spectacle of the interaction itself qualifies this process in both participants, analytic thinking is abandoned and a reverential language adopted. J. L. Moreno, for example, describes the meeting of two persons, or therapist and patient, as a *Begegnung*, encounter, and coins the word *Zweifühlung* on the analogy of *Einfühlung*. He translates this as togetherness and a sharing of life. 'It is an intuitive reversal of roles, a realisation of the self through the other; it is identity, the rare, unforgotten experience of reciprocity. The encounter is extemporaneous, unstructured, unplanned, unrehearsed—it occurs on the spur of the moment.'[32] This is the counsellor's version of 'communion'. The language and imagery tries to be new, but the referents are those of occidental and oriental mysticism. Silvano Arieti writes, for

[32] In *Progress in Psychotherapy*, Ed. by Frieda Fromm-Reichmann and J. L. Moreno, New York, 1956, p. 27.

example, that young therapists find it difficult to learn a professional skill when the instructions 'at times consist largely of "intuitional improvisations" or of "mystical" and "unscientific" procedures'.[33] Writing about psychotherapy of schizophrenics he admits that 'it would almost seem as if the exquisite therapeutic sensitivity of some therapists in relating to schizophrenics were an irreducible or untransmittable quality...'[34] and compares the therapist-patient relationship to 'an I-Thou relationship in Buber's sense'.[35] He regards the establishment of this kind of relatedness as an 'absolute requirement for successful treatment' though, of course, 'treatment entails much more' in addition to this requirement. No one need question whether the technical and theoretical equipment of the therapist-counsellor is a requisite of successful therapy. Apart from happy and rare exceptions it probably is an essential requisite. But the point here is that according to Arieti, a faculty member of the William Alanson White Institute, the Buberian relatedness is an *absolute requirement*.

Writing in the same volume, H. F. Searles, senior psychiatrist and training analyst, repeats the same 'technical' specification: he believes that 'frequently—though by no means always—various manifestations of feeling participation by the therapist which in the past have been regarded as unwanted countertransference will be seen to be *inevitable, and utterly essential*, components of the recovery process'.[36] (My italics.) Then proceeding to describe 'the ingredients of this relatedness' Searles explains, 'These lie in the realm of the therapist's acceptance of the deep dependency, including even—at one crucial phase of the work—a symbiotic kind of mutual dependency, which he naturally comes to feel towards the patient; his acceptance of a mutual caring which amounts at times to adoration; and his being able to acknowledge the patient's contribution—inevitable, in successful therapy—to his own (the therapist's ... *sic*) personal integration.'[37]

All this may be most unsatisfactory for the 'scientists of counselling'. They would think it is only a matter of time before these

[33] *Psychotherapy of the Psychoses*, Ed. by A. Burton, New York, 1961, pp. 69–71.
[34] *Ibid.*
[35] *Ibid.*
[36] *Op. cit.*, pp. 283–284.
[37] *Ibid.* Also see A. Burton on p. 173 and especially on p. 185 where Burton unqualifiedly stipulates, 'this is the framework within which all therapeutic effort must be set'.

'mystical'-sounding processes are broken down into quantifiable phases or motions. They will reflect with Irving Sarnoff that 'Psychology ... does not yet possess any systematic way of describing the *simultaneity* of interpersonal behaviour. Until it acquires such tools, psychology will be powerless to deal with that which may be the most crucial aspect not only of psychotherapy but of many other contexts within which direct social influence is taking place.'[38] One question is, of course, whether the act of faith—necessary to maintain that a 'systematic way of describing' will eventually be discovered—is of a less arbitrary character than the one that is necessary to maintain that it will *not* be discovered. It is not for me to answer this question but to say that the counsellors behave and write so as if they wished to maintain that there is no such 'systematic way'.

Another writer, H. Racker, explains in *The Psychoanalytic Quarterly*[39] that 'to be cured and to cure is to integrate the patient's psyche by integrating one's own, re-establishing the equation *non-ego*(you) = *ego*. To understand, is to overcome the division into two, and to identify oneself is, in this aspect, to restore an already pre-existing identity. *To understand, to unite with another, and hence also to love prove, at root, to be one and the same.*' (Italics added.) The painstakingly serious pursuit of this idea in an important psychoanalytical journal is not without interest. In fact, these psychoanalytical excursions into mysticism are not just instances of exceptional obscurantism or neurotic lapses, which a short spell of return into training analysis might correct. Nor are they symptoms of an 'antiparty' diversionism or rebellion against institutionalised psychoanalysis. They are displayed as the inevitable consequences of devoted practice in one of the most scrupulous forms of counselling, psychoanalysis.

There are some interesting variations on this theme, though all of them are about experiences of mutuality. W. P. Kraemer calls the simultaneous transference and countertransference relationship 'partnership transference',[40] implying that the fact of partnership may well be something in addition to the separate facts of transference and countertransference. One could, of course, be cynical

[38] *Personality Dynamics and Development*, New York, 1962, p. 423.
[39] 'Psychoanalytic Technique and the Analyst's Unconscious Masochism', 1958, Vol. XXVII, pp. 555–562.
[40] 'Transference and Countertransference', *The British Journal of Medical Psychology*, 1957, Vol. XXX, pp. 63–74.

about this, and call the twosome *une névrose à deux*, but name-calling would not clarify the situation. The reverential labels, such as, for example, 'consubstantial union' and *unio mystica* are hardly more helpful. Yet there is an important philosophical difference between the complimentary and not so complimentary interpretations. The former reflects our desire to transcend ourselves in love and togetherness, and to overcome our separative limitations. In this, there is always a movement towards 'limitless fusion' and an aspiration to 'something greater and more lasting than we are'. The not-so-complimentary interpretations of empathy range from the neutral to the explicitly inhuman. An example of the first is given by Arnold Eisendorfer in a paper in *The Psychoanalytic Quarterly*[41] where he defines empathy as 'the capacity for reciprocal identification between the participants in the interview, i.e., an ability to identify'. This does not assume more than what we would do if we were to say, 'some people can draw, some can sing, and some can identify'. An example of the 'reductive' and unflattering kind is the interpretation according to which empathy is an instance of regression to a primitive or infantile state of being. Though the counsellor's faith in communion is professed time and again either by unostentatious deeds or by guarded implications, it is equally often denied in blunt or even rude words, or prescribed dispassionately as a 'technique'. Sometimes the counsellors seem to protest guiltily that they are innocent of the virtue of personal love, and deny that the good and creative kind of responsibility which they are able to sustain has anything to do with compassion. Often they severely proclaim that the only interest they have is that of the investigative scientist, and that therapy is an accidental by-product of their investigative activities or of their wholly objective concern for truth. Freud himself is quoted as saying : 'I only want to feel assured that the therapy does not destroy the science.'[42] Thomas Szász chides those who like to fancy that '... Freud was, after all, a physician (who) was for ever trying to perfect his ways of healing sick people'. In Szász' view this is 'a sentimental rewriting of the history of psychoanalysis'.[43] Szász

[41] 'The Selection of Candidates Applying for Psychoanalytical Training', 1959, Vol. XXVIII, pp. 374–378.
[42] 'On the Theory of Psychoanalytic Treatment', *The International Journal of Psychoanalysis*, May-August 1957, Vol. XXXVIII, Parts 3–4, pp. 166–182.
[43] *Ibid.* And also cf. Menninger, K., *The Theory of Psychoanalytic Technique*, New York, 1958, p. xi.

believes that Freud was not principally interested in being a physician and in curing patients, and that he was passionately devoted to increasing his own understanding and to grasping more firmly the facts of human growth. It would seem that this strenuously tough-minded conception of the searcher for truth augurs ill for him for we are told time and again that the discovery of truth depends on our ability to empathise![44] The counsellor is expected to observe the patient objectively, listen to his own feelings and also listen to the two processes with a 'third ear'. Unless he can do all these things, as it were stereoscopically, the facts will not show themselves plastic and tangible.

It can be seen in spite of the documentation I am presenting in these pages that, on occasion, the counsellor displays a strong aspiration to couch his descriptive account of the counselling experience in metaphorical terms which suggest something more matter-of-fact than he, in fact, experiences. *Malgré lui* he is dissatisfied with the mechanistic account of what he is doing because he suspects that the account has a self-stultifying effect on his practice. So he lapses into a poetic discourse the message of which he promptly disowns when challenged. 'At a recent case presentation made jointly by a psychoanalyst and two social workers,' we read in the journal, *Social Casework*, 'the accusation was made (and it seemed definitely an accusation) that they were too identified with the patient and hence over-protective and even "loving". The patient was a badly neglected, utterly deprived child, and it seemed to me,' the writer of this paper, S. W. Ginsburg noted, 'that a perfectly adequate theoretical case could have been constructed for the techniques employed. But what interested me more was the need of several of those who participated in the discussion to find some technical justification for such feelings, some sanction for them in dynamic terms, as if just loving the child was somehow suspect.'[45]

It would appear that, in the fusion of deliberate manipulation with tenderness, tenderness absorbs manipulation. So as to avoid the appearance of sentimentalism and with it, the therapeutic error of indulging in his own fantasies, possibly at the expense of the patient, the counsellor seeks 'technical justifications' for his spon-

[44] *Ibid.*
[45] 'The Impact of the Social Worker's Cultural Structure on Social Therapy', 1951, Vol. XXXII, pp. 319–325.

taneous tenderness. The counsellor's roomy sympathy, gentle flexibility, and generously listening-waiting posture are either not analysable into mechanical skill-operations or, if they are, the counsellor must forget this, so as to protect his total personal approach from fragmentation. Sometimes he suspects that the genealogy of his sentiments goes back to an ancestry which is no less decisive for its being only vaguely known; sometimes he pulls himself together and, dismissing these fancies, talks of his tenderness as 'mature genitality'. But even those psychoanalysts who most consistently retain the biological frame of reference disclose a 'subtle shift' in their argument, a shift from biology to metaphysics, from manipulation to the total imagery of personal love. 'In the classical psychoanalytical situation,' writes L. Stone, a training analyst, 'we have an instrumentality of unique scientific productiveness, also of tremendous psychodynamic range and power. It can, however, be improved, not only as a therapeutic instrument, but in a genuinely scientific sense, if we accept confrontation with certain ineluctable, if not as yet well-formulated, psychological realities. For these are always, by common agreement, more important than formulations as such, however convincing the latter may seem in primary logical encounter...'[46] These are the concluding words of a painstakingly positivistic psychoanalyst's book, the epigraph as it were, and the crowning wisdom. According to Stone, 'purely technical or intellectual errors can, in most instances, be corrected' but 'a failure in a critical juncture to show reasonable human response which any person inevitably expects from another on whom he deeply depends, can invalidate years of patient and largely skilful work'.[47] Most counsellors would be apprehensive of pursuing this line of thinking and some would even quarantine themselves against the virus of sentimental over-simplification. Yet, I think, this anxious defensiveness is of no avail: the documentation in this book presents a stark close-up of the counsellor's reliance on the ineffable.

When Paul Tillich is invited to write for a prominent casework journal one suspects an editorial nostalgia for older explanations of these sentiments. Tillich identifies himself with the social workers and says, 'We (he means social workers and others who care)

[46] *The Psychoanalytic Situation*, by L. Stone, New York, 1961, pp. 108 and 111.
[47] *Op. cit.*, p. 55.

tried one of the great laws of life, the law of "listening love".[48] This referring back to theologico-poetical authorities and making their *charisma*, their evident gift of grace, work for counselling thought, as a kind of inspirational aid, is now becoming a regular practice in journals and books. Even the relatively non-clinical school 'counselors' (the American variety) follow this line. C. Gilbert Wrenn, charged by the American Personnel and Guidance Association to look into the future role of the American school-'counselor', concludes his report with Kahlil Gibran's *credo*, 'Work is love made visible',[49] and declares that the counselor's joy in communicating this to his clients is his most effective contribution. And so we are not a bit surprised when Father Biestek, a member of the Society of Jesus, embraces the 'intellectual and technical discipline' of social casework and diligently practises it under the banner, 'love is the skill'.[50] One only has to exchange the clerical black for the clinical white to arrive at the psychiatrist's C. L. C. Burns' verdict that, 'the difference which really counts and is vital to the child is not one of theory and conscious practice so much as one between those who have the gift of sympathy, understanding, and all the qualities contained in what may be called "therapeutic love", and those who have not'.[51]

Here the psychiatrist altogether resigns from technical expertise, from the authority of special professional knowledge and skill. As if the counsellor had been irresistibly driven to admit that neuro-psychiatry and social psychology come to nought in the absence of love for those who seek help. The counsellor writes only too often as if he wished to puncture the balloon of positivistic conceit and to act as a witness to a creed of love. One could, of course, say that there may be other explanations. That, for example, the counsellor does not prefer anything unscientific, and that he only makes a bid to evoke overtones of feeling in others who—unlike him—are still under the spell of numinous symbols and reverential images. Indeed he often protests that these traditional images call up sentiments which are analysable in terms of the positive categories of his psychological theory. He uses the traditional and inspira-

[48] 'The Philosophy of Social Work', *The Social Service Review*, March 1962, Vol. XXXVI, No. 1, pp. 13–16.
[49] *The Counsellor in a Changing World*, American Personnel and Guidance Association, Washington, 1962, p. 182.
[50] *The Casework Relationship*, by F. P. Biestek, London, 1961, p. 191.
[51] 'Psychiatric Treatment of Children in a Residential Setting', *The British Journal of Criminology*, July 1960, Vol. II, No. 1, p. 422.

tional language on some occasions only because this language well identifies certain configurations of sentiment for which his science has not yet found labels. Knowing the psychological theoretician's well-known absence of restraint in coining neologisms, this does not seem to be a very plausible excuse. In fact, the cynical excuse that the sceptical counsellor uses the inspirational language calculatingly carries no conviction; on the contrary, it suggests that the counsellor is ashamed to admit the sincerity of this language and that he actually means what he says. Just the same, there are some hard souls among them who face this and deny this.

These will insist that when psychiatrists speak of 'love', psychoanalysts talk respectfully about 'communion', and psychiatric social workers prescribe 'mothering', these counsellors are merely using inherited labels for what there are scientifically respectable notions available. They may say that these things are errors of naming, slips or careless wording; but surely such a plea as this in *this* company would be rather telling! At any rate, what are those scientifically respectable notions which could replace sentimentalism and mysticism in counselling? The rest of this section will be devoted to seeking an answer to this question.

Writing about 'Love in Infant Monkeys', H. F. Harlow presents his, by now famous, tale of motherless rhesus monkeys, and concludes, that 'there appears to be no reason why we cannot at some future time investigate the fundamental neurophysiological and biochemical variables underlying affection and love'.[52] Clearly, there is at least a promise here—also implied in psychoanalysis but entirely forgotten there—of penetrating into the very structure and molecular make-up of the response-system called 'love', which, I am sure, will be agreed even today, is a human experience of some moment. There are no vague notions of spirituality in this psychology or allusions to 'communion' or 'union'. The total or molar and personal experience is equated with the sum of its parts which are discoverable and will be discovered. The analytic dismemberment of experience is a necessary and worthy enterprise which the retention of total and personalistic imagery would only obstruct. There is no confluence of dynamic psychology and theology possible here, no convenient merger presents itself, such as for example the one between the psychological entelechy of 'libido' and the fervent affirmations of love. The Harlows, in another

[52] 'Love in Infant Monkeys', *Scientific American*, June 1959, pp. 68–74.

paper, speak of an 'affectional system' as if it was a plant, like the cardiovascular system or the alimentary system. And speaking of systems they imply that these things consist of identifiable parts or elements. But by retaining the concept of 'system' as a necessary concept they also admit that there might be something specific about the 'system' which the sum of the parts does not possess. The thesis is briefly this : love is an analysable response system consisting of parts which in themselves are not love but certain specifiable mechanical events—items of sensory stimulation and no more.

In H. J. Eysenck's *Behaviour Therapy and the Neuroses*, there is an abundance of illustrations of what happens when therapeutic action is carried out with this mechanical notion of love in mind. One of the contributors, A. A. Lazarus, for example, reports on the case of a nine-year-old girl, whose mother 'stated that she had read an article which stressed that one should refrain from giving a nine-year-old child any overt demonstrations of love and affection (such as hugging or kissing the child), since these practices supposedly hindered the development of "personality and maturity". The therapist vehemently condemned this contention and provided *"handling instructions"*, which emphasised the necessity for deliberate and overt *love and warmth'*.[53] (Italics mine.) There are some urgent questions demanding answers : is 'handling' instrumental to convey 'love and warmth', and if so, how do the behaviour therapists define this 'overt love and warmth'? If the mode of thought of this psychology is that it advocates 'handling instructions' when, in fact, it means to advocate love, might we not find that a piecemeal obeisance to it will elicit *handling*, in the sense of manipulating, and not *love?* Whether there are 'do-it-yourself-kits' of loving behaviour or not is a psychological question, but the paradoxical thing is that even if there were such things, by virtue of our knowledge of their existence we would lose our respect for this sort of behaviour. Truth may well be self-stultifying by being made known. It is, to say the least, open to doubt that a literal execution of prescribed motions, prescribed 'handling', will induce a satisfactory change in unloving mothers or in hurried and harassed institutional staff. Nor is it likely to succeed in the training of counsellors whose tenderness and compassion has been widely claimed to be essential to their professional efficiency.

[53] 'The Elimination of Children's Phobias by Deconditioning', *Loc. cit.*, London, 1960, p. 117.

But perhaps the claim for there being other things too besides 'handling' and 'manipulation' is unfounded? Perhaps, it is a symptom of muddle-headed, sentimental thinking, unable to free itself from the religious imagery and the tender pieties of a potent past? Let us now see what sort of reports we get from those who are firmly convinced to have emancipated themselves from these frailties. For not all those who practise therapy would, like the counsellors, admit to relying on therapeutic theories of 'relationship' and 'love'.

Ever since Pavlov there has been a firm conviction among some clinical workers that the *machine man's* psyche requires only machinists for maintenance and repair and that all therapy of the psyche must therefore be pursued in the businesslike spirit of the garage mechanic. All pretences to their being non-mechanical tools are regarded as sheer self-deceptions and signs of naive obscurantism. Even the 'use of the person of the therapist' is interpreted as the use of a complex but analysable stimulus system. In Joseph Wolpe's words, 'when fundamental psychotherapeutic effects are obtained in neuroses—no matter by what therapist—these effects are nearly always really a consequence of the occurrence of reciprocal inhibition of neurotic anxiety responses, that is, the complete or partial suppression of the anxiety responses as a consequence of the simultaneous evocation of other responses physiologically antagonistic to anxiety'.[54] In simpler terms : if human relationships were erstwhile anxiety-producing and the relationship with the therapist or counsellor is reassuring then the response 'anxiety' to the stimulus 'human relationship' will be inhibited by the rewarding response of reassurance. It might be argued that to choose between the notions of 'healing power of love' and 'reciprocal inhibition of anxiety' is a matter of taste and not a matter of more or less workable hypotheses about reality. Whether this is a valid plea or not, will be decided by the relative fruitfulness of the two hypotheses. For the time being, I shall be obliged to show that the 'behaviour therapists', or as I prefer to call them, the 'mechanotherapists', themselves appear to be unsure of the outcome when they try to enforce consistency in their conceptual scheme. For we are led to discover again and again that, against their better judgment, the model of the machine tends to become vitalised.

[54] 'Reciprocal Inhibition as the Main Basis of Psychotherapeutic Effects', *Loc. cit.*, p. 88.

Indeed, the more objectively and conscientiously the model is used, the more it partakes of the conscientiousness of its applier and the more it is permeated by his personal humaneness. 'The final explanation of our therapeutic successes,' writes A. A. Lazarus, 'must necessarily incorporate elements of . . . non-specific reciprocal inhibition via the interpersonal relationship between patient and therapist (common to all types of psychotherapy).'[55] It is, at least, possible that the 'non-specific' influence will never be entirely specified and that this is so because the personal and total agent of inhibition is not analysable with the tools of a mechanistic-physiological psychology. Even Wolpe, when writing about 'abreaction-therapy', finds it consistent with his own concepts to speak like this, 'It is only when the patient can feel the impact of the therapeutic situation, e.g. the therapist's sympathetic acceptance of him, that beneficial abreaction can occur.'[56] One could, of course, think of this 'sympathetic acceptance' as if it was a complicated, yet analysable, set or *Gestalt* of discrete sensory stimuli, offered by counsellor to patient as deliberately as an actor or public speaker might deliberately contrive to present entertainment or a show of conviction. The point is, can sympathetic acceptance be fragmented into sensory stimuli and yet remain an unfragmented total pattern to provide the client with the necessary therapeutic influence? And, in any case, how can the mechanotherapist afford the luxury of terms such as 'sympathetic acceptance' when he does not believe in its existence? By retaining the reverential terms, isn't he trying to have it both ways? And doesn't he thereby concede that the separate and discrete sensory stimuli acquire a new and heightened potency of influence by virtue of their pattern and simultaneity? And, finally, does he claim that his scientific categories are adequate to describe the emergent love in terms of the constituent sensory stimuli? For the verbal reinforcements would not bring about a change without the therapist showing 'a basic respect for the individual needs and integrity of the patient'.[57] E. J. Shoben documents the thesis that the mechanotherapists are 'personally warm and concerned in their clinical dealings' by quoting the mechanotherapists' use of concepts such as 'endeavour to establish

[55] *Loc. cit.*
[56] Wolpe, *Op. cit.*
[57] 'Learning Theory and Psychotherapy: Biotropic Versus Sociotropic Approaches', by E. J. Murray, *Journal of Counselling Psychology*, 1963, Vol. 10, No. 3.

good rapport' in their behaviour-therapy or their administering of 'reassuring stimuli' to the patients. A. A. Lazarus recommends to the 'behaviourist or objective psychotherapist' the usual instruments of the counsellor such as, for example, 'support', 'guidance', and 'catharsis',[58] and quotes A. Salter, another mechanotherapist and critic of psychoanalysis, who says that 'cure comes through learning healthy personal relationships now, and not by stewing over past emotional frustrations'.[59] Presumably the patient is to learn healthy personal relationships in the personal relationship with the mechanotherapist. But the mechanotherapist does not admit making use of any such instrument at all! We must seek some reconciliation in this paradox or repudiate the claims of the mechanotherapist. Either it is true that 'support', 'sympathy', 'sympathetic acceptance', and the like, are mechanical reinforcers as food-pellets are to the albino rat, or that they are essentially different. The mechanotherapist's constant harking back to the complex and molar terms, the terms of tenderness and radiance, cannot but persuade us that he behaves as if he did not believe his own premises. He seems to conduct himself professionally as if he needed his disbelief in molecular explanations, and as if, for therapeutic reinforcement, he needed the molar notions, the notions of unanalysable emergent things, such as sympathy or love. Throughout the whole volume of *Behaviour Therapy and the Neuroses*, paper after paper records the need for 'support', 'sympathy', and so on, and contains reservations such as, 'it is not claimed that the approach based on learning theory is solely responsible for the patient no longer suffering from her original very distressing symptoms ...'

The literature of learning theory and especially of behaviour therapy makes frequent references to 'social reinforcers'. A close scrutiny of a recent definition of social reinforcers would lend further support to our suspicions about the mechanistic pretences of this concept. The definition by S. Rachman is this: '... social reinforcement may be regarded as any event mediated by a person which has the effect of increasing the strength of the behaviour which immediately preceded it. By definition, then, most reinforcers would be social in nature.'[60] So it has to be mediated by a *person*, and as most reinforcers are social so most reinforcers must be

[58] In *Op. cit.*, by Eysenck, p. 145.
[59] *The Case Against Psychoanalysis*, New York, 1953.
[60] 'Learning Theory and Child Psychology: Therapeutic Possibilities', *Journal of Child Psychology and Psychiatry*, 1962, Vol. III, No. 3–4.

mediated by persons. Just what this means in terms of a behaviour-istic and non-personalistic psychology is not very clear. What they call 'clinician contact' is inevitable anyway but we are now being told that, in fact, it may be precisely this obtruding presence of an uncontrollable variable which may have to be credited with prac-tically all that is achieved. And one must remember that these observations are not made by psychoanalytically indoctrinated counsellors, but by tough-minded experimenters and clinicians who are contemptuously critical of the counsellors' appeal to 'support-iveness' or 'mothering' or, indeed, to soulful notions of 'love'. They indignantly repudiate the counsellors' view that the mechano-therapists' success is really due to transference, suggestion, and sup-portiveness, but in reporting their own treatment-cases display a remarkable lack of control over these very processes. For example, reporting a single case in some detail, Wolpe tells us that in the course of 60 lengthy interviews no more suggestion was used than that at the outset the patient was told : 'I am going to use a treat-ment that may help you...'[61] Knowing of the average psycho-neurotic patient's need for encouragement, it is difficult to regard this testimony as convincing. Perseverance with 60 interviews must be sustained by rewards which would make the obviously repetitive and probably tiresome process of 'desensitisation' acceptable to a disturbed patient. A pale remark at the outset of 60 lengthy inter-views (comprising 36 'hierarchies' and 1,491 'presentations') could not have sufficed! Nor is it at all conclusive evidence of the irrelevance of transference that six desensitisation sessions out of the 36, from the 18th to the 23rd, could be successfully conducted by a medical student in Wolpe's absence for a week. Wolpe let the student conduct the 15th session under his supervision and cor-rected the student's errors by silently passing him written notes. A learning theorist, well acquainted with the concept of 'stimulus-generalisation', can in these circumstances, surely not discount the power of his personal influence through the *locum tenens*!

The literature of behaviour therapy and its practice seems to be at variance. The advocacy by word is rigorously mechanistic; the advocacy by deed is manifestly not. The mechanotherapists are often capable of supplying the 'non-specific social reinforcement'

[61] 'Isolation of a Conditioning Procedure as the Crucial Psychotherapeutic Factor: A Case Study', *Journal of Nervous and Mental Disease*, 1962, Vol. CXXXIV, No. 4.

and are very willing to supply it in an unanalysed, global, and personal manner.[62] They also manage to shelter this manner from the fragmenting discipline of their thinking. They take the total personal relationship 'as read', and apply mechanotherapeutic techniques against its secure background. The inclusion of suggestion and hypnosis among the devices used only adds to our suspicion that the person-to-person factor is the backbone of this whole operation. Nor will it enhance our confidence in these techniques when the factor of so much therapeutic significance remains largely unanalysed by the behaviour therapists in spite of their commitment to an analytic dismemberment of the behavioural process. On their own showing, it is not possible to determine what measure of their claimed success is due to the personal presence of the mechanotherapist and due even to his personal supervision of a regimen of austere manipulations. One cannot help feeling that the mechanotherapist conveys to the patient some of the faith in the ultimateness and desirableness of the goals which he, the mechanotherapist, envisages as a result of his endeavours. He cannot help communicating his concern when pleading for the patient's co-operation, and when encouraging him to put his trust in the proceedings. G. B. Shaw said once that 'what really flatters a man is that you think him worth flattering'; we might say of all counsellors *as well as* of mechanotherapists that what really helps a man seeking their help is that they think him worth helping.

The faith of the mechanotherapist is plainly more than a faith in the contemporary categories of scientific thought, and, especially, of mechanics. It is more than the faith of the logical positivist for whom the only defensible account of human experience is a mathematical-mechanical account. It is not surprising that the intellectual scrupulousness of the mechanotherapist leads him to think of his scrupulousness as a mechanical lever or lubricant, and that he should regard his own complex presence as of the same kind as the tricks and stratagems of his conditioning and deconditioning moves. What is surprising is that the mechanotherapist refuses to admit the crucial limitations of his basic categories of thinking about the total and global personality. He believes that personality's functioning can be analysed in mechanical terms, and without an important remainder, failing to see, that were this to

[62] 'The Therapeutic Object: Men or Machines?' by E. J. Shoben, Jr., *Journal of Counselling Psychology*, 1963, Vol. X, No. 3.

become possible, it might transform his very conception of the 'mechanical', obliterating the difference between the counselling and mechanotherapeutic modes of thinking.

This book is not about the mechanotherapists, who would certainly object to being bracketed with the counsellors. I have nevertheless included this digression so as to show that, if the counsellors have faith in love, this is not an outcome of an obscurantism and sentimentalism special to them. The mechanotherapist should be deprived of the pretence of 'being more consistently scientific' : if anything, he is even guiltier than the counsellor of importing uncustomed goods into his territory. One is especially aware of liberties such as these being taken when, for example, Soviet Russian psychotherapists speak with some warmth of the therapist-patient relationship. 'The dry and pedantic utterances of a tired physician will not cure a single patient. But suggestions—disturbing, arousing, *inspiring* (*sic*) suggestions—represent a complex and *dynamic* (*sic*) system of words and meanings, imagery and motions, as well as a functionally psychological and consequently, physiological totality capable of combining a *dynamic* form and a *significant* content.'[63] (Italics mine.) The pathos and the reverential language is supposed to be warranted by Pavlovian physiology, which is not only assumed to accommodate 'dynamic totalities' but would also, presumably, account for things like 'significant content' and processes such as are 'inspiring'. Of course, the plea that these words are marginal lapses into a conventional and sentimental language could be made. It is another matter whether the plea would succeed in getting much sympathy.

The charge of sentimentalism has also been levelled against the author, a sociologist, a mere observer of the counsellor and of the mechanotherapist. It was said[64] that I had attributed to the counsellors more 'sentimental' views about their professional performance than they would admit to having. My finding is that the counsellor universally admits to relying on positive sentiments for the performance of his professional work, but that he self-consciously declines to examine the nature and extent of his reliance. On the evidence of his own admissions, the counsellor

[63] V. N. Miassischev (Leningrad) in the first and key-note paper read at the Moscow, 1956, Congress of Soviet Russian Psychotherapists. (From *Psychotherapy in the Soviet Union*, Ed. R. Winn, London, 1962, p. 12.)
[64] Cf. 'Love or Skill', by P. Halmos, *New Society*, 19 March 1964, and also correspondence in subsequent numbers.

could be said to rely on these positive sentiments as much as on skill or expertise. But whilst the development and refinement of skill and expertise lend themselves to scholarly treatment in papers and books the positive sentiments will only shrivel and die in the glare of any publicity. The charge of sentimentalism levelled against the sociologist may be inspired by anxiety felt about this possible loss.[65]

Summary of the argument in this section. The counsellors have been shown to profess, openly or by implication, that they consider their warm personal attachment to the help-seeker as a vital instrument of helping. So that this attachment be related to the psychological theory of their practice, at first, they interpreted their attachment as a deliberate offer of parental care and tenderness to those whose childhood grossly lacked these. The counsellors who proved especially sensitive to the emotional needs of others were called 'good empathisers', and the term 'empathy', and even 'communion', were now frequently used to describe the intimate rapport into which they were expected to enter spontaneously. The counsellors have been in the habit of characterising their professional relationship with their clients as 'sympathetic', 'accepting', and 'supportive', and from time to time some counsellors would comprehensively refer to the relationship as *'loving'*. At this point of my account it was necessary to compare notes with the behaviour therapists to see whether they have been able to dispense with the total, composite, or mosaic image of loving by simply listing the colour and position of each individual constituent piece of the whole image in terms of sensory stimuli and responses. Of course, the behaviour therapist has not been able to accomplish this, nor has he been able to convince us that he would ever accomplish it. Meanwhile he has amply volunteered the information that, though he does not profess a faith in love, he cannot do without its works.

Faith in the Triumph of Love Over Hatred

The revivalist tone of this section title may put off some readers. This would be regrettable for it accurately reflects a strong, though implicit, doctrine in the faith of the counsellors.

[65] Cf. *The Informed Heart,* by B. Bettelheim, London, 1961, p. 24.

No one would seriously question that the counsellors master techniques and use skills. All that the previous section tried to document was that counsellors also confess to a close reliance on their warm personal concern and affection. The frequent stipulation that the counsellor should use his personality in addition to using skills does not suggest that skills do not matter. But slogans, like 'love ·is the skill', at least imply an intimacy between care and skill in which the latter needs the sustenance of the former. But this hypothesis of the pre-eminence of care, concern, or love over other, less positive, sentiments would appear to the psychoanalytically indoctrinated counsellor as starry-eyed, and certainly superficial. The personal involvement of the counsellor in the client is acknowledged by psychoanalytic thought but this involvement is invariably described as through-and-through *ambivalent*. The involvement comprises both love and hatred of the client-patient and is called *countertransference*. Whilst in 'transference' the patient expresses his erstwhile filial loves *and* hates and addresses them to the counsellor, in countertransference the counsellor transfers his own positive *and* negative infantile feelings to the patient who, in a certain oddly plausible manner, can embody the rewarding or frustrating 'good or bad parent images' in the analyst's unconscious.

Some writers would restrict 'countertransference' to the counsellor's responses to the patient's transference. I do not think this distinction of much use for it is not possible to set aside responses which are from those which are not of this kind. Nowadays, we are led by psychoanalytic writers to believe that, in fact, countertransference is not only inevitable, but also has an important function in therapy provided it is appropriately handled. Now, this countertransference, we are told, is inescapably ambivalent. Ambivalence, the alternating and telescoping duality of love and hate, is a sound enough conception, and, no' doubt, the analyst's countertransference can be legitimately defined in terms of this ambivalence and nothing much else. The neglected point is, however, that this 'balance' is in fact a lop-sided balance, and that the counsellors speak, write, and act *as if* love's prevalence over hatred was an essential characteristic of it. Far from being a gratuitous assumption, this, I think, is a necessary premise, for without it the success of the counselling enterprise would not be credible. That the counsellor implicitly proclaims *love's prevalence in ambivalence*, and that his idea of this ambivalence is not like an idea of a fortuitous see-saw, or of a dialectic of equally matched forces, is borne out by his own dedication and care, prevailing even in the most discouraging and unlikeable cases. Yet the counsellor strenuously refrains from giving himself moral credit for displaying this prevalence in his professional perseverance.

Let us see whether the literature of counselling does testify to this admirable modesty, itself unaccountable in terms of the principles affirmed in that literature.

It appears from psychoanalytical literature that there are many ways in which the counsellor may make countertransference work for him. 'Countertransference is a necessary prerequisite of analysis,' writes Annie Reich, 'if it does not exist, the necessary talent and interest is lacking. But it has to remain shadowy and in the background.'[1] Presumably the same talent and interest which is responsible for the countertransference will also do the service of keeping it shadowy and in the background. This service is a positive service of care and concern; it could not be performed by ambivalent agents, but only by agents whose care and concern is stronger than their ambivalence, or whose ambivalence is 'lopsided'. Another analyst goes a long way towards acknowledging that this is so: Margaret Little writes about 'the analyst's real feeling for the patient, and his desire to help (there has to be some feeling, whether we call it sympathy, compassion, or interest, to prompt the starting and continuing of the analysis), these need to be expressed clearly and explicitly at times when they are appropriate *and are actually felt*, and can therefore come spontaneously and sincerely'.[2] This does not read like a recipe for what the counsellor *ought to* feel, for a cooked-up sentiment, but rather like a description of what the counsellor does in fact feel by virtue of his being engaged in counselling. The 'real feeling' is there 'spontaneously' or it is not there. *Nor is this 'real feeling' a mere arithmetic half of an ambivalent whole, for it is expected to preside over the use to which the ambivalent whole is put!* Margaret Little explains that countertransference used to be regarded as something hazardous, and even perilous, but she adds that 'nowadays it is even respectable', and, so long as the analyst shows 'flexibility,

---

[1] 'On Countertransference', *The International Journal of Psychoanalysis*, 1951, Vol. XXXII, Part 1, pp. 25–31.
[2] '"R"—The Analyst's Total Response to his Patient's Needs', *The International Journal of Psychoanalysis*, 1957, Vol. XXXIII, Parts 3–4, pp. 240–254.

reliability, and strength', he can make and should make use of it, so much the more, as it is 'unavoidable'. But how does he do this if his own professional attitude is to be explained entirely in terms of countertransference and ambivalence?

Maxwell Gitelson, yet another psychoanalytic writer on counter-transference, observes that in spite of his training analysis 'the analyst may bring into the analytic situation interfering emotional factors' such as, for example, 'identification with his own analyst', 'narcissistic power motives', 'unconscious instinctual aims', and so on. Gitelson explains that the only safeguard against the inevitable backsliding is an interminable self-analysis, a kind of 'listening with the third ear'. Gitelson goes on, 'Thus, a "third ear" directed towards himself, maintains the continuing prospect of resolving the analyst's own interfering emotions while coping with those of his patient. This, perhaps, is the most important technical qualification of the analyst.'[3] It is remarkable how far the notion of 'technical' will stretch. In fact, by now the term has ceased to signify any-thing reminiscent of manipulation and, therefore, serves, for the practising counsellor, merely as an instrument of self-deprecation and modesty. The standard line of argument seems to be that the very conscious attempt at overcoming the distorting influences of 'power motives', of 'voyeuristic curiosity', and the like, ultimately comes from the same energy sources which generate distortion. *The ultimate prevalence of these sources works out in a positive way and, therefore, it is extraneous to the ambivalence which is supposed to dominate the counsellor's attitude to the client.* The psychoanalyst Leo Berman describes this prevalent positive attitude as comprising '... a dedication of the good leader and good parent and that this makes an analyst's attitude of kindly acceptance, patience, and so on, genuine and effective'.[4] On the whole, the question of where the professional sublimations may come from has been left in a nebulous state. To avoid sanctimoniousness, the analyst, and the counsellors in general, will disclaim knowledge of the nature of these sublimating agents or dismiss pleas for their study as fruitless. Nonetheless he will, refrainlike, mention the presence of these categories, lying outside the closed dualism of ambi-

[3] 'The Emotional Position of the Analyst in the Psychoanalytic Situation', *The International Journal of Psychoanalysis*, 1952, Vol. XXXIII, Part 1, pp. 1–10.
[4] 'Countertransference and Attitudes of the Analyst in the Therapeutic Process', *Psychiatry*, 1949, Vol. XII, No. 2, pp. 159–166.

valence, and do so in the manner described in the previous section.

To enable these categories to prevail, there are some frequently uttered warnings to the counsellors about using the counselling situation exploitively. The counsellor must not get 'involved'. It is surprising how brazenly hypocritical we can be about this issue of involvement. On the one hand, we find it necessary for the more sensitive performance of the professional task; on the other, we condemn it as a device of selfish gratification. Time and again we hear or read the severe counsel, 'Don't try to solve your personal problems with the help of your professional work! Don't seek personal satisfaction from your professional relationships with clients, patients', and so on. We come across these demands in other professions too, for example, the spinster nursery school teacher is warned off maternal satisfactions in the same way as the social worker is warned off mutuality of relationship with a client. But what rewards if any should energise their perseverance in seeking solutions to the problems of their charges? How are these professional workers to succeed without a perpetually purposeful application of their own personalities and without unconsciously staking a claim for some kind of personal satisfaction? When we carefully examine the rules relating to this abstemious caring, and to this utterly selfless control of caring, we find that the rules are not so unambiguous as they appeared at first. There are some instances when explicit licence is given for gratification on a plane which seems to be regarded by the writers in question as a 'higher' one. R. Schafer, for example, suggests that whilst 'the empathiser's implicit aim is to understand, to enhance the reality of the other person through his own inner experience and awareness of that person ... that *he thereby enhances his own inner world does not detract from the object-related nature of empathy ...*'[5] (Italics mine.) Thus the warning, 'don't get involved!' is flagrantly contradicted here, for what else could 'enhancing one's inner world' mean but a considerable self-involvement? So long as the account of involvement is couched in the reverential language ('inner world') the reward earned by the counsellor is legitimate. Yet, an ascetic and severe point of view is also expressed, according to which the counsellor 'has to forego any immediate gratification derived from his ability to understand and to function correctly in an egosyntonic

[5] 'Generative Empathy in the Treatment Situation', *Psycho-Analytic Quarterly*, 1959, Vol. XXVIII, pp. 342–373.

way'.[6] To put it bluntly, this might be interpreted as meaning also that the counsellor, though not at liberty to get a kick out of understanding and mastery, is still allowed to get a kick out of being able to stop himself from getting a kick out of counselling. Because of the possibility of this 'infinite regress', the warning, not to seek personal gratification, is impossible to heed, for even the cultivation of restraint and severity is not without substantial rewards. It is instructive to watch the theoreticians of counselling trying to stop this 'infinite regress' by makeshift barricades of arbitrary principles which are really sustained by acts of faith and not by their own strength. Paula Heiman, a psychoanalyst, does this especially innocently. She writes, 'the aim of the analyst's own analysis is not to turn him into a mechanical brain which can produce interpretations on the basis of a purely intellectual procedure, but to enable him to *sustain* his feelings as opposed to discharging them like the patient'.[7] But how does analysis 'enable to sustain'? The egosyntonic acceptance of self without blindness to the defects of the self, is what the analysand, trainee or patient, must learn from the analyst. The analyst's acceptance of the patient is the patient's model for his acceptance of himself, as well as of others. The ultimate category which 'enables to sustain' is this acceptance and not the countertransference with its ambiguities of love and hatred. *There must be a prevalence in the positive polarity of ambivalence if this outcome is to be secured.* Certainly, the analyst also strives for a cold therapeutic objectivity which he has to balance with his striving for a non-rational and non-objective communion of warm acceptance and affection : who or what is striving for the balancing of these two? The analysts often evade this question by invoking a mysterious 'professional attitude'. The conventionally respectful and secular-moral connotation of this enables the analyst to sound matter-of-fact and not at all mystical or metaphysical. D. W. Winnicott, for example, tells us that 'a professional attitude may, of course, be built up on the basis of defences and inhibitions and obsessional orderliness.[8] There are several comments one would want to make on this. *Firstly*, if it 'may' be built on these, may it not be built on other, entirely dif-

---

[6] 'Further Remarks on Counter-Transference', by A. Reich, *The International Journal of Psychoanalysis*, 1960, Vol. XLI, Parts 4–5, pp. 389–395.
[7] 'Counter-Transference', *The British Journal of Medical Psychology*, 1960, Vol. XXXIII, Part 1, pp. 9–15.
[8] *Loc. cit.*

ferent, foundations as well? This 'may' obliges Winnicott to explain what these other things might be. *Secondly*, even if defences, inhibitions, and obsessional orderliness actually give rise and energise a 'professional attitude' this attitude—judging from the analyst's respectful reference to it—is a good deal more and other than the defences which have given it impetus and sustenance. We must either claim that we can make silk purses out of sow's ears, or we must prove that there is no difference between the silky and the swinish. On the other hand, if the 'professional attitude' is respectfully postulated as an extra, as an addition to what one has already described, then there is an admission of some moment here. Lurking shyly behind the cloak of a dispassionate prose and a technical language, the admission is that the emergent human quality cannot be fully explained in terms of its antecedents. One may go as far as to suspect the intellectual scrupulousness of the analyst's conclusions for they too must have been arrived at while engaged in using defences, inhibitions, and obsessional orderliness. One could not help having one's trust undermined in conclusions which have been arrived at with the help of these distortive and deceptive mechanisms. I do not doubt that we often do the right thing for the wrong reason but unless this happens fortuitously—a contingency itself suspect to the psychoanalyst—the conversion of distortive defences into a non-distortive 'professional attitude' will have to be accounted for by the definition of what has been brought into this process from elsewhere and added to it. If, on the other hand, the theory of counselling has defined the categories which are responsible for the emergence of a 'professional attitude' why is it that the counsellors can speak of the distortive defences only, and only vague and infrequent allusions are made to the vital category? Winnicott declares, 'I want to state that the working analyst is in a special state, that is, his attitude is professional';[9] but what does it mean *psychoanalytically* that the analyst's state is so 'special' and that his attitude is professional? Is this supposed to be something extraneous to the psychoanalytic theory? H. Guntrip very aptly remarked that 'difficulties concerning Winnicott's views arise mainly over the fact that his Freudian foundations do not really support his own superstructure'.[10] But

[9] *Loc. cit.*
[10] *Personality Structure and Human Interaction*, London, 1961, pp. 411–412.

Winnicott is by no means alone among his colleagues who are in this predicament. Hermann Nunberg, for example, argues that the analyst's relationship with the patient is 'professional', that is, it is not only influenced by emotional factors but also by technical principles which must be 'scientific, accurate, and objective as his profession demands...'[11] But the vital factor, the loyalty to the professional demands and the energies necessary to sustain this loyalty comes from 'prohibited infantile sexual curiosity', the compassion for the sufferings of others arises from guilt, and parental solicitousness is the outcome of identification with the father, the fantasied figure of protectiveness, dominance, and restitutive power. Thus the counsellor's resources consist of defences, defences, and defences. Social concern is supposed to be a reaction formation of antisocial inclinations, and presumably love a reaction formation of hate. And thus positive orientations are more often than not derived from negative ones neglecting the fact of their being so derived at all: for the frequency of converting the resources of Thanatos to serve the needs of Eros can only be explained with reference to the higher authority of Eros, the prevalence of Eros. But the Freudian dualism neglects to stress this and in the careful perusal of the literature of psychoanalytically oriented counselling we learn only of the balancing of love and hatred, of the universality of ambivalence, and hardly anything of love's prevalence. Even love itself, or as much of it as there is at birth, is described as narcissistic. It is not explained how this could be a dominant characteristic when the infant's self-love includes the entirely uncompromising demand for the love of another: for how can the love of another be so absolutely desired unless that other was also desired and, therefore, loved? The whole egotistical interpretation of primary love collapses when one perceives that it is in the desiring of the love of another as a complement of our self-love that the distinction between self-love and love of the other vanishes. Winnicott, Nunberg, and others may not wish to insist that the 'professional attitude' consists only of defence; or that love, care, and sympathy are not central to it; but they are so very much taken up by the urgency to warn other practitioners against the pitfalls in their work that the positive categories are

[11] *Practice and Theory of Psychoanalysis*, Nervous and Mental Disease Monographs, No. 74, New York, 1948, p. 178.

left to be indicated by the vague and general terms, such as, for example, 'professional attitude'.

One ought to add here that the love-hate dualism of ambivalence is not always the context of choice : sometimes one has to choose between love and indifference or between concern and neutrality. It is said that the stance of unhurried patience and waiting neutrality, or even a deliberate *façade* of indifference may be at times necessary for the patient's progress. On occasions, there are some very plausible technical reasons why the patient should be challenged by the stress of having to take, a few steps at least, without the crutches of the counsellor's concern. In this sense the counsellor's indifference—seeming indifference—can be described as therapeutic. The same would be true if the patient's reactions to indifference had to be worked through and these reactions had to be produced deliberately. But weaning a child or teaching him independence is not the same as abandoning him and the intermittent pauses of neutrality must occur in the context of concern so that the rationing of neutrality is in a warm and sensitive rapport to the learning capacity or growth potential of the patient. For example, H. F. Searles says that when the patient needs from the counsellor 'responses of inscrutability, impassivity, and, on many occasions, what can be called indifference', these the analyst must provide 'although it may indeed severely threaten his sense of humanness.'[12] To put it with much less sophistication : 'one must be cruel to be kind', one's humanness must carry and sustain the gambit of indifference and this indifference must be *administered* with care and compassion. One notes that Searles does not wish to invalidate the thesis of 'the therapist's responsiveness', which he regards as essential, but to provide a 'necessary counterbalance' for it.[13]

One should not take it for granted that the very decision—which the counsellor has to make—whether to suspend manifest concern and make the patient fend for himself, is a decision reached in alert attendance to the needs of another, in brief, whilst caring.

Another warning concerns a special aspect of the counsellor's involvement. Inevitably, the counsellor seeks confirmation of his own worth by wanting to succeed with the patient. In other words, the counsellor has a therapeutic ambition. But he is asked to renounce

12 'The Place of Neutral Therapist Responses in Psychotherapy with the Schizophrenic Patient', *International Journal of Psychoanalysis*, January 1963, Vol. 44, Part 1, pp. 42–56.
13 *Ibid.*

this ambition too. Freud wrote about this to Ophuijsen: 'I would advise you to set aside your therapeutic ambitions and try to understand what is happening. When you have done that, therapeutics will take care of itself.'[14] Does this advice take into account all the psychological facts that bear on it? 'Trying to understand' may be a working-out of intellectual curiosity, but it is a curiosity for things human, as distinct from things non-human. The aspiration to come near to the innermost realities of other human beings may seem to express itself in an objectively explorative, problem-grappling, and mastery-seeking curiosity, in short, in an egotistical curiosity, a curiosity which seeks conquest and power as much as knowledge or anything else. Were it no more than this, the counsellor would fail to enter into empathy with the patient-client, nor could his arid and unsympathetic curiosity sustain the work of a prolonged, in fact interminable, counselling process. The 'game of problem-solving' may be diverting, and it is true that an impersonally playful curiosity does lead to the solution of scientific and mathematical problems. But to continue throughout the 'dog-days' of counselling interviews, endure provocations, enticements, and obstinacies of the patient-client, and yet be ever ready to ferret out the significant detail, could not be done without the perseverance of a therapeutic ambition. In the final resort 'trying to understand' is inseparable from concern for the improvement of the patient. Once again, Freud's warning against the *furor prophylacticus et therapeuticus* was necessary and timely, but in showing up the excesses of healing zeal he also discouraged all desire to heal, for healing—in his view—will have to take care of itself. And so, in keeping with the intellectual climate of our times, the *furor therapeuticus* has been replaced by the *furor logicus*. There is for the intellectual more dignity in denying himself the certainty and conceit that there is an ultimate benevolent category in him which works itself out in creative and therapeutic ways. The counsellor believes that he is not entitled to these certainties, and that there is more dignity in an abstention from emotive declarations of faith in his own goodwill than in any faith at all. For him it is a sign of strength, and not a failing in virtue, to be able to cohabit with declared uncertainty and a sign of weakness to hanker after this being wedded to doctrine. The odd outcome of all this painstaking

[14] Quoted in *The Anatomy of Psychotherapy*, by H. L. Lennard and A. Bernstein, New York, 1960.

non-involvement, is that its conscientious care is justified by its help-fulness to others. They seem to be saying that the best way of helping others is to deny the virtue of having the desire to do so.

There is yet one more special warning on non-involvement which is frequently given. This is related to the choice of career as a counsellor and to a lesser extent to the actual practice of coun-selling. The counsellor candidate, so the warning goes, must not seek this vocation as a means of self-therapy and self-realisation. An absurdly and paradoxically purist view, for *all* vocations are 'self-realising' and were they not they could not be 'vocations'. Certainly, the striving towards self-realisation may take on a quality of greed, of obsessed voracity, and these would make functioning as a coun-sellor problematic if not impossible. One hopes, of course, that ten-dencies in this direction can be halted and reversed in the course of training or, indeed, that applicants for training as counsellors who show signs of marked and deeply ingrained tendencies in this direction can be advised to choose another career. We must not pretend not to have noticed that the candidates for training analysis display an obvious readiness, and indeed a warm desire, to benefit personally from the therapeutic component of their training. This is neither unexpected nor is it entirely new: 'The sages of old', says Chuang Tzu, 'first got Tao for themselves, then got it for others'. In the case of the counsellors this may mean that the voca-tional choice was dictated by an intense desire for self-clarification, often enough to justify a warning about this. 'To what degree,' Eisendorfer asks, 'has the applicant (for training as a psycho-analyst) awareness that his need to treat others stems from an inner need for self-therapy?'[15] Here too the creed of scrupulousness and selflessness manifests itself in the warning. For it would seem that progress in sensitivity and understanding others depends on pro-gress in sensitivity and understanding oneself; and the latter must be propelled by a desire for self-therapy, for without this it could not succeed. In an intriguing sense, self-care and the care for others is indissolubly merged in the counsellor's professional atti-tude. Charlotte Towle produces an especially outspoken testimony for this in the case of social workers: 'To what extent *educable* social workers have been misunderstood children who, out of per-sistent need for understanding now strive to understand others, is

[15] 'The Selection of Candidates Applying for Psychoanalytic Training', *The Psychoanalytic Quarterly*, 1959, Vol. XXVIII, pp. 374–378.

not known. To what extent they have been lonely individuals, who in this work vicariously seek intimate relationships, is not known. Nor is it known to what degree educable social workers have been hurt children who, out of their persistent need for pity, now are sensitive rather than susceptible to the sufferings of others.'[16] Towle recognises the inevitable usefulness of these motives and advocates, as all trainers of counsellors do, more self-knowledge about these motives.

It seems then, that the candidate for the profession of counselling often enough discloses a strong desire for self-clarification and self-understanding. One may in fact say that this is a *necessary* desire to have if one wants to be a counsellor and that it would be senseless to proscribe it. The crux of the matter is that when the counsellor reflects on this desire he arrives at a value-judgment and an affirmation according to which self-knowledge is a good thing. His faith in this value and affirmation is a constituent element in the Faith of the Counsellors.

Another aspect of self-involvement and self-realisation consists in a seeking of the experience of *giving*. A social casework theoretician portrays this seeking in the following words: 'The infant and child takes from his mother and at the same time gives her her capacity to be a mother through her function as one, just as anyone who takes a present gives at the same time to the giver his capacity to give, to be a giver. This is what clients do for the social worker. By using our services they give us a place in society which wants this function performed and has created the agency to perform it.'[17] The ancient circularity of 'blessed are the givers' is obvious enough, yet one gasps to see it appear in a 'technical' paper, in *Case Conference*, a journal mainly devoted to social science as well as to the administration and technicalities of social casework. It needs little perspicuity to see that this passage plainly means : 'the service of counselling is a service rendered no less to the counsellor than to the client'.

The abstemious rules—according to which the involvement of the professional worker vitiates his therapeutic influence—originate from clinical, and in particular, from psychoanalytical counselling practice. Here, as I have stated before, the issue is not that self-involvement is simultaneously or alternatingly selfish and unselfish but that it is *equivalently* selfish and unselfish or, indeed, that it is

---

[16] *The Learner in Education for the Professions*, Chicago, 1954, p. 80.
[17] 'Casework and Agency Function', by C. Winnicott, *Case Conference*, January 1962, Vol. VIII, No. 7.

equivalently loving and hating. The psychoanalytical technical literature, the casework literature, and the counsellor's literature in general implies this equivalence, and the counsellor's vocation contradicts it. So it is that the counsellor's theory remains silent on the significance of this : it says nothing about the disparity between love and hate or about the prevalence of love over hatred.

So far the specific warnings about involvement which I have discussed, the exploitation of the dependent patient, therapeutic ambition and power drive, and surreptitious seeking of self-therapy, do not exhaust all possibilities of involvement, though go a long way towards filling in the important details. Now, in all these instances, the counsellor is enjoined to handle the temptations in certain disciplined and critical ways and to observe a careful watch over backsliding. Here too, we may note the strangeness of the modern doctrine which has done so much to disillusion us of the eighteenth-century fiction that man is a fundamentally rational creature and which now turns out to be the very doctrine to demand of the counsellor that he should make the rationality of his insight the final arbiter of what he can allow himself to do. He is then not the plaything of ambivalence and his countertransference is subject to a control by something which is extraneous to countertransference or ambivalence. In fact, by enjoining the counsellor to conduct himself according to certain principles, a moral language is used imperceptibly mingled with a positive psychological language. I much agree with A. C. MacIntyre's comment on Freud's habit of mixing the language of rationality and mechanicalness with the language of responsibility and purpose.[18] 'Where *Id* was, there shall *Ego* be', is how Freud sums up the objective of psychotherapy. But in his appeal to analysts he asks them to apply this rule to their own countertransference so that their work should fare better. So the 'shall' in the Freudian enunciation is not a mere positive future tense, a mere prediction of the automatic blossoming-out of the *ego*, but a moral imperative, an inspiring preference. We feel obliged to agree with Philip Rieff that Freud's mind often communicates to us as the moralist's mind would and that his 'Helmholtzian vocabulary of forces' is a mere 'rhetorical mask for the ethical direction of his thought'.[19] The subtle mingling of the two kinds of discourse is not just a symptom of carelessness

18 *The Unconscious*, London, 1958, p. 92.
19 *Freud, The Mind of the Moralist*, London, 1959, p. 21.

but also of a deep desire for an affirmation of value. In the literature of counselling this merging of assertion of facts with reverential expressions of ideals has been a recurrent feature, especially in texts dealing with the vocational commitments of counsellors. One could cite volumes of illustrations for this telescoping of different levels of language and meaning. One example, however, will suffice, both because the writers are highly respected and because the writing is comparatively recent. J. Dollard and N. E. Miller in their book, *Personality and Psychotherapy*, begin by affirming the following scientific standards for the study of psychotherapy, 'We believe that giving the solid, systematic basis of learning theory to the data of psychotherapy is a matter of importance. Application of these laws and the investigation of the conditions of learning which psychotherapy involves should provide us with a rational foundation for practice in psychotherapy analogous to that provided by the science of bacteriology to treatment of contagious diseases.'[20] Thus psychotherapy is conceived of as an applied science the truth-standards of which are analogous to those of the experimental sciences. This declaration of faith is on page *8*. Now on page *413* of the same work we read : 'The therapist *must believe*—and, better, believe on the basis of his own experience—that repression can be evoked and that neurotic conflicts can be eliminated. How else can he have *courage* to drive and to help the patient along the blind way he must go? He *must believe* in the patient's capacity to learn. We must agree with Rogers that *faith* in the patient is a most important requirement in a therapist.' (My italics.)

'Courage' and 'faith' are reverential and even worshipful terms which are brought into the proceedings of a mechanistic learning theory rather as *émigré* royal dukes are invited to serve on the board of directors of dubious business organisations. These noble qualities which the therapist-counsellor *'must'* have cannot be fully accounted for in terms of a mechanistic learning theory without loss of nobility. For if the realities to which these terms of pathos and ancient reverence relate are mere mechanistic 'response systems' why make use of their conventional respectability and address them in all solemnity to the counsellors? Yet I believe that the authors' solemnity is not a sign of hypocrisy but an unconscious admission by them that they have the same kind of faith and courage as they expect of the counsellor about whom they are

[20] New York, 1950.

writing. I should describe the condition in which they and so many other psychological writers and thinkers are today as a condition of inverted hypocrisy. If the hypocrite is someone who professes what he does not believe, these inverted hypocrites are too shy to profess what they in fact believe. (Or indeed they profess not professing a faith at all.) An unspiritual and mechanistically fully accountable universe has no room for 'faith', nor have imperative noises such as 'must believe' any significance or meaning in that universe. The counsellor's passion about truth and rationality does not extend to truth about the passion, for if it did, the passion would abate.[21] In fact, the paradox is that the counselling theoretician's interpretation undermines the authority and very credibility of the standards which seem to inspire his investigative rigour.

In the recently published Freud-Pfister correspondence there are some interesting traces of the moral-positive hybrid language to show that the arch-counsellor's defiance of sentimental, or just tender, principles had its moments of weakness—or, perhaps, moments of truth. Writing about the resolution of the ambivalent transference and countertransference, Freud concludes, 'what then remains of the transference may, indeed should (sic), have the character of a cordial human relationship'.[22] Presumably, a *cordial human relationship* is a non-psychoanalytic category which is no more to be saddled with thoughts about the ubiquity of ambivalence. Freud's reluctance to speak of the paramountcy of love, and its emancipation from ambivalence, touchingly ceases when he speaks of his own personal relationships. In his letter to Pfister on 10 May 1909 he wrote, 'a remarkable man who came to see me one day, a true servant of God, a man in the very idea of whom I should have had difficulty in believing, in that he feels the need to do spiritual good to every one he meets'.[23] And having described his friend, Pfister, in these words, he added, 'You did good in this way even to me!' In another letter to Pfister he says, 'I kept reminding myself of what a good, kind person you are.' But what do the epithets, 'good', 'kind', and 'spiritual' mean to the psychoanalyst who uses them here in an obviously affectionate and respecting manner? If they are only consolidated sublimations of

[21] Cf. *Sigmund Freud's Mission*, by Erich Fromm, London, 1959, Chapter I.
[22] *Psychoanalysis and Faith, The Letters of Sigmund Freud and Oskar Pfister*, Ed. by H. Meng and E. L. Freud, London, 1963, p. 113.
[23] *Op. cit.*, p. 24.

the sexual libido, we should have to regard Freud's sincere laudatory messages to his friend as either no more than personality diagnosis in everyday language or as meaninglessly hypocritical compliments. Surely, he was not indulging in conventional compliments nor was he at all insincere. He meant what he said and he expected them to be accepted without reference to his theoretical views about sentiments of this kind.

And so it would seem that the theoretician—and of course the counsellor too—must be allowed freedom from his theories so that he can have as much abundance of life as anybody else and this includes the experience of using reverential and moral language, as well as the experience of meaning what this language conveys.

Summary of the argument in this section. To recognise the divided nature of man and his ambivalence needs sustained courage. The counsellor's intellectual scrupulousness dictates that he faces the facts of human frailty and that he refrains from embellishing these facts. Yet with all the anomalousness of the human soul, with all its disillusioning weaknesses caused mainly by his dividedness in ambivalence, he believes in the prevalence of love over hatred.[24] He believes that his unpretentious sympathy will survive, and will not be deadened, even after all disillusionment about man has been faced and thoroughly assimilated. It is, after all, comparatively easy to cultivate a concern which is hedged round with grand deceptions and lofty thoughts about the noble deservingness and spirituality of its beneficiaries. The counsellor's prevailing love of his charges is a truly informed 'love of sinners' and thus it is far from being a defection from the ancient paradigm of 'forgiveness' : it is, in fact, a modern refinement of it.

I have tried to show that, *according to the counsellor*, it is not ambivalence but the prevalence of love, which is the ultimate explanatory principle used to control the involvement of the counsellor in the client. The ascetic scrupulousness of self-criticism, and almost a cult of merciless sincerity, are brought to bear on the counsellor's work so that he avoids any kind of self-indulgence, tries not to fulfil therapeutic ambition, or refrains from exploiting his professional function for self-therapy.

To make this discipline possible the counsellor seems to adopt a paradoxical philosophical position concerning the nature of his ultimate motives. On the one hand, he relentlessly unmasks his own

[24] Cf. The quotation from Freud facing the first Preface.

rationalisations and attempts at claiming virtues and will treat his own indulgences with pitiless candour. On the other hand, he cannot but betray his kindness, concern, and idealism about man in general because of the aspiration for insight and rationality, and above all, because of his determination to procure more happiness for others.

The Counsellor's Objectivity and Neutrality: The Fiction of Non-directiveness

One of the central ideas of the counselling ideology is 'non-directiveness'. According to this ideal the counsellor must do his work without ever violating the personal initiative, uniqueness, and freedom of the patient or client. It is necessary to stress at the outset that this 'must' does not follow from the psychological theories of the counsellor and, indeed cannot follow from them, for there can be no logically defensible entailment from the propositions of a theory about facts, about what 'is', resulting in the confirmation of what 'ought to be' and 'must be'. It is a commonplace in philosophy that one cannot derive an 'ought' from an 'is', and the counsellor's 'ought' is no exception. But this is not the only instance of counselling thought flying in the face of well-established philosophical principles. For example, it is pointless to demand that one ought to do something one cannot do, this too is generally accepted in moral philosophical thinking as fundamental. Yet such is the ideal of non-directiveness that it is an instance of such an 'ought': it is unattainable. The questions whether non-directiveness is in fact possible, and if possible, desirable, are usually treated in conjunction with each other. I propose to separate these two and consider the facts before the values.

In any ordinary social relationship between two people there will always be some assimilation of each other's qualities. 'The more frequently persons interact with one another,' writes G. C. Homans, 'the more alike in some respects both their activities and their sentiments become.'[1] If this is true of ordinary social relationships so much more is it true of the counselling 'dyad'. In their truly valiant

[1] *The Human Group*, London, 1951.

experimental study of 120 tape-recorded psychotherapeutic sessions, involving the classification of more than 40,000 verbal propositions along several dimensions, H. L. Lennard and A. Bernstein ascertained the directiveness of psychotherapy by using the 'interaction process analysis' devised by R. F. Bales.[2] They came to the conclusion that personality change in the patient is strictly influenced by the available model, the therapist. They write, 'Traditional theories of psychotherapy have always maintained the view that the patient, like Peer Gynt, should become more "himself" in the course of therapy, rather than be transformed into a facsimile of the therapist. Our findings (with respect to specific aspects of therapist and patient communication patterns) can be interpreted as bearing out Homans' hypothesis that interacting individuals tend to become more alike as time passes.'[3] Indeed, we could entertain the notion that non-directiveness is possible only if we accepted the contradictory propositions that a human relationship can continue to be intimate and deeply communicative and, at the same time, it can be free from directiveness. This is partly what E. J. Shoben had in mind when he wrote recently, that 'given the model *l'homme machine* of the patient as a computer gone defective, it *is* ridiculous to talk of ... "freedom" granted to the client'.[4] Unless we mean therapy to be therapeutic and, therefore, determining and directing in important ways, we can hardly expect to be helpful. Even in the so-called 'Oh? huh!' method of treatment the therapist's comment is not entirely withheld; at any rate the obviously inevitable physical presence of the therapist-counsellor will exert its influence in surreptitious ways. In an interesting experimental study the influence of the comment of 'Mm-hmm' and of 'good' on the responses of interviewees and listeners was carried out by D. C. Hildum and R. W. Brown who found these grunts and monosyllabic notes powerfully reinforcing. This cannot but undermine our confidence in the possibility of 'not influencing'.[5] There are other ways which are easily overlooked: a spontaneous bursting into facial grimace, a nod, gesture, grunt, or sigh, and so on, are utterly inevitable; and even the counsellor's taste in furniture, in clothes, his choice of

---

[2] *Interaction Process Analysis*, Cambridge, 1950.
[3] *The Anatomy of Psychotherapy*, New York, 1960, p. 90.
[4] *Op. cit.*
[5] 'Verbal Reinforcement and Interviewer Bias', *Journal of Abnormal and Social Psychology*, 1956, Vol. LIII, pp. 108–111.

pictures on the wall of his consulting room, the outward physical signs of his domestic circumstances, the status and other symbols of his consulting room, his publicly reported statements, and several other signs of his activities, will make the ideal of non-directiveness impossible to achieve.

It is also difficult to see how any professional service can be stripped of the motive or desire to be *instrumental* in bringing about a change by doing a service. The counsellor's desire to be 'instrumental' in this way is an integral part of his professional motivation. No doubt this desire may push itself forward too excessively but it is certain that far from being harmful, or even only superfluous, it is a necessary condition of effective service. A perfect non-directiveness would be a negation of this motive or desire. What seems to be happening is that the carefully cultivated and painstakingly observed non-directiveness is the form which the counsellor has chosen to allay his anxiety about 'being found in possession' of moral preferences. The scrupulous and sometimes ostentatious non-interventionism of counselling is obviously doctrinaire. And 'a doctrinaire permissiveness which tries to give identical encouragement to every individual'[6] either advertises moral relativism or equalitarianism, or both.

The counsellor's faith in non-directiveness is merged with his professional commitment to *direct* the patient to health, no matter how obliquely. Of course, those who write for counsellors are ready to proscribe the cruder methods of imposing 'health' on the patient; for example Dollard and Miller say about this 'that almost all therapists talk too much or, rather, too loosely. They find it hard to subordinate themselves to a listening role. They interrupt the patient, prompt the patient, give him unnecessary reassurance, paraphrase his statements without essential clarification and otherwise socialise in a useless manner.'[7] No doubt, Dollard and Miller look upon these as errors which can be rectified by learning and self-discipline, and thus they help to consolidate the belief that the ideal of non-directiveness is at least realisable.

For the large majority of counsellors, who cannot afford to devote several hundred hours to the same client, the ideal, and the belief that the ideal can at least be approximated, may become the

---

[6] L. J. Cronbach: 'The Two Disciples of Scientific Psychology', *American Psychologist*, 1957, Vol. XII.
[7] *Personality and Psychotherapy*, New York, 1950, p. 412.

source of self-deception. For example, John Bowlby said recently that it is 'imperative to refrain from exceeding the client's mandate ... It is for the client ... to decide whether or not he wishes the problem which has been revealed to be dealt with.'[8] But could the client be consulted on how much of the problem he wishes to have revealed? Is it for him to decide what should be revealed and at what rate? And even more important than these : 'to be dealt with' means that a certain amount of the counsellor's time and supportiveness will be used. The client does not and cannot know in advance how much of this he can count on, or for that matter, how much of this he will need if he agrees to a problem's being dealt with. Surely, this is not a contract freely entered into by both parties : if the client's mandate is given, more often than not he does not know what this mandate has been given for.

No matter how much care is taken to allow people spontaneity of growth along the lines of their own choosing, it is simply not true that arbitrariness of influence on them can be avoided. The social realities of counselling—underpaid and overworked counselling staffs of statutory and voluntary bodies, too many clients in urgent need of some help, lack of co-operation by other, non-counselling services and the clients' resistance too, as well as many other factors, physical illness, for example—will inevitably limit the counsellor's potential of behaving non-directively. These limitations are not understood by most clients at the time when they are supposed to be giving their mandate to a counsellor to help them. The client does not know how much of his eventual disclosures will be absorbed in supportive contact, and how much of these will be left stranded, like the fisherman's unmarketable catch, which may as well be thrown back into the stirred-up muddy waters. 'When case loads are too high,' writes Helen Harris Perlman, 'sustained contact with clients becomes impossible and only "hit and run" visits can be made.'[9] Can we really maintain that in these circumstances we have a clear enough notion of what the client's mandate is? There is no doubt, that vital decisions will have to be taken without consulting him.

Thus intervention is irremovably there when counselling is undertaken and the therapeutic intention is, as it were, stated in the

[8] Foreword in *The Caseworker's Use of Relationships*, by M. L. Ferard and N. K. Hunnybun, London, 1962.
[9] 'Are We Creating Dependency?', *Social Service Review*, 1960, Vol. XXXIV, pp. 323–333.

very act of the first encounter with the patient. The name of the institution for which the counsellor often works either has an explicit moral purpose, or the client's fantasies about it having such a purpose, are not effectively dispelled. Only the quality and potency of the intervention can be varied and this only within the range which is limited by the humanity of the counsellor and of his client.

In addition to the reasons so far given for unavoidable directiveness there is now a theoretical feature in counselling thought which, in practice, necessitates the *prescription* of directiveness. In current psychoanalytical thinking much stress is put on *ego*-therapy and, in general, on reinforcing the *ego*, irrespective of whether there is an increase in insight or not. It is now freely promised that improvement can occur without insight and that insight may even exacerbate the patient's condition.[10] This is a hazardous departure from the relatively objective point of view of a reductively working psychoanalytic therapy. According to this therapy, the patient's personality is reorientated because he increases his full effective understanding of his own motives and, as a result, acquires spontaneous and unsuggested preference for different feelings and actions in the future. How can a process of 'ego-reinforcement', say, in social casework, claim that it can retain the same measure of objectivity as a reductive psychotherapy of some duration might have? If there is a genuine reinforcement of the *ego*, it is likely to be a selective reinforcement. Some defences will be singled out for favour, and others may be less encouraged. No doubt, there is almost always a sincere and energetic attempt at clarifying the patient's *own* views to him, highlighting for him his preferences and aversions to show the pattern they may make, but it is impossible to engage even in this act of clarification without implying certain stresses, emphases, and preoccupations.

Whether in the special processes of ego-reinforcement or in counselling generally, the counsellor *means* to direct the patient towards health and will include in his direction his own personal and idiosyncratic version of health. In some cases this will exact from the patient or client either a measure of conformity and compromise, or it will impose on patient or client the counsellor's own special brand of non-conformity. In social casework for

[10] Cf. Theodore Lidz in *Progress in Psychotherapy*, Ed. by F. Fromm-Reichmann and J. L. Moreno, New York, 1956.

example, the frank departures from non-directive handling have become more frequent. When G. L. Bibring outlined her 'Psychiatric Principles of Casework' in the *Journal of Social Casework*[11] she gave pride of place to what she called 'manipulation'. No, it is not 'the undesirable attempt of the worker to force his concepts and plans on the client', social caseworkers would use the term in a more positive sense than this. 'After listening to and observing the client,' Dr. Bibring continues, 'we may use our understanding of his personality structure, his patterns, his needs and conflicts, and his defences in order to "manipulate" him in various ways.' Dr. Bibring presents a formidable list of the ways in which this 'manipulation' may occur. 'We may make suggestions as to what steps may or may not help this individual to cope better with his problems; we may plan with him as to his emotional, professional, and recreational activities; we may give appropriate advice to members of his environment; ... or we may purposely activate relevant emotional attitudes in the client for the sake of adjustive change. It is in this specific sense that we use the term "manipulation".' It is just this sweeping *un*specificness which makes the alleged standard of non-directiveness fictional.

But the assumption of radical initiative is not restricted to the 'brief therapies' of counselling. Remarkably enough it is in the pages of *The International Journal of Psychoanalysis* that we read, 'we cannot be neutral in our daily work as therapists; the research on countertransferences has shown that this attitude is virtually impossible to maintain. New methods of therapy may be indicated *putting more stress on guidance and re-education.* We must not regress to primitive methods of suggestion and persuasion,' the writer surprisingly stipulates, *'but we have to realise that psychoanalytic therapy has always been directive, and that the directive force is the personality of the therapist and his value judgments ...* Last but not least, the so-called spiritual values (*sic*!) have to be treated more respectfully and the "nothing-but" attitude subjected to vigorous analysis.'[12] (Italics mine.) In another article in the same journal the same retreat from non-directiveness is announced, 'there comes a moment in analysis when "neutrality", so superstitiously observed, has to be replaced by an

[11] June 1949, Vol. XXX, No. 6, pp. 230–235.
[12] 'Value Judgments in Psychoanalysis', by N. Nielsen, July–October 1960, Vol. XLI, Parts 4–5, pp. 435–429

attitude of presence . . .'[13] Now, 'presence' is an interesting category though its relationship with the psychoanalytical system of concepts is not entirely clear. Certainly, it elicits an image of power and influence, and not one of impartiality and neutrality. In a later paper of the same author this image is more elaborately presented and because of its great relevance to the central ideas of this book I will quote the key passage of this paper in full. There is another and equally important reason for doing this in the context of a discussion on non-directiveness : the passage draws attention to the connection between loving and directiveness on the one hand, and not-loving and non-directiveness on the other. It will also serve as an example of how the separately listed 'elements in the counsellor's faith' in this chapter are really aspects of the same 'authentic benevolence',[14] the same Faith. The passage could have been cited to document the first section on the oddity of calling tenderness and concern a skill; here it will accomplish the added function of showing that, according to the counsellors : 'the words of the analyst (and counsellors in general) and the interventions that he makes are only effective (and presumably directive) . . . and the interpretations he gives . . . are of value to his patient' if, what S. Nacht calls the analyst's 'gratifying presence', constitutes a 'deep-down attitude of availability and hearty attentiveness'.[15]

> 'For the patient to be able to let himself go in that special kind of deep union which he unconsciously desires, it is more than ever necessary for the analyst to bring a certain *quality of presence* rooted in inner availability and openness. This quality can only be beneficial if it arises from an authentic inner attitude; any semblance of it would be without value, without bearing, without significance. What significance would such an attitude have, and what would be its efficacy, if it were not based on a truly profound interest on the part of the doctor for his patient, a constant and unconditional understanding?'[16]

I have already discussed the vanity of considering this quality of personal presence a 'skill', and the ideology of 'matter-of-

[13] 'The Pre-Object Universe in the Transference Situation', S. Nacht and S. Viderman, *The International Journal of Psychoanalysis*, July–October 1960, Vol. XLI, Parts 4–5, pp. 385–388.
[14] and [15] 'The Non-Verbal Relationship in Psycho-Analytic Treatment', by S. Nacht, *The International Journal of Pychoanalysis*, July 1963, Vol XLIV, Part 3, pp. 328–333.
[16] *Op. cit.*, p. 331.

factness' which encourages this belief. Here I am trying to show that the counsellor not only takes his influential presence as a therapeutic tool for granted, but that he thinks it to be a most powerfully directive presence.

One wonders whether passages and articles of this kind are allowed space in *The International Journal of Psychoanalysis* either because of a casual or a liberal-minded editorial policy or because, if truth be told, psychoanalysis has not committed its followers to some of the most fundamental tenets of the theory, namely those which insist that therapy should be reductive so that the patient should be able to resolve the present in terms of the objective insight he gains into the past, and not in terms of either a mystical and spiritual communion with the analyst, or in terms of directions and value-judgments coming from him. These passages with their oblique references to spirituality flagrantly ignore the fact that the concept of spirituality either has no place in psychoanalysis or, if it appears there, it would be described by the theory as a sign of the operation of some defence mechanism. Surely, these adventurous departures from the tough-minded, scientifically committed, psychoanalytic mentality, occurring with increasing frequency in places which one might consider 'official', are not accidental lapses. They are certainly not rare or inconspicuous, nor would the plea of 'mere lapses or careless phrasing' be regarded by this journal of all journals as of no evidential value. Are the Editor, the subscribers, and the sponsoring International Association of Psychoanalysis confessing to uncertainty on these matters? Or are they confessing to indifference whether or not they are taken to have authorised the use of 'the directive force of the therapist's value judgments' as a legitimate part of reductive analysis? If they accommodate views of this nature in the official international organ of the profession does this mean that there is at least an element of doubt in their minds about basic principles? Yet if such concepts and language are flagrantly confusing or useless to them how can the papers containing them be accepted for publication? Assuredly, one could no more claim here that a liberal editorial policy must allow for a divergence of views than one could claim it, in some other scientific journal, in respect of a paper which disregards the use of scientific principles.

But this orientation of thinking and sentiment is widespread. Not only is it apparent in the journals of psychotherapy and psychiatry, in the professional journals of social work, but it is also restated in the more definitive works of leading counsellors. Karl Menninger, one of the more distinguished among these, comes to the following conclusion, 'We cannot ignore the fact that what the psychoanalyst believes, what he lives for, what he loves, what he considers to be good and what he considers to be evil, become known to the patient and influence him enormously not as "suggestion" but as inspiration'.[17] Here too, directiveness is given a reverential testimonial : it is not a mechanical suggestion and manipulation, but 'inspiration', a process with obvious spiritual associations. Menninger openly deplores the over-anxious avoidance of directiveness and complains that 'in some psychoanalysts this attitude of non-judgment becomes almost a religion'.[18] Of course, the situation is paradoxical, and Menninger sees this,[19] for both the meticulously enforced care not to violate the integrity of the patient, and the dedicated care to direct him to health can, especially in their simultaneity, 'become almost a religion'. Another no less prominent training analyst, Thomas S. Szász, confesses, 'we cannot ... forever hold fast to and profit from the morally judgmental and socially manipulative character of our traditional psychiatric and psychoanalytic language without paying a price'.[20] If this is to what a staff-member of the Chicago Institute of Psychoanalysis has to testify, it is likely to be based not only on Szász' own therapeutic work but also on his assessment of his colleagues' work.

Of course, Freud himself envisaged that at times 'the pure gold of analysis will have to be diluted by the copper of suggestion',[21] but this was to be a temporary expediency to be got out of the way when more analytic knowledge will make this possible. At the same time other therapeutic systems do not promise the atrophy of suggestion in the glare of 'more knowledge'. If anything, they prescribe direction even more unambiguously than the psychoanalytical examples so far cited. H. S. Sullivan maintained that the analyst must not be a mere detached observer but a 'participant observer'. The Adlerian, for example, speaks of *encouragement* as an integral part of therapy, and looks upon moral re-education as part of his therapeutic task. The Jungian regards *education* as a

17 *Theory of Psychoanalytic Technique*, London, 1958, p. 91.
18 *Ibid.*, p. 97.
19 *Ibid.*, pp. 27 and 94.
20 *The Myth of Mental Illness*, London, 1962, p. 4.
21 *Collected Papers*, London, 1946, Vol. II, pp. 400–402.

normal phase of psychotherapy. And outside these identifiable systems, where psychotherapy merges with the practice of medicine, in the professional literature of psychiatry, there are even fewer signs of squeamishness about direction, exhortation, and suggestion. For example, in the book, *Personality Patterns of Psychiatrists*, directive assertiveness is bluntly prescribed without any apologetic reservations : '... psychiatrists must at times be active and directive people who have authoritarian personality structures(!) and a need to dominate(!)', and the authors add that these 'are perhaps not so unsuitable as they are considered to be for psychoanalysis and psychotherapy ...'[22] The implication here that one could speak of 'more' or 'less' directiveness or of different 'levels' in directiveness will be followed up later. What concerns us here is that psychiatrists are 'counsellors' whose primarily and predominantly *medical* education is not in the majority of cases supplemented by any systematic training in counselling. In view of this notorious deficiency in the training of psychiatrists, the otherwise legitimately manipulative—surgical and medical— approach to the patient will inevitably retain its sway over the psychiatrist's manner. 'Teachers of medicine sometimes rephrase the distinction,' write H. S. Becker and B. Geer, 'between clinical and pre-clinical years into one between cynical and pre-cynical years.'[23] They add that 'psychological research supports this view, presenting attitude surveys which show medical students year by year scoring lower on "idealism" and higher on "cynicism" '. Certainly, the evidence for this requires some strengthening but it is at least probable that the very desirable regimen of scientific rigour in medical training and the laudable insistence on the utmost technical scrupulousness leave very little margin of sheer time and energy for the cultivation of empathic curiosity and sensitivity.

The medical career-image of the average grammar or high school young person is in keeping with the scientific-technological standards of the medical training process. Once, in a study of career-choices, I put a questionnaire before some English sixth formers, who had declared their resolve to pursue a medical career, and asked them to choose a career on the assumption that entry

[22] By R. R. Holt and L. Luborski, Imago, London, 1958, p. 262.
[23] 'The Fate of Idealism in the Medical School', *American Sociological Review*, February 1958, pp. 50–56.

into the medical profession would be barred to them. A significantly higher number chose 'research scientist' and similar impersonal careers than ones which would entail a personal service. Naturally, the choices open to them—with a 'science-sixth' education behind them—were probably limited for all sorts of reasons. Yet was it not at least possible that in these circumstances there would be many manipulative and object-oriented youngsters who would opt for this course and career and not only those who were person-oriented?

It would not be a fruitful query in the present context, at any rate, to seek an answer to this question. Let it suffice that the *medical* background 'in the counsellor's professional history is not an asset in developing the non-directive stance or realising its ideals.

In my listing of the 'counselling professions' I did not include the general practitioner. This may seem anomalous at first, but is justifiable. The practitioners of medicine give their first attention to physical diagnosis and therapy. They would mostly decline to be called 'counsellors' in the sense I have given this term. Nonetheless, some recent developments show that at least a minority of doctors are beginning to agree with the view that 'all good medical practice . . . has been and is to some degree psychotherapy'.[24] This minority of doctors—their numbers unknown—is already beginning to make its influence felt on the ideology of counselling and their practice as well as their interpretation of their counselling function is beginning to be important for my portraiture of the counselling creeds.[25] This is especially true in respect of the issue of moral directiveness.

In the past, the general practitioner tended to be brazenly and self-assuredly directive. His views about considered psychological techniques were contemptuous and often paranoid.[26] During the last three or four decades considerable changes have taken place in the physician's attitudes to psychological medicine and psycho-

[24] *The Social System*, by Talcott Parsons, London, 1952, p. 478.
[25] There are many striking illustrations available to show up the nature of this change, for example, 'Mrs. Challock called her doctor at 2.30 a.m. for her husband, who was supposed to be very ill. The doctor, sensing some sort of emotional crisis, sat down and let the patient talk for an hour and a half. He went next day again and carried on listening.' From *Night Calls*, by M. B. Clyne, London, 1961, p. 137.
[26] 'The Psychology of the Psychotherapist', by E. Glover, *The British Journal of Medical Psychology*, 1962, Vol. XXXV, Part 1, pp. 47–57.

therapeutic handling. The psychologising G.P. is no longer a rarity. Yet although the cultural climate of medical practice has changed, and the moral tone of the medical man's intervention, *qua* counsellor of patient or his family has changed, there has not been and could not have been a marked change in the personal mental health of the practising family physician. There is no new assurance available that the contemporary practitioner is better suited to be trusted with part-time psychotherapeutic experimentation than his predecessors were at the beginning of this century. Glover listed the general practitioner's reactions, whenever he functions as a counsellor, as reactions of a 'magical, or persuasive, or exhortative, or negativistic' kind and presumably what Glover calls 'peremptory system of gingering' was a constant standby of their technique. Naturally, in these circumstances we could hardly feel assured that wilful advice will not be given whether the patient asked for it or not.

Today, however, some general physicians assume much more sophisticated roles and act as counsellors only after some thought and preparation. These would regard themselves as counsellors, in my sense of the term, and this warrants their inclusion here. Dr. Michael Balint has, in fact, undertaken to train general practitioners as counsellors, and by now, there is some literature available on this enterprise from which we can obtain Balint's views as well as the views of those he has trained. One of Balint's pupils, Dr. Primrose, for example, has recourse to what he calls 'forceful psychotherapy'. Whatever this may mean, in reading Primrose's little book,[27] one is persuaded to disregard any claim for this method's non-directiveness. Balint himself reports that some of the general practitioners of his following apply 'rather forceful methods to bring about the change from physical to psychological illness'.[28] The therapist-doctor who, according to Balint (a senior psychoanalyst), has an 'apostolic function', will look at the physical complaint of the patient, and if it is his view that the physical condition is a presenting problem, camouflaging a real problem which is psychological, then he will set aside the physical problem and proceed to the examination of the underlying psychological causes. The patient may, of course, consent to this procedure without

[27] *Psychological Illness, A Community Study*, London, 1962, p. 40.
[28] *The Doctor, His Patient and The Illness*, by M. Balint, London, 1957, p. 184.

knowing one important implication of it, that is that the physician's time does not allow a thorough exploration of his condition and that at an arbitrarily chosen point he will have to 'seal off' the exploration, leaving the patient at a stage of reorientation, at which he may not have chosen to be left in preference to the condition with which he has started. One might argue that the blank cheque the patient is required to sign before an operation is a consent of the same order. This analogy, however, will not stand up to close examination. The protection of the patient's *physical integrity* demands primarily if not exclusively scientific expertise and manipulative skill, whilst the protection of his *personal integrity* requires qualifications of a somewhat different kind.

In all these instances, in all the areas of counselling so far surveyed, even when the doctrine of non-directiveness and non-judgmentalness has been openly abandoned, there are still gestures and reservations to the effect that the 'constructive' potentialities of the client-patient will be given full scope and that whatever 'encouragement', 're-education', or 'ego-reinforcement' is undertaken, it will take due notice of these potentialities. Necessarily, the counsellor will have the unenviable responsibility of judging what is constructive and creative and what is not. As a consequence of this, from time to time, contemporary literature breaks out into rashes of protest against the tendency to direct people towards conformity, and there is often a cry against the 'adjustment-cult' of some 'reactionary' counsellors.[29] The protesters rightly stress that adjustment to an inept society is a greater evil than the stress of maladjustment to it. The critics of counselling say that the counsellor tries to induce the client to want what the counsellor wants.[30] Yet some will try to defend the counsellor by saying that there are forms of intervention which do not amount to directiveness. For example, Roger Wilson defends the social worker by suggesting that non-judgmental attitude includes helping people 'to achieve the conformity which we assume, with some reason, most people want most of the time'.[31] But will this defence stand up to scrutiny? Even if we rashly assume that most people want conformity most of the time, and equally rashly conclude that leading people back

[29] *Prescription for Rebellion*, by R. Lindner, London, 1953, is a vivid example of this kind of protest.
[30] *Social Science and Social Pathology*, by B. Wootton, London.
[31] 'Uniformity in the Affluent Society', *The Sociological Review*, November 1960, Vol. VIII, No. 1, pp. 119–128.

to conformity is, therefore, a legitimate professional goal in counselling, we still have not reached a firm enough foothold. For
which of the many conformities available in a complex society is
the counsellor to countenance? Divorce or monogamy? Women
going out to work and relegating maternal tasks to others, or
women staying at home? Earning more money stressfully or managing on much less and have peace? In an age of rapid transition
conformity itself is too elusive to be cited as a guide. It is true that,
as Dr. Bibring remarks, 'we may modify our attitude and approach
to (the client's) problems', which is a genuine enough promise but
somewhat difficult to accept as 'collateral' for the large credit
which the authority for this direction and manipulation will no
doubt require.

My contention in this section has been that even in those cases
in which deliberate influencing is made explicitly part of the
therapeutic service, a core of the fiction of non-directiveness is preserved. I should like to stress, however, that I do not question the
partial success of the counsellor's effort not to be dominating, and
authoritarian, and his equally well-known effort to elicit as much
spontaneity from the client as possible. But this success conceals
important areas of failure, and it is these areas which make the
doctrine of non-directiveness ideological, though the very success
of the effort contributes its share of the ideological too : in it the
counsellor affirms the value of individual uniqueness. The counsellor is a respecter of persons, and the client's specially individual
brand of personhood must be safeguarded against too deep incur-
sions of advice and persuasion.

I do not focus attention on the judgmentalness of the counsellor
because I wish to be reproachful about it. It is an element in the
counsellor's faith, and it had to be given its due. People who are
ever keen to rehabilitate the notion of 'moral responsibility' should
not complain if the counsellor assumes it in the presence of need
for care and love. There is no breach of humanity in using all our
resources to liberate people from what they can't very well endure,
especially when our conscience tells us that they ought not to be
expected to endure it without our efforts to alleviate and help. Of
course, there is an arbitrary moral initiative taken here, but counselling is a moral initiative and all moral initiative is arbitrary.
The intervention in counselling is not an error that can be avoided.
Yet, paradoxically, it is desirable to cultivate the fiction of total

non-intervention, so that the most could be got out of each unique instance of humanity. At the same time, it would be a mistake to allow the ideal of non-directiveness to perpetuate a fiction of its total possibility.

At its lowest estimate, the counsellor cannot sustain the activity of healing another or helping another with perseverance, and scrupulously avoid communicating the idea that concern for the welfare of others is worthwhile! The therapeutic attention is a moral stance, no matter how much effort is expended on the most cautious non-directive self-control. And indeed even this, the conscientiousness of it, the painstaking tactfulness of it, and so on, will hardly escape the attention, no matter how unconscious and intuitive, of those who are helped. The whole performance is inevitably personal, and biased in some most important sense. The truth lies not in disowning this bias but rather acting on it with full awareness and frank admission. The real bias is to think that we can care and remain unbiased, that we ought to be unbiased even in the 'I and Thou' relationship of persons, or that counselling does not need that kind of relationship.

Summary of the argument in this section. I began by explaining that the principle of non-directiveness is a moral principle and not a psychological proposition, and I continued to argue that, in fact, the ideal of non-directiveness cannot be realised. All human relationships cause those who take part in them to assume the characteristics of each other, and the counselling relationship has this nature too, which is enhanced by the therapeutic intentions of the counsellor. It is almost as if to restrain directiveness was incompatible with giving help, for the empathy and prompt sensitivity, as well as the support, and initiative required of the counsellor will make the aspiration to non-directiveness unrealistic and, perhaps, even self-defeating. The counselling literature was quoted to show that the counsellors believe in the necessity of using their personal presence and, indeed, their fundamental preferences in values. They regard personal dedication to the cause of counselling as fundamentally paradoxical : both affectionate concern on the one hand, and keenly interested neutrality and non-involvement on the other, are necessary for success in counselling. They realise that absolute neutrality would neutralise the therapeutic influence itself. But there is little danger of this occurring, for a moral attitude is implicit in the very advocacy of mental health in general.

And in the singling out of specific symptoms, response-systems, and behavioural elements for attention, interpretation, and discussion, the counsellor's moral influence is made quite specific and detailed.

Psychoanalysts, psychotherapists, and social caseworkers, are all shown to admit that they believe in the 'armed neutrality' of the counsellor. For some the arms are much in evidence, they are powerful and they are there to impose. For others the discipline of restraint and neutrality is the thing that is most conspicuous about them. But all share the paradox of a non-involved involvement, and a non-judgmental directiveness. I have shown that counsellors sometimes attempt to represent their directive influence as somehow 'inspirational', 'educational', or mysteriously 'available', and I have argued that these are by no means the signs of deception, but of an idealistic aspiration, which is itself an important asset and virtue of the counselling function. Of course, there is not enough time for each client, and there are not enough counsellors; and if the counsellor is to help he must make some decisions. What is wrong is not that he takes them but that he may find it necessary to deny this. This section is not a 'supplement' to Barbara Wootton's chapter on the counsellor's 'arrogant psychiatric interpretations' of plain material distress. I do not criticise the counsellor's directiveness, only present reasons why he is wrong to deny it or even to underestimate it.

In this section I have also shown that counsellors with a medical training are especially susceptible to overlook their own decisiveness and imperativeness. It is not easy to live down the surgeon's or apothecary's habit of simple instrumentalism. The psychiatrist untrained in counselling and the occasional family doctor half-trained in it, are both too busy to notice themselves relapsing into sheer manipulation of an authoritarian kind.

Finally, there are the charges about conformity and reactionary influences. Here too, I tried to show that the counsellor's defence against these charges may be weak but it reaffirms his faith in the integrity and uniqueness of those he is committed to help. And this reaffirmation helps to keep his intervention within reasonable bounds. Thus, the fiction of non-directiveness is, to some extent, a necessary fiction, a necessary guide.

The Fiction of 'Applying Science'

And thus the counsellor is made to realise that he must work in an archetypal fellowship bond, that he must allow himself to be involved in the professional-personal relationships of counselling, and that he must confess to be an influential moral agent. Yet he must dispassionately watch himself being all these things, and apply insight as well as a sociopsychological science to the control of his work. The trouble is that the very concept of an 'applied sociopsychological science' is somewhat blurred at the edges. At the centre, where things are sharper, we may observe that an 'applied science' is a system of theoretical generalisations about certain tools and procedures which can be used to modify part of our universe. The essential point is that in the various 'technologies', for example, in engineering or medicine, the theoretical generalisations are usually verified before they lead to the construction and use of tools, or to the manipulation of substances, whereas in counselling, the theoretical generalisations often lead straight to action, even when they have not yet been verified. Or in other words, in the technologies there is no doubt that what we apply is *science*, whilst in counselling there is a great deal of doubt. In the previous sections I have cited the views of several prominent counselling theoreticians explicitly stating that the counsellor is not only an applier of science, but also of his own person, and that undue emphasis on science is detrimental to the counselling process. On the other hand, the system of generalisations about personality and about human relationships, which we regard as constituting our sociopsychological science, is itself at a grievous disadvantage. To most experienced and sensitive counsellors many of these generalisations will appear plausible, yet only a fraction of these could be regarded as 'verified' in the conventional sense of the term.

And so, from time to time, critics of the 'arche-theory' of counselling, psychoanalysis, overflow into books and articles about the excessive claims of psychoanalysis for the status of 'science'. The counsellors, using psychoanalytic procedures and mental tools, whether fully trained by psychoanalytic institutes or not, are often painfully aware of the forbidding difficulties in the way of securing for their working assumptions the kind of verification we, and they too, expect to have in the experimental sciences. Naturally, what constitutes evidence for verification and what does not will have to remain the concern of the philosophy of science; here in the area of *giving help*, of urgent and morally inevitable acts, assumptions without verification often seem to compel the counsellor to intervene. Not unexpectedly, counsellors who intervene act on assumptions about human growth which they regard as valid. These assumptions compel the counsellor to act especially when, through the therapeutic analysis of his own personality, he has come to discover certain causal relationships in his own life-history. These relationships seem to him to be verified by the vividness of his own recollections and by the startling unambiguity of their disclosures. To propose to him—as is often done—that these recollections are at least contaminated by the suggestions of his own therapist, or by his own reading and training in an intellectual climate of doctrines and premature certainties, is to offer him an explanation for his certainties which he will find unacceptable : he *knows* that the anamnesias are his own, and that his insight is the product of private memories, and not of doctrine or persuasion. To some extent, he now '*knows*' his own mind, and methodological scruples about the credentials of this knowledge only tend to irritate him. In these circumstances whether to delay action, to procrastinate until some 'hard evidence' will convince the counsellor's critics that the assumptions are true, is a moral decision and not a logico-intellectual one.[1] That he can and should decide in favour of acting on the subjective evidence available to him, when he may not consent to his surgeon acting in this manner, is proof of his moral resolve to act on *faith*.

This does not mean that the psychoanalytically oriented counsellor need despair of the prospects of verification for his assumptions. So long as it is perfectly possible, and not too difficult, to translate many of the tenets of psychoanalytic personality-doctrine into the language of modern learning theory, or some other behaviour theory, some measure of scientific agreement on the fundamentals of this doctrine can reasonably be expected.

---

[1] Cf. 'Social Science and Social Work: a Theory of their Relationship', by E. Greenwood, *The Social Service Review*, 1955, Vol. XXIX, No. 1, pp. 20–33.

It is, however, not my present task to ascertain whether the counsellor's system of assumptions is a scientifically respectable system of hypotheses. Though this task is an important one, it lies outside the scope of my present business, which is to explore whether the profession of counselling relies on certain acts of faith which are demonstrably extraneous to science. Here I am not going to ask whether there is a science where it is claimed to be, but rather to enquire whether the counsellors *admit* to relying on premises, which—on their own showing—lie outside the field of science. No doubt, if there is no science, nor even the possibility of it, one could argue that the counsellor's claim to be applying one, and his illusion that a system of dubious generalisations amounts to science, would be an act of faith. Yet my task of clarification is not to be the rather hackneyed one of arguing with the counsellors whether their psychology is valid, whether their account of personality development is the true account, and whether any particular dynamic theory is more plausible than any other. The task I set myself is to show that, entirely *outside* the framework of any conceivable empirical science, the counsellors, on their own admission, depend on acts of faith, on moral affirmations, and on *a priori* digging-in-of-heels, rather than on the technological and instrumental wielding of discursive, scientific, and mathematically expressible knowledge or, for that matter, of any kind of empirical knowledge. In this book I have put forward the view that counselling is in fact readily and freely described by its practitioners as not only a technological and manipulative operation, an operation analysable into mechanical phases, into molecular events, but also an unanalysable personal and molar performance.

Nowadays, when social workers are often teased for their seeming ambition to be 'the poor man's psychoanalysts', and when it is widely held that the counselling professions have derived most of their theoretical premises from psychoanalysis, it is proper to go to the source and enquire whether there are any unequivocal admissions by psychoanalysts, occurring with sufficient frequency, to preclude the thought that the admissions are accidental. I have suggested before, and must repeat it here, that the psychoanalytic therapeutic literature furnishes a constant source of theoretical clarification and justification to the rank and file of the various counselling subgroups. Most counsellors, no matter how different their clinical and social background, develop their ideas under the influence of published psychoanalytic reflection. It is easy to show how an insight or a new explanatory concept in therapy is passed down the line, usually starting with psychoanalytical reappraisals, and ending with the social casework theoreticians translating the thing into the idiom of the social caseworkers. Even if in their eclecticism many of the counsellors have explicitly claimed to be independent of the psychoanalytic counselling fraternity, they still receive powerful suggestions and potent concepts from this arche-theory and proto-theory of counselling. And although much of my documentation is psychoanalytical, the views expressed reflect thinking far outside the comparatively small psychoanalytical *élite*. Indeed, this influence reaches the general cultural orientation of our communities.

Thus the repeated admissions in the literature of the inner circle rapidly reach the peripheries and take hold there as guiding principles. The psychoanalytic teachers of social workers, of doctors, and so on, carry the pupils with them and the pupils too are not slow in documenting their allegiance to the principles of their mentors. And so, we can follow with ease the counselling ideology of psychoanalysis which reappears in the professional journals of social work. There too, amidst avowals of fidelity to science we find confessions of a total personal and spiritual committedness. Let us then take representative illustrations of the views of counsellors on the regard they show for science. There will be two major trends discernible: one points to an open renunciation of a complete scientific rationale for counselling: the other consists in an attempt to obliterate distinctions between objective and subjective observation, a distinction of some significance to the progress of science.

One need only peruse the leading official paper of psychoanalysis, *The International Journal of Psychoanalysis*, to collect, with surprising ease, a rich selection of weighty testimonies. W. D. R. Fairbairn, writing 'On the Nature and Aims of Psychoanalytic Treatment', observes: 'No disparagement of the scientific aspect of psychoanalysis, any more than that of medicine, is implied in the contention that concern over the scientific aspect of a therapeutic method can be carried too far. For, if this concern is too exclusive, the human factor in the therapeutic situation (as represented by individuality, the personal value and the needs of the patient) is only too liable to be sacrificed to the method, which thus comes to assume greater importance than the aims which it is intended to serve.'[2] We are first reminded that psychoanalysis has a scientific aspect, not that it *is* a science. Then we are told that this aspect is not to be allowed exclusive control over the method of therapy. No, the method must be guided by moral aims and by moral considerations for 'the human factor', which he elaborates to mean the 'individuality, the personal value, and the needs of the patient'. One may, of course, complain that, surely, the therapeutic methods, appropriately defined and conscientiously applied, should necessarily serve 'the human factor', and that a conflict of what comes first, science or human concern, can't arise. After all, how can anyone possibly sacrifice these human values, having mastered the 'best method', unless there is something vitally important which is *extraneous* to the 'best *method*'? We could not make much sense of what Fairbairn is saying here unless we were willing to agree that, in addition to learning the articulated elements of method, the counsellor must also respond with some mysteriously basic application to and reverence for the personal presence of a needer of help and a seeker of counsel. Or is this mere respectful talk about the inviolability of the *person*, so that the tender-minded will not take the technicalities too much to heart? Or is Fairbairn appealing to something outside the analytically definable potentials of the counsellor, and is he 'backsliding' into a vague moralising and metaphysical language? Surely, one cannot be blamed for thinking that, in fact, Fairbairn appeals to forces which exist outside the psychoanalytical country, in an area with which Fairbairn's homeland has no diplomatic relations!

I am further sustained in my belief that my interpretation might be correct by the following illuminating passage in the same paper: '. . . it must be recognised that the practising analyst is "not primarily a scientist, but a psychotherapist", and that "the adoption of a psychotherapeutic role *ipso facto* involves a departure from the strictly scientific attitude" '.[3] As clear an admission of faith as one need look for to prove that the counsellors' base of operation is not the laboratory and that they are by no means appliers of science. This admission involves more than an acknowledgement that the counsellor cannot rely on science alone: it implies that relying on science alone is incompatible with coun-

2 *The International Journal of Psychoanalysis*, Vol. XXXIX, Part 5, pp. 374–385.
3 *Ibid.*

selling. Counselling, properly conceived '*ipso facto* involves a departure' from scientific rigour.

Another contributor to *The International Journal of Psychoanalysis*, H. W. Loewald, phrases the same line of thought in this way : 'the analyst may become a scientific observer to the extent to which he is able to observe objectively the patient and himself in interaction. The interaction itself, however, cannot be adequately represented by the model of scientific neutrality.' And he adds that identification between analyst and patient 'has nothing to do with scientific detachment and the neutrality of the mirror'.[4] The interaction is not separable from the patient and analyst in interaction; scientific methods of studying them as separate entities must extend to the interaction or they are not scientific methods. The contradiction in the passage is possible only because of the obvious dissent from a positivistic world-view : science *is* renounced as a way of thinking about human relationships. There are, of course, attempts at escaping the painful responsibilities of this renunciation. I should like to illustrate two of these, one naive, the other sophisticated and imaginative.

The first of these is brought to mind by a gambit of C. P. Oberndorf in the *Psychoanalytic Quarterly*, another leading journal of psychoanalysis. He writes, 'the attention of most investigators dissatisfied with their own results has centred about the question of technique, with the hope that improvements in technique, especially the analysis of transference, would bring about better results. Fortunately the analyst as well as the patient are human and fallible, for were either an automaton it is unlikely that the tremendous force of the transference could be mobilized and utilised in the interest of therapy . . .'[5] According to the psychoanalytical theory, and indeed, according to all 'scientific psychological theories' we *are* supposed to be automata, and were it not so, psychological generalisations could not be used, and predictions could not be made about personality development, about counselling, and about transference phenomena in particular. Yet this psychoanalytical writer is prepared to have it both ways : generalisations about behaviour and determinism all round, and then a bow to the other side by introducing the emotively loaded term

[4] 'On the Therapeutic Action of Psychoanalysis', January–February 1960, Vol. XLI, Part 1, pp. 16–33.
[5] 'Unsatisfactory Results of Psychoanalytic Therapy', 1950, Vol. XIX, pp. 393–407.

'automaton' and cordially assuring the other side that, of course, no one thinks that we are automata. Apart from allowing some metaphysical premises to stand there unsupported—a legitimate practice—the psychoanalytic theory most certainly insists that the mechanistic determinism of the universal causal law, and nothing else, shall explain how we behave and experience what we do. In these circumstances, a psychoanalyst, Oberndorf, merely gives expression to his non-discursive and pre-logical affirmation, to his *Faith* that the principle of disjunction is false, that the logical principle of contradiction is not sovereign over men, and that the machine that is man, can overrule itself by the very principles which gave rise to it, and which keep it going. The machine can override its own calculableness and this is what makes it essentially human. The basic paradox of human existence comes into view here again and we have little justification for crying angrily, 'hypocrisy' or 'double-think'. We are simply enjoined to cultivate faith in a 'non-automatic automaton', and are left standing there dazed, mystified, yet also a little hopeful that there might be a 'third truth' concealed by the paradox.

The second illustration makes greater demands on our attention and offers us something more palatable though, of course, not necessarily more digestible. The more scrupulously the psycho-analyst pursues the path of impartiality and rigorously positivistic thinking, the more striking are his ultimate confessions that this impartiality and rigour are, somehow, not enough, and indeed that something else is indispensable to both success in counselling and in acquiring more knowledge about counselling. L. E. Tower, a psychoanalyst of some standing, observes in her searching paper on 'Countertransference'[6] that 'interpretations as such do not cure, nor will any analyst ever be remembered primarily for his interpretive brilliance by any patient with whom he has been successful'. The ultimate insufficiency of the discursive and cognitive spelling out of facts, and the aridity of just conveying information about them, are recognised here. And yet, paradoxically, she goes on to say that, 'this is not, however, to depreciate the importance of interpretation in the analytic procedure. Obviously, only through the patient's verbal communications, and the painstaking, dispassionate, interpretative efforts of the analyst is it possible, little

6 *Journal of the American Psychoanalytical Association*, 1956, Vol. IV, pp. 224–255.

by little, so to peel away the defences that those insights and communications can be obtained that we know to be the essence of the curative effect of the analytic process.' So it seems that interpretations are not everything and yet they are : 'the "overscientific analyst" is twin to the "unscientific" one' remarks Mark Kanzer in the *International Journal of Psychoanalysis*.[7] This heroic effort to combine the attitude of healing concern with the scientific attitude of criticism and rigour is bound to remain only partially successful. The aims of such effort as this are incompatible, and *The Psychoanalytic Situation*[8] or the 'counselling situation' is inevitably paradoxical. To serve these two ends simultaneously the counsellor seems to receive inspiration from a context of faith which is extraneous to science. Dr. Tower, however, offers a scientific rationale for reconciling the antithetical aspirations and does it, unbeknown to herself, with so much awe and admiration for the vast cosmic scope of science, that it is worth reproducing here in full as an especially up-to-date poetic instance of the counsellor's faith :

'I would conjecture that the development of countertransference neurotic structures in an analyst over a long period of time might be something like Einstein's theory of relativity. This theory has to do with the fact that light is supposed to travel in a straight line from one point to another, and actually does so in our own little world and with our short distances of measurement. However, when light travels the gigantic distances known to us in terms of millions of light years, other factors previously never understood or even conceived of enter into the picture and Einstein proved that over these vast reaches of time and space, there is a drift from the straight line in the beam of light. So, too, the hypothetically perfectly trained and perfectly analysed analyst should be able to pursue an utterly straight course of avoiding all those countertransference pitfalls which his personal analysis should have taught him to anticipate and avoid. And undoubtedly, by and large, he is increasingly able to do this and over a considerable period of time. Ultimately, however, it would appear that even under the most ideal circumstances there are bound to be certain drifts, so to speak, from the utterly

7 January 1963, Vol. XLIV, Part 1, p. 108.
8 Cf. The book of this title by L. Stone, New York, 1961.

straight direction of the analyst's performance, and understanding of the case, and it is these very slow almost imperceptible drifts which develop in him in unconscious response to hidden pressures and motivations from his patient . . .'[9]

So the 'drift' from the objective, rational, and positivistic account of what the analyst is doing is not to be tolerated; a *scientific-sounding* account is offered instead. It is hoped that the cosmic metaphor will convince us that there is a psychological equivalent of Einsteinian mathematics and physics and that the drift from the positivistic account of the counsellor's work need not really occur. Images of infinite distances of space are conjured up to illustrate the infinite objectivities of the analyst's care. Well, not quite *infinite* objectivities : after vast distances of straight travelling the course of objectivity is bent. And, what is implied by the Einsteinian metaphor is that *this departure too* is subject to a scientific-objective account. One may plead that Dr. Tower's argument should not be cited to document the renunciation of a full scientific account of the counsellor's work. I don't think I should allow this plea, for the immensities marshalled by Dr. Tower do not offer a scientific hypothesis but constitute a highly reverential and evocative appeal to trust and proclivities of belief. Of course, the renunciation of science is implicit only but there are so many instances of explicit resignation from the pure scientist's role that the presence of this element in the counselling ideology cannot be doubted. 'There can be no wholly scientific approach to psychotherapy because no man is wholly scientific',[10] is the sort of terse disclaimer one is not at all surprised to meet from time to time, and Dr. Tower's elaborate and ingenious construction is the exception not the rule.

Clear and determined renunciations of the 'scientific attitude' abound though these are more frequent in the writings of psychoanalysts who have taken refuge in the poetic unclarities of existentialism. R. D. Laing, for example, styled as a 'research psychiatrist' and working at a psychoanalytically oriented institution, the Tavistock, puts forward without any visible embarrassment that 'Too many psychotherapists find it necessary to betray their

9 *Loc. cit.*
10 Alexander Reid Martin in *Progress in Psychotherapy*, p. 173. Compare this with the following: 'Medicine can never become fully scientific unless it becomes completely inhuman' (R. T. V. Pulvertaft in *The Lancet*, 1952, p. 839).

experience when they seek to convey it, under the entirely confused and mistaken impression that they have to pay their tribute to the idol of what they suppose to be scientific respectability. Our experience addresses no one except you and me. It finds its validation when, across the gulf of our idioms and style, our mistakes, errings, and perversities, we recognise in the other's communication, a certain common experience of relationship, that we are all seeking to convey, knowing that we shall never entirely succeed.'[11] So it would seem that science has nothing to say about what happens at the core of the counselling experience because it is ineffable and essentially incommunicable! And this is the conclusion of a 'research psychiatrist' working at a leading psychoanalytically oriented institution of treatment and research.

The explicit disowning of scientific neutrality and objectivity crops up in all sorts of psychotherapeutic and psychoanalytic contexts again and again. It is as if the ethical and metaphysical substance of the therapeutic effort were so bulky that it could no longer be concealed, in spite of frantic protestations that the counsellors were innocent of mysteries, that they were scientists or appliers of science, mere technologists or possibly only craftsmen. Some counsellors try to escape from the dilemma by pleading, rather thoughtlessly, that they practise an art, forgetting that, were it so, no generalisation about their practice would have more than either an aesthetic, and, therefore a morally ambiguous, or even only trivial, significance. The theoreticians of counselling who resign from the scientist's role put an end to the expectation that eventually the process of counselling could be broken up into minute and discrete stages of engineered learning, or rather unlearning and relearning, and that the techniques of managing this process in counselling, that is prompting it, sustaining it, and concluding it, could be similarly broken up into discrete and learnable elements. I have no desire to complain about this development: my task is to show that the development has been taking place. The plain fact for all to see is that, at least until now, the counselling literature has everywhere included observations and admissions about the unbreakable total front of the personality's holistic function, and about the unanalysable nature of the counsellor's love for his patient.

11 'Psychotherapy: the Search for a New Theory', *New Society*, 1 October 1964.

This, the counsellor's renunciation of science, was my first theme. The second one, the blurring of distinctions between objective and subjective observations, has yet to be documented.

It seems that we are now invited to look again very closely indeed to see whether 'understanding' and 'knowing' people are not fundamentally different from 'understanding' and 'knowing' things and non-personal events. We are now invited by the theoreticians of counselling to make a distinction here. All our perception of people—even, sometimes, of animals—inescapably comprises egomorphic, that is to say, projective elements whereas the observation of things and thing-events are relatively free from this. The subjective bias in our perception of people has been a well-known and, indeed, a commonplace reason put forward for distrusting it. Yet, paradoxically, we are now being strongly persuaded to revise our views about this and entertain the idea that in fact we cannot know enough, and cannot understand enough, without a 'feeling-into', a 'rapport', an 'empathy', with the other person. In brief, fellow-feeling may be a requisite of more vivid objectivity, a condition of discovering the truth. This is a strikingly new departure in the methodology of a social or psychological science. The *scientist* of human behaviour and experience is called upon to use sympathy as a research tool, and compassion as an instrument, of scientific method. Moreover, he is warned to watch out for the exact measure of the sympathy required, because an error either way will convert the aid of sympathy into a hindrance. That sympathy may be a condition of the discovery of truth about man and, therefore, a condition for the establishment of a psychological science, would be regarded as grossly objectionable by the 'behavioural scientists'. Nonetheless this is a proposition which is now underwritten by a good many thoughtful and reputable specialists of much experience and discrimination.

I will begin my documentation of this with an instance in which the writer sensed the hazards of this line of thinking and tried to anticipate criticism. However, the equivocal way in which he tried to shield himself in advance merely increased his vulnerability. In his Introduction to Sylvia Brody's *Pattern of Mothering*,[12] René Spitz gives a strikingly good specimen of the ambiguities involved in this issue. He begins by commending Brody's book 'for the author's sensitivity and empathy'. Then he attempts to rectify the

[12] New York, 1956.

impression of there being more empathy than scientific objectivity in Brody's work, and continues, 'Yet my use of the word empathy should not be misunderstood; the observations are carried out in the spirit of commendable scientific detachment, which obviously is a prime requirement for a study such as the author has undertaken. As I have stressed on frequent occasions, the only way to carry out scientific observation is to avoid getting emotionally involved, by identification or otherwise, with one's subjects. One should behave as the psychoanalyst does when he handles the countertransference: he performs brief identifications with the subject for the purposes of empathy and no more.'[13] I should have thought that to perform brief identifications *is* to get 'emotionally involved', especially if the purpose of these 'brief' moves is a continuing state of empathy. It seems to me that, in spite of his reservations, Spitz remains vague about the nature of the empiricism he would require: 'empathy', however disciplined and restrained, is not a controllable process. In empathy the self is used, and contributes or adds to the situation from its own resources in a non-cognitive way by generating an affect in the observer and thus conjuring up images in the observer about the observer which will appear to be true about the observed person. But this is by no means the whole of Spitz's difficulty: the very idea of painstakingly controlling and modulating these spells of identifications, so that they do not get out of hand and obscure the picture gained through empathy, must credit the controlling and exquisitely conscientious observer with using this empathy for control! In other words, the proper control of empathy will depend on the empathic tie itself!

The literature is teeming with declarations of faith in the virtues of empathy. Yet the praises sung are accompanied by signs of apprehension, even perhaps of guilt. The writers seem to be aware of the anomalousness of this notion and remind themselves that they must not sing so lustily after all. So the formula is a kind of balance: invariably bearing the burden of a paradox, empathy used to control empathy. There are many styles and languages, many conceptual devices used to formulate, to pin down this restless and undisciplined idea, and the documentation which will follow should suffice to display the Gordian knot which the counsellors invariably slash through with the sword of faith.

13 *Op. cit.*, pp. 15–16.

One of the more recent statements on this was made by no less an authoritative body than the Scientific Committee of the World Federation for Mental Health. 'It appears to us,' the document reads, 'that sympathy between human beings may be a universal phenomenon, and in any interpersonal relationship a minimum sympathy must exist before empathy can be established. Many people will make an antithesis between sympathy and objectivity of attitude, and may regard objectivity as a lack of sympathy. We do not accept this view. Sympathy may interfere with strict objectivity, but it is likely that objectivity without sympathy may not be truly objective because it may lead to distortions in the estimation of emotional values.'[14] Recently impressive empirical evidence has been reported by C. B. Truax to the effect that when one assesses the performance of psychotherapists their 'empathic understanding' is 'dependent upon first obtaining at least a minimally high level of unconditional positive regard for the patient. To be deeply sensitive to the moment-to-moment "being" of another person requires of us as therapists that we first accept and to some degree unconditionally prize this other person'.[15]

The telescoping of the empirical, cognitive, and logical with the intuitively introspective, affective, and pre-logical is not a scientific operation in the currently accepted sense of 'scientific'. To say this is not necessarily to condemn this method of getting at facts but to draw attention to certain distinctive qualities of the process. '... For a considerable proportion of analytic time,' writes W. R. Bion, 'the only evidence on which an interpretation can be based is that which is afforded by the counter-transference.'[16] Bion explains how his own subjective, free-floating fantasy can yield up information about the patient and how self-perception is made to disclose facts about another.

Thus objectivity, a cornerstone of the scientific edifice, is henceforth to rest not only on the solid ground of objective external-empirical observation but also on the ground of countertransference, positive regard or fellow-feeling. I for one will not rush to

[14] *Identity—Mental Health and Value Systems*, Ed. K. Soddy, London, 1961, p. 206.
[15] 'Effective Ingredients in Psychotherapy: An Approach to Unravelling the Patient-Therapist Interaction', *Journal of Counselling Psychology*, 1963, Vol. X, No. 3, pp. 256–263.
[16] 'Language and the Schizophrenic' in *New Directions in Psychoanalysis*, Ed. by M. Klein, P. Heimann and R. Money-Kyrle, New York, 1955, p. 224.

assume that the second ground is more likely to subside than the first, but I am well aware that we have always been enjoined to believe so. It is not at all helpful to say these things, almost casually, and pretend that views, such as these, do not amount to profound categorical innovations about the nature of truth, of science, and of human knowledge in general. Nor is it helpful to conceal that the professors of views, such as these, profess a faith in their total and personal functioning as a means of truth-getting. The 'science of counselling' is not after all only an applied science, in the accepted sense of the term, but, though it is that, it is also a system of categorical affirmations of values by mature, sensitive, and critical, moral agents in a morally still infantile civilisation.

The key-note of these testimonies is that the counsellor must balance between objectivity and subjectivity. The Balints, for example, say that 'every form of psychotherapy requires this biphasic effort',[17] and assume that objective and subjective perception take turns or alternate, one phase obediently following the other—and this, presumably, without any distortive carry-over. More frequently, writers on psychotherapy describe this effort as one aimed at fusion or bifurcation of two disparate ways and not as an orderly oscillation of logic and sympathy. So that the counsellors in social work see the pertinence of all this to their field of operation, Gordon Hamilton's widely used textbook on social casework will remind them that 'it is very difficult and perhaps impossible to become aware of the nature of organic reality, or what the social worker would call the "reality situation" without entering into it, directly experiencing it, and he would say "interpreting it through sympathy" '. And Hamilton continues, 'While the social worker who relies wholly on intuition to understand another person may become lost in mysticism, it is possible also to over-estimate the intellectual approach to life as yielding real meaning'.[18] One cannot help wondering how the momentousness of such precepts as these could have escaped the attention of the more critical counselling theoreticians? Surely, the point is not whether one should or should not be *entirely* lost in mysticism for, evidently, according to Gordon Hamilton, the social worker must be half-lost in it if he is to interpret the situation accurately.

[17] *Psychotherapeutic Techniques in Medicine*, by M. and E. Balint, London, 1961, p. 135.
[18] *Theory and Practice of Social Casework*, New York, 1951, p. 41.

Some incisive writers have not only openly recognised that *subjectifying* is an aid to gaining new insight for the furtherance of an *objective* social science, but they have diagnosed the condition of those who would have nothing to do with this development as one of alienation, and their intolerance of subjective psychologising as a defensive reaction. They are now challenging the objectivists to examine their motives! A. H. Maslow, for example, using the psychoanalyst's own weapons, most aptly explains this point of view in these words, 'Impersonal science can sometimes be a flight from or defence against the personal within oneself and within other human beings, a distaste for emotion and impulse, even sometimes a disgust with humanness or a fear of it.'[19] Set over against this, we find writers, very much aware of the demands of counselling for rapport, empathy, and the like, who now sound the alarm and prescribe 'built-in controls of scepticism', and 'questionmindedness'.[20] The anxiety about an inroad on our intellectual honesty and about consequent material errors is understandable enough, and also salutary as a corrective to too effusive sympathies, which the faith of the counsellors may inspire but—to say the least—it is doubtful that work in any of the helping professions, even outside counselling, could continue efficiently were it kept under the ubiquitously watchful eyes of scepticism. Human misery, problems and pain, are miserable, problematic and painful to the observer, who cares to, and dares to, seek full knowledge of these things. The counsellors would probably say that not even the manipulatively objective surgeon would be doing his best by relying on built-in controls of scepticism when only contemplating and attempting to assess the recuperative powers of a potentially surgical patient.

But this see-saw between objectivity and subjectivity settles little. The alternative emphases which appear in the literature merely reflect the ambiguity, the hesitation, and uncertainty. Those, who find this too painful, escape into a reverential language about the counsellor's need to eke out the ordinary empirical observation by using his 'person', or entering into a 'communion', and so on. In examining the relationship between the notion of 'skill' and 'love' I have already shown how much importance is

[19] 'Are Our Publications and Conventions Suitable for the Personal Psychologies?', *Report No. 8*, Western Behavioral Sciences Institute, 1961.
[20] 'Evaluation of Social Work', by R. Huws Jones, *Social Service Quarterly*, December 1961–February 1962, Vol. XXXV, No. 3.

attached to the images these reverential terms elicit. 'The therapist's personality is the most important agent of the therapeutic
process',[21] was the conclusion with which we were left there. Here,
in this present section, we are to consider the same formula, but
this time in an entirely different context. The formula in the new
context is this : the counsellor must use his *personality* to find out,
to understand, and to learn. Or as the psychoanalyst S. H. Foulkes
puts it, 'The therapist is himself the instrument of observation and
treatment, and psychotherapy depends on "experience", understanding, and communion (*sic!*) such as is only possible between
two fully engaged persons.'[22] Were it not for the reluctance of
analysts to admit to the implication of their not altogether scientific
credo, one might find this kind of hobnobbing with spirituality
leading them to some startling philosophical conclusions. And this
is not mere musing about remote possibilities! Dr. Saul, a training
analyst of the Philadelphia Institute of Psychoanalysis, does believe
that there is something special about a human relationship of
counselling, in which one human being has not only his *Id*, *Ego*
and *Superego* but also his *soul* to bare. Dr. Saul speaks of the
'spiritual' as if it was a recognised part of the Freudian 'anatomy
of the mental personality'.[23]

It is in Erich Fromm's recent writing that the process of 'understanding' is taken right out of the orbit of scientific thinking. 'The
only way of full knowledge lies in the act of love,' he declares.
'Only if I know a human being objectively, can I know him in his
ultimate essence, in the act of love.'[24] And, indeed, 'the problem
of knowing man is parallel to the religious problem of knowing
God'. Here, in addition to the fusion of 'knowing' and 'feeling' we
also have this fusion at its best equated with the mystical communion. Fromm, himself a trainer of counsellors, proclaims an
ancient conviction here, an instance of the perennial philosophy,
which, it seems, encompasses the *Faith of the Counsellors* in our
time. I have no doubt that there is also a *Science of the Counsellors* and that during the last five or six decades a multitude of
brilliant generalisations have been formulated about personality

[21] 'Dynamics of Countertransference', by Therese Benedek, *Bulletin of
the Menninger Clinic*, 1953, Vol. XVII, No. 6, pp. 201–208.
[22] 'Psychotherapy', *British Journal of Medical Psychology*, 1961, Vol.
XXXV, Part 2, pp. 91–102.
[23] *Technic and Practice of Psychoanalysis*, by L. J. Saul, Philadelphia, 1958.
[24] *The Art of Loving*, London, 1957, pp. 31–32.

growth and change, a significant number of which have been verified. Of course, the counsellors apply this science, and it is not the
purpose of this section to deny this. But we must take notice of their
repeated and insistent confessions—usually made at the end of a
working day which had seemed to consist of ratiocination alone—
that their science was of no avail without their faith.

It is as well to realise that the incompatibilities between objectivity and action plague all human relations and are not peculiar
to counselling. *Firstly*, in practice of any kind the ideal of objectivity is itself such that the standard of objectivity applied to it
would destroy it; *secondly*, action in all fields must be undertaken
even when the knowledge of the circumstances is incomplete, and
knowledge is always incomplete. Action of a helping kind has a
quality of urgency about it, and when this action consists in the
counsellor making himself benevolently available, offering his
presence and his attentiveness, the modesty of his scientific
resources cannot and, of course, should not put off his intervention. At any rate, social science will never free us from the necessity of making moral decisions, nor can we hope that social science
will ever catch up with the always differentiating and refining
moral concerns of man. In all probability—to be able to help
others—there will always be a 'social science lag' between what we
feel we must assume and what we can verify.

The predicament is not new : it has been known to a profession
older than that of modern counselling. In the book on *The Student
Physician*[25] doctors are pressed to remember that they 'must maintain a self-critical attitude and be disciplined in the scientific
appraisal of evidence. *But:* they must be decisive and not post-
pone decisions beyond what the situation requires, even when the
scientific evidence is inadequate.' There seems to be no way of
getting round the conflict between the cultural climates of a
scientific and a professional way of thinking and acting, and also,
incidentally, between a scientific and professional education. To
act on insufficient scientific evidence is discouraged by the moral
climate of science, whilst to act intuitively in possession of insufficient evidence or information when human sympathy dictates that
we act, is both enjoined by convention and commanded by spontaneous inner urges.

[25] Ed. by R. K. Merton, G. G. Reader, and P. L. Kendall, Harvard,
1957, p. 73.

Summary of the argument in this section. Here I have asked : is the counsellor a matter-of-fact, dispassionate, and impersonal applier of a social science? And, as we are told by the counsellor that he is not that alone, so the question is, what else is he? In treating this problem I refused to get involved in the quarrel about which of the counsellor's psychological propositions are verified and which are not. In fact, I did not question that there was a science to apply. What I was concerned to show was that the counsellor was so much impressed by the insufficiency of his science, and by the potency of his personal presence, that he repeatedly demanded to be recognised as a good deal more than an applier of science. To document this I presented some counsellors' explicit renunciation of science as the ultimate arbiter of what they did professionally, and I showed some other counsellors—all distinguished and thoughtful witnesses—arguing, that objectivity without sympathy was not sufficient to yield knowledge. Finally, I drew attention to the frequency with which writers on counselling made understanding and knowledge dependent on an unspecific 'use of their person', on 'communion' with their patients, and on so-called 'spiritual' aspects of the counselling relationship. The appliers of science themselves say that they need all these things.

The Faith in Shortcuts and Expediencies

The principles and policies, which counsellors have been putting forward for the guidance of the selection and training of the counsellors, themselves reflect the uncertainties and ambiguities I have been discussing.

There are two preliminary reminders necessary here.

Firstly, we ought to discriminate standards (of skilfulness, objectivity, care, etc.) which are made possible for the counsellor by a full therapeutic training ('training analysis'), and standards, which had to be achieved without this kind of training. This is not the place to attempt the admittedly very necessary task of examining the concept of 'training analysis' in great detail. It is certainly a unique training procedure which comprises the 'full' psychotherapy of the candidate-counsellor. The principle, which dictates it, is simple and plausible : unless the counsellor himself is relatively free from the conditions he is asked to treat in his clients, and unless he has had the experience of being treated for similar conditions, his professional work will suffer and his counselling intervention may even be pathogenic, and not therapeutic to his clients. We must then consider that, if this therapeutic training is to be regarded as essential to the training of the counsellors, then social caseworkers, clinical psychologists, general practitioners of medicine, psychiatrists, and some others, constantly engaged in counselling, are not in fact qualified to be so engaged.

Secondly, we ought to discriminate between standards (of skilfulness, objectivity, care, etc.), which are made possible by the exceptionally generous concentration of attention characteristic of private practice in psychoanalysis—and in psychotherapy too—where there are few limitations of time to force the analyst to intervene judgingly or to threaten with termination, and those standards, which are possible to observe in social casework interviews, in a general practitioner's consulting room, or during an interview by a psychiatrist in a busy psychiatric outpatient clinic. Clearly, counsellors in these situations must have recourse to therapeutic measures of an almost makeshift, and possibly peremptory, kind and, through persuasion and dissuasion, aim and achieve goals which must be regarded as arbitrary unless proved otherwise. Through the inevitable fragmentariness of these contacts, the themes selected for discussion, the points of time selected for intervention, and especially the degree of depth fixed as a limit of operations, will all be arbitrarily decided. For the reduction of arbitrariness requires time, and of this there is never enough.

The purpose of this section is to disclose acts of faith of the counsellors who, by these acts, and not by the theory or science they profess to apply, make decisions on shortcuts, on expediencies, and on treatment policies. Individual counsellors and institutions employing counselling staffs make policy decisions on the 'levels' on which they propose to train or treat, and, in this section, I will try to highlight the paradoxical results of these decisions.

(1) *The Expedient of 'Levels' in Training Counsellors*

In counselling there is ample scope for using techniques which have a deep penetrative power, or which can be otherwise exploited and even sadistically used. Possibly, sublimated residues of these tendencies are inevitable, and even necessary, components of effective therapeutic performance. Yet certainly, so long as a personal therapeutic analysis is not regarded as an essential requisite of qualification—and it is not so regarded in the majority of counselling subgroups—these therapeutic motives will continue to have at least some arbitrary influence which it would be pointless to underestimate or deny. Generally it would seem that less self-knowledge in the counsellor will mean less self-knowledge in the client. Now the training requirements laid down for psychoanalysts make a determined bid to secure the maximum self-knowledge for psychoanalysts, through the training analysis, which they must undergo to qualify. To what measure training analyses increase the analyst's self-knowledge is not known, but there is no doubt that two or three years of intensive 'working-through', as well as of being 'on the receiving end', must considerably enhance the sensitivities of the counsellor so trained. Of course there are psychotherapists whose professional associations do not oblige them to undergo this therapeutic training as a condition of accrediting them. Many of these profess to apply psychological principles which are much the same as those of the psychoanalysts, and therefore, their relinquishing this condition constitutes an act of expediency unaccountable in terms of their psychologies.

But the practice of this expediency goes far beyond the usages of the not-analysed psychotherapists. It is interesting to observe that psychoanalysts themselves play a prominent part in the induction of psychotherapeutic auxiliaries, in the training of social workers, general practitioners, psychiatrists, human relations consultants, and some others, and that their leadership in the training field has not been entirely thrust upon them. One may be forgiven for feeling some momentary, and perhaps indefensible, sympathy for those critics of psychoanalysis, who may now say, that these expensive and exclusive counsellors must have developed a sense of guilt about the smallness of the number, and the relative opulence, of their patients. Be that as it may, it now appears that at least some of them have now resolved to 'write large' the technique, the orientation, and the ideology of their vocation, and make a modified, abbreviated, and 'paper-back' version of these acceptable to those counsellors who, of necessity, are much more pressed for time than the psychoanalyst. It is remarkable that psychoanalysts, themselves often engaged in excessively prolonged analyses of private patients, and having themselves received training analyses of at least 600 to 800 hours' duration, should now generously lend their services in the training of social workers, general practitioners, and others without imposing on them the stringencies of their own erstwhile training. They now readily join in the training of people with a view to equipping them as counsellors or therapists, whilst fully realising that these people may not be suited, or adequately prepared to use their personalities, in a consistently and safely therapeutic manner.

There are four areas in which concessions, compromises and expediencies are most noticeable and where a faith in the counselling mission is necessary to advocate them. These are, (a) selection of counsellors, (b) the shortcut of 'instruction', (c) the shortcut of 'supervision', (d) the shortcut of 'group methods' in training.

(a) *Selection of counsellors.* In the absence of the lengthy and expensive personal analysis of the counsellor, we might think it possible to enhance standards of the antithetical yet exquisitely balanced virtues of detachment and sympathy by appropriately stringent selection methods, but these in turn could only succeed if we knew more precisely what qualifications we do, in fact, require. In selecting with that air of judiciousness, we much too often pretend that at least we can make certain basic distinctions reliably. We do this whilst conceding elsewhere that making reliable psychological distinctions outside the prolonged therapeutic process is always risky. To combat conceit and a notorious pose of perspicuity, it is well to repeat this here again. If, on the other hand, a reliable diagnosis for selection purposes is not to be had, we may as well admit that in assessing candidates without treating and thus exploring them first and in crediting one candidate with more suitability for training than another, we are guided by intuition and by acts of faith.

I know of no systematic and genuinely objective procedures of selection to courses in which counsellors receive training. All we know are requirements stated in general terms, such as, for example, that a candidate for training to be a counsellor must possess some marked potentials of social intelligence, sensitivity, and security. But how are we to assess whether a candidate for counselling possesses this remarkable complex of virtues? After careful weighing of what has been found out about aptitudes for a counselling career, it turns out that the very prescriptions for this have a baffling paradoxical character. Take intelligence, for example. There are some good reasons to think that great and exceptional intelligence will lead away from clinical and inter-personal interests to impersonal, scientific, and scholarly interests. In fact, in a study of *Personality Patterns of Psychiatrists* it is openly stated that in respect of intelligence at least one trainer of psychiatrists prefers '. . . those in the last part of the first third or the second third of the class. Those with the highest grades are likely to be bookworms who are introverted, are not good teachers, and do not make good psychiatrists.'[1] It does not seem at all promising that we can establish a positive correlation between intelligence and counselling aptitudes among those who are already in the field. Naturally counselling, like all complex professional activities, will demand at least a good above-average intelligence, but how are we to select the suitable candidates from among the large number of unsuitable ones who, in fact, possess a good, above-average intelligence?

'The most pessimistic criticism of psychotherapy I have ever heard,' James Glover told the British Psychological Society in his presidential address in 1925, 'was the opinion of a medical col-league that no one ought to practise psychotherapy unless he had the wisdom of Socrates and the morality of Jesus Christ. In my view,' Glover went on, 'the advancement of psychotherapy requires the development of a psychotherapeutic technique demanding only the wisdom of any intelligent medical graduate and the morality of the Hippocratic Oath he takes on graduation.'[2] I believe, per-haps somewhat misguidedly, that the intelligent medical graduate possesses no more wisdom for work of this nature than intelligent social work graduates, sociology graduates, psychology graduates, and some others. Nor do I think that the Hippocratic Oath is a sacrament warranting a trust in the unique appropriateness of medical qualification for the job of counselling. In fact, in an earlier section I tried to show that there might be some reasons to think that a training in physical medicine may so reinforce a manipulative-authoritarian attitude that it cannot be regarded as

---

[1] By R. R. Holt and L. Luborsky, Imago, London, 1958, p. 257.
[2] 'Divergent Tendencies in Psychotherapy', *British Journal of Medical Psychology*, 1962, Vol. XXXV, Part 1, pp. 3–73.

the most appropriate avenue of approach to counselling. No doubt, knowledge of physical medicine and especially experience in its connections with the general state of the total personality are valuable but not indispensable qualifications. Already Freud saw this clearly enough.[3] We must not be misled by the 'mana' of the medical profession and its magical therapeutic potentials, and give credit for an expertise which they have not been afforded the opportunity to acquire. In the present state of medical education, the qualified practitioner possesses no more knowledge of the total personality and of its development that what he has managed to retain after a long course of drill in the physical mechanics and anatomy of the organism, and what he has managed to pick up in the course of his subsequent career. Once again, I must stress that no particular professional training in the empirical knowledge of physical facts, processes, and technologies will equip the trainee with aptitude for training in counselling. At any rate, in the modern welfare state, health and welfare administration has increasingly been put on a team-basis, and non-medical counsellors could be trained to seek appropriate medical checks on the physical condition of their clients whenever necessary.

In fact, a university degree in medicine or in any other field of objective study, including sociology and psychology, is no special indicator of suitability. Is it then at all possible to isolate a personality trait which would reliably call attention to this suitability? Once again the facts will warrant a paradoxical answer. I hope to be able to show the compelling nature of these facts.

Whether people are suitable to be trained as counsellors, or not, naturally depends on their initial willingness to undertake the exercise, but possibly not on their zealous overwillingness to undertake it. They are supposed to be intelligent and perspicuous but not obsessively reflective and speculative; they are expected to be curious about themselves and about other people but their curiosity must always be tempered by warm sympathy and sensible tolerance. Glover uses 'wisdom' to describe the precious quality we must look for. In their reflections psychoanalysts often choose explanatory notions of a numinous or mystical quality. The term 'wisdom' too has accumulated a quality of nebulous loftiness over the centuries, and so, it is not likely to help us here. We shall be well-

[3] 'Postscript to a Discussion on Lay Analysis', *Collected Papers*, London, 1950, Vol. V, p. 206.

advised to be somewhat more explicit and less sweeping. We can demand in general terms that a candidate for training to be a counsellor should show signs of his educability in social under-standing and sensitivity. But how are we to define these qualifications? There is no doubt that some people, probably a few only, are the fortunate possessors of qualities such as this complex comprises, and that, perhaps unfortunately for us, the majority of these don't aspire to be counsellors. But even so, even with those few who would come forward, we cannot be sure that we can recognise them, for certain of their 'disqualifications' are, in fact, their strong points. *Great serenity and exceptional freedom from neurotic symptoms may preclude understanding of, and sensitivity to, those who have many such symptoms.* According to Fritz Red-lich 'the psychiatrist doesn't have to be a paragon of mental health',[4] and we are also informed that 'overnormality' is a contradiction for psychoanalytic training.[5] It seems then that in addition to not wishing to have the very intelligent candidate, we ought not to be in favour of the candidate who shows no signs of emotional instability whatsoever.

The ubiquity of paradoxical specifications in the selection of counsellors is impressive. In the absence of clearly defined preferences no general principles will help us very much. But even if we had some general principles on which we could rely, in the absence of a sufficiently objective testing instrument it is difficult to see how, otherwise than in intuitive ways, aptitude could be assessed initially. One cannot help suspecting that the trainer in search for suitable personalities 'responds' favourably to candidates who 'respond' to him, and that whatever analytic spelling-out of this response is eventually offered to us to justify the trainer's judgment of the candidate, in the ultimate resort it is the non-analysable rapport or communion of trainer (selector) and candidate-trainee which decides the fate of the candidate, and that the analytic *raison* given for acceptance may well be a rationalisation. Here, at least sometimes, the faith of the counsellor is cloaked in the technicalities of objective personal assessment. On the other hand, if rapport and sympathy are the conditions of objectivity and understanding, the counsellor-selector is at least consistent in the application of his basic assumptions. After all, what he claims

4 Holt and Luborsky, *Op. cit.*, p. 257.
5 *Ibid.*, p. 264.

to be able to do in an initial assessment interview is what he claims to be able to do in therapy: understanding through empathy. There is no promise of a controlled study of this kind of assessment and there are no reservations made to say that, perhaps, the empathic assessment may not be reliable. Writing about a difficult patient of one of the doctors in his seminar for general practitioners, Michael Balint observes, 'Not every general practitioner could even think of accepting such a case. D. H. had a special flair for psychotherapy and in a way she had "green fingers".'[6] No gardener has ever been successfully prevailed upon to divulge for us what this mystical quality of possessing 'green fingers' might be, if it is to be something else and more than an extensive knowledge of the botany of the English back garden. One cannot help remembering this when reading Dr. Balint's way of describing one of his students' aptitude for counselling, and one cannot help wondering whether it was any more dependable than the gardener's compliment.

(b) *The shortcut of 'instruction'*. With training analysis, an essential and in fact central component of training, a therapeutic 'amendment' of the candidate-analyst's personality is expected with some reasonable confidence. Without the training analysis, and relying on didactic imparting of theory and practice, the trainer would find himself in an odd position. He would have to include in his didactic operation the teaching that such operations are useless. Indeed, no one who is familiar with the radical scepticism of the psychoanalyst about so-called 'intellectual insight' could be expected to regard a mere instructional or didactic technique as at all adequate for training in counselling. For the consistent Freudian, training analysis is not a perfectionist complement of training but its very spine. Some Freudian trainers would not hesitate to describe the didactic course, the teaching, lecturing and paper-writing part of training, as a conventional paedagogical ritual, and possibly as a gesture of reassurance that an authoritative and fatherly guidance is available. The psychoanalyst believes that 'learning' to be a counsellor is radically different from almost all other kinds of learning a skill or acquiring knowledge. The central part of this learning, its core subject matter, is learning about the self, and to teach this the way one would teach law, architecture, or even medicine is simply not possible.

6 *The Doctor, His Patient and The Illness*, London, 1957, p. 193.

And yet today, the psychoanalytically trained counsellors and trainers of counsellors, have second thoughts on this, and show a surprising degree of liberality about the use of straight instruction and its training value. Nowadays they enter into compromises about 'minimum requirements' in which instruction, possibly combined with other substitutes, such as group-methods and supervision—both of which I will consider below—will have to make do *in lieu* of a personal training therapy. The lowering of training requirements by those, who themselves have received most severe training, tends to be justified by expediency. 'You don't use a sledge-hammer to crack a nut', is what they are saying. There is no doubt that social caseworkers cannot and need not be required to undergo a prolonged training analysis to qualify for their counselling work, or that practitioners in most other fields of counselling could not be recruited if we were to stipulate that they must be lengthily treated before they can qualify. Trainers of counsellors fully realise this and respect the social necessity of creating and supporting all kinds of rapid and sketchy training methods. The kind of argument advanced in support of these is that it would be both uneconomical and unnecessary to require more intensive training standards for those who would be dealing with simple, stereotyped, and standardisable cases, and who would not be asked to do more than relatively brief supporting tasks or clarifying tasks without too much exploration of the past. Writing about the psychotherapeutic cushioning of 'normal' people against the stress of anticipating major surgery, and against the stress of post-operative pain and anxiety, I. L. Janis formulated some policies on these compromises which will well illustrate my point. Janis says that

'it is probably a serious mistake to assume that all that is needed to expand this type of activity (pre- or post-operative psychological care of surgical patients) in modern society is to communicate a set of simple guiding principles to all interested professional workers who are in a position to make use of them, irrespective of their psychological training, talents or experience. But, on the other hand, it would probably also be a mistake to assume that the amount of talent, training, and experience necessary for becoming a practitioner in this field will prove to be of the same order of magnitude as that required for qualified practitioners of psychotherapy . . .'[7]

Naturally, the compromise in training standards seems reasonable here as, in fact, it is in a good many comparable settings, yet the point at issue is not openly faced in these cases. This is that in the *first* place, the compromise, the expediency, cannot be derived from the counselling principles; for these compromises and expediencies are the outcome of recognising social needs and meeting them with tactical and moral decisions, with policy decisions, which the counselling principles do not entail. And *secondly*, the actual professional operations of counsellors, who were trained in these abbreviated ways, are still conducted under the same banners of 'objectivity, sympathy, non-directiveness, non-involvement, and so on', which were handed over to them by their trainers themselves who were, perhaps, more entitled to carry such banners than hand them over. There is no doubt about the paradoxicality and dividedness of psychoanalytic leadership when it presides over the training and functioning of social welfare and health personnel, themselves not trained psychoanalytically. Whilst the didactic methods which this leadership now licenses are entirely justifiable on grounds of social necessity, in terms of psychoanalytic principles, these methods will accomplish no more than the suggestion of counterphobic attitudes, the encouragement of changing of defences, and the displacement of the candidate's fixations by new ones. At other times and in other places, the psychoanalytic mentors will mercilessly condemn these devices as worse than no insight-giving at all!

Of course, it is by no means certain that a sharp dividing line can be drawn between instruction and therapy. It is the psychoanalytically oriented counsellors who assume that there is a sharp division here. That this doctrine compromises its own history is almost entirely overlooked: it isn't only that Freud himself was obliged to dig himself through his resistances without anybody tunnelling for him at the other end, but that the first trainees of Freud received from him no more than very brief and superficial training analyses. These were much rather like seminars or tutorials, in which far more straight instruction and teaching took place than personal therapy. Today's general theoretical premise, 'no insight

[7] *Psychological Stress: Psychoanalytical and Behavioral Studies of Surgical Patients*, by I. L. Janis, New York, 1958, pp. 382–383.

without prolonged therapeutic relationship', did not quite apply then in the training of the first counsellors. Teaching, and perhaps indoctrination, was acceptable because it was impossible to treat so many eager and sometimes impecunious candidates at great length, and 'the message had to be got across' to candidates who, according to present-day standards, were grossly unsuitable to be counsellors. According to the basic principles of the theory it was wrong to try to 'get it across' in this hasty and superficial manner at all. Yet the eventual world-wide dissemination of the counselling ideology proves that it could be 'got across' with considerable seminal influence on the clinical, scientific, and moral culture of our times. Thus, and in this sense, instruction was effective. But this effectiveness cannot be accounted for in terms of psychoanalytic thinking. In fact, the theory which denies the radical penetrative and therapeutic power of instructional and persuasive techniques, and then justifies them out of expediency, is either in error in its premises or in its warrant for expediency!

Psychoanalysts, the proto-theorists of counselling, do not succeed in resolving the paradoxical nature of their standards. *They seem to meet the intractable real-life situations with compromises which their theoretical premises cannot support.* They advocate these compromises, which are the outcome of moral resolve, of faith, and not of scientific theory about human behaviour. The writers on counselling let it slip out—in spite of some explicit denials—that they do not really underplay the significance of ultimate and unanalysable personal influences, which they hope to use constructively and creatively with or without elaborate training analyses of candidates. Their concession to 'instruction' is thus helped by their theoretical concessions to the 'total use of the analyst's person', to the use of 'supportiveness', and other non-analytical conceptions discussed in the previous sections.

(c) *The shortcut of 'supervision'.* Training through 'supervision' has long been known, especially in the training of social workers, and it is a complement of training even of psychoanalysts who also undergo training analysis. In those cases, when supervision is complementary to other methods of training, it is a valuable and necessary adjunct, and not a 'shortcut' to evade the more exacting and costly training analysis. The essence of supervision is simple : the candidate-counsellor proceeds with a case of counselling and reports back to a senior training-counsellor with whom he discusses what transpires in the counselling of the patient and how the training process affects the novice personally. The ambiguities and paradoxes of this method come to the forefront when it is to be the core of the training process, with instruction added but *no personal training analysis* to go with it. R. E. Ekstein and R. S. Wallerstein have made out a painstakingly argued case in the defence of such a method as this.[8] B. D. Lewin who wrote the Preface to their book on this subject calls this didactic method, somewhat pleonastically, a 'preceptorial tutoring in therapy'. The authors of the book recognise the legitimacy of instructional training and openly write off training analysis as a necessary complement of training. 'There are quite a number of supervisors', they explain, 'who at bottom believe that personal psychotherapy of the student is indeed the most forceful instrument of teaching. Such supervisors take this notion from early psychoanalytic training in which it was assumed that the personal analysis constituted the real training of the analyst-to-be, while all other aspects of psychoanalytic training were but embroideries that imitated the established academic (but useless) pattern of training. This notion of psychoanalytic training lingers on as a phantom in some of the abandoned closets of psychoanalytic institutes but essentially of course has been given up.'[9] That training analyses should be regarded as a phantom-requirement is a most remarkable thought to have issued from the Menninger School of Psychiatry, an institute of well-known psychoanalytical orientations, where the authors worked and wrote. But this is not all : the authors of the book assert that a trainee physician *asking* for psychotherapy, as a part of his training, is one who displays a rationalisation of his difficulties in didactic learning ! It does not occur to the writers that this is itself, in fact, for the most part a desperate rationalisation for an expediency. Here too, the aspiration to justify a more economical mental health programme leads to professions of faith, which are unsupported by theory. To do this, the theory about rationalisations is used to arrive at a conclusion, which is incompatible with the theory as a whole. For the psychoanalytic theory, on which the conception of counselling is largely based, clearly and repeatedly stresses, that without the analyst's understanding and control of his own ambivalent reactions to the patient, and

[8] *The Training and Learning of Psychotherapy*, Imago, London, 1958.
[9] *Op. cit.*, p. 90.

without a control of his own infantile reactivations, the analyst's handling of the situation will not only be distorted, but will become pathogenic. The theory, which the counsellors have adopted, and adapted to their various uses, explicitly lays down that under-standing and control commanded by the counsellor is a function —to a substantial degree—of the therapeutic training-treatment of the candidate counsellor.

In scrutinising the meaning of compromises, and their incon-sistencies, we should not be influenced by what we think is prob-ably essential for training but rather by what the senior coun-sellors specify as essential. In citing their views I have no intention to plead with them that they should take back training analysis or that they should abandon their concessions. I am solely concerned to disclose the inner inconsistency of their position, an inconsistency in terms of a theory they accept, and to show that their dedicated loyalty to paradoxical positions is a stance of faith.

To continue the documentation : the next item is even more telling than the previous ones have been. Social casework tutors using the technique of supervision have often rationalised their training method by claiming that supervision is a kind of therapy but that it involves the trainee's *professional self* only. Ekstein and Wallerstein also adopt this gambit and put forward that 'the change ostensibly sought is limited to one area, that of the manner of use of oneself in a psychotherapeutic relationship but within that area the change desired may be equally far-reaching and "deep"'.[10] Such fanciful compartments of the 'deep'—a professional and a private compartment—are unknown to psychoanalytical theory, which has furnished the whole *raison d'être* of the exercise of counselling even according to these two authors. Nor is there any evidence for this compartmentalisation from any other source. And that this is so, is in fact admitted by these writers when they say later on that: '... in certain individuals both learning problems and problems about learning are so pervasive and tenaciously rooted in the ramifying complex of personal problems that it will be possible to pay fruitful attention to them (the learning prob-lems) only after considerable resolution of the underlying personal problems. Such individuals should not do therapeutic work, whether supervised or not, until after a preliminary period of

[10] *Op. cit.*, p. 138.

personal therapeutic help.'[11] Surely this is not a qualitative but a quantitative difference, as Freud so often stressed.[12] An initial diagnosis of suitability will be highly suspect for these quantitative distinctions cannot be reliably assessed at all (once again cf. Freud[12]), and a plausible guess cannot be made without some exploratory therapy. Supervision is not a substitute for this kind of therapy for it makes a division of the personality along lines (the 'professional and the non-professional sectors') which have certainly no reality in terms of the theory professed by these counsellors.

Of course, training analysis as a requirement in professional training is not stipulated by the majority of counselling subgroups and it would be unfair to attach responsibility for *all* the rationalisations that have so far been mentioned in favour of dispensing with the personal therapy of the candidate to Ekstein and Wallerstein. There are many leading counsellors today who see no serious inconsistency in practising an explorative and reductive analysis of some sort and not prescribing this treatment for their pupils as a condition of their qualifying to practise the same kind of analysis. Carl Rogers, for example, believes that a reasonable receptiveness, sensitivity, and insight, combined with skill acquired from instruction and supervision, is all that need be reasonably expected as a minimum qualification. In all these less exacting schemes of training we are expected to feel assured that 'acting-out' by neurotic candidates, over-identifications with patients or members of their families, being exploitive, punitive, or over-protectively indulgent, to mention only a few of the more obvious interferences, are safely anticipated and averted. *And we are invited to believe this by a theory which tirelessly impresses on us that these types of behaviour are ubiquitous, stubborn, and yield only to the most persevering and time-consuming therapies.*

(*d*) *The shortcut of 'group methods'.* When group-psychotherapeutic methods were first used they were justified on grounds of economy as well as on the grounds that certain advantages were to be gained from treating patients in a group-setting. These arguments have since been extended to the use of groups and seminars in the training of counsellors, as well as in the training of professional personnel with some counselling functions. In the docu-

[11] *Op. cit.,* p. 139.
[12] 'Analysis Terminable and Interminable', *Collected Papers,* (1937), London, 1950, Vol. V, pp. 316–357.

mentation of the counsellor's faith, I have singled out the expediencies and compromises of training and it would seem to me that the use of these methods represents yet another instance of a compromise, reflecting certain convictions which are extraneous to the avowed principles of counselling. Here I will consider two areas of counselling activity in which the points I have been raising receive some useful emphasis. I have in mind Dr. Michael Balint's seminars for family doctors[13] and the group-psychotherapeutic sessions of leading managerial and professional personnel conducted mainly under the aegis of the Tavistock Institute of Human Relations.[14] There are other similar new enterprises in which the psychoanalytically fully committed leadership tries to spread the benefits of insight into motivation beyond the narrow confines of the 'fifty-minute hour'. These two illustrations will highlight different aspects of the faith of the counsellors, and my account will consist in singling out and pinpointing the most telling admissions and testimonies.

The first of these two 'glossaries' concerns Michael Balint's reverential language and mystical implications. These suggest, to some degree at least, that the readiness with which these compromises on training can be accepted is prompted not merely by economies, by the clinical expediency and certain special virtues of the group methods, but rather by an unadmitted realisation that core-experiences falling within the orbit of the paradigmatic human relationship of fellowship are being fostered. Balint, a senior psychoanalyst and training analyst who uses group-methods of training doctors to be counsellors, casually remarks, 'I have to apologise for borrowing so many terms from theology; my excuse is that they describe exactly what I have in mind'.[15] And indeed they do. Balint introduces the concept, 'The Apostolic Function of the Family Doctor', by which he seems to mean a kind of moral-spiritual committedness to personal service. Then he attempts to deflate this concept by proposing, rather unexpectedly, that this Apostolic Function consists in 'relying chiefly on his common sense, which is just another word for apostolic function'. But the point is that the notion of 'common sense' is kept plain, sober, and arid by very well-known connotations, whilst the phrase

[13] *The Doctor, His Patient and The Illness*, London, 1957.
[14] Cf. *Explorations in Group Relations*, by E. L. Trist, C. Sofer, Leicester University Press, 1959.
[15] *Op. cit.*, p. 226.

'apostolic function' is evocative, sublime, and numinous. They simply do not mean the same things and, by trying to persuade us to believe that they do, Balint discloses his own faith in the reality of the paradoxical. 'There are many fields in present-day medicine', he writes, 'where science is of little help to the practitioner and he has to rely chiefly on his common sense, which is just another word for apostolic function.' Thus he revolves around this idea most unhelpfully. Surely, at best, this is a euphemism and an inverted euphemism, depending on which side one is standing, much like calling the King our brother at one moment and calling every man a king in another.

To illustrate what he means, Balint explains that whenever the doctor regularly visits the chronic invalid for whom he can no longer do anything 'objectively' because he is beyond curing, there is still 'psychological justification' in calling and giving reassurance, comfort, and inspiring hope. I don't quite know what to make of the phrase 'psychological justification'. In the first place the concept of 'justification' is a *moral* and not a *psychological* concept, especially in the hands of one who is engaged in exercising an 'apostolic function'. Secondly, the language of 'suggesting', of 'manipulating' is not a little at variance with the language of 'inspiring hope' nor is the latter an accidental outcome, but a spontaneous preference for words of respect. When Balint speaks of 'conversion to the "psychosomatic faith"' (p. 191) and when he measures psychotherapeutic progress in terms of the warm and trusting relationship between doctor and patient (p. 126), he deepens the significance of his theological language. Having recourse to the language of the creeds he testifies that he needs the meanings which this language is capable of carrying. The language is hardly accidental; on the contrary, it is used to convey the immediate and non-psychoanalytical confidence in the healing power of certain types of counselling relationships, and their usefulness in training counsellors. The festive and evocative images are deliberately though, no doubt, unconsciously produced 'to certify' therapeutic processes as sound, although according to the theory they are not sound, or, at any rate, they do not proceed along the lines the theory could map out for us. In fact, were we to rely on the theory exclusively, we would be obliged to concur with one of Balint's critics, quoted by Balint himself, 'that the kind of psychotherapy by general practitioners with which...

(Balint and associates) were experimenting was dangerously irresponsible and ambitious...' (p. 204). I believe that this is an unrealistic, as well as a morally weak, criticism, uttered as it was in the contemporary situation of great and urgent need. Yet, if one were to rely on the prescriptions, standards, and rules of psychoanalytic therapy exclusively, one would have to accept this criticism.

The trainers of counsellors realistically respond to the needs of the times when they construe and try to operate compromise procedures of training. These expedients and shortcuts may have good moral credentials but are certainly not justifiable by the moral principles underlying psychoanalytic practice. The unvarnished truth of this is not concealed by Balint: '. . . the practitioner can take considered risks with his patients, risks which cannot be taken by a psychiatrist... What is inadvisable, impossible, or unthinkable for a psychiatrist can be perfectly plain sailing for a general practitioner.'[16] One wonders how Balint's colleague Bowlby would apply the general principle of 'not going beyond the patient's or client's mandate' to this bit of licence? And yet, if the trainer or the practitioner abandons the pretence of objectivity, of impartiality, of 'scientific credentials and nought else', and so on, there *are* good moral justifications for intervening in the 'risky' way Balint suggests.

This mentality of expediency is further illustrated by the tendency of thinking in terms of 'levels' of treating and training. 'General practitioners who are interested and have acquired some professional skill in psychotherapy may go further and experiment in their practice with *minor* psychotherapy,' Balint recommends (p. 125 italics added). As if psychotherapeutic expertise could be stratified in the same way as, say, obstetrics, where the run-of-the-mill, standard, and therefore, simple cases can be dealt with by midwives, and a doctor—let alone a consultant obstetrician—would be called in only in case of complications. Is there a comparable division between 'minor' and 'major' psychotherapeutic tasks? Does not the general practitioner arrogate to himself a not inconsiderable moral responsibility when deciding whether to intervene—untrained or half-trained as he is—or not to intervene, having already taken upon himself to decide whether it was a

16 *Op. cit.*, pp. 58–59. Balint must have meant 'psychoanalyst' as well as 'psychiatrist' in this context.

'minor' or a 'major' case? I think that if he justifies his intervention on the rationalistic grounds that he is applying a science, he
would certainly act arrogantly, and, therefore, his action may bear
the marks of this blemish. If, on the other hand, he faces the fact
that all intervention in the personal life of the other is a major
moral intervention, his action need not be impaired in this way.
A slackening of technical rules and standards even for the so-
called 'minor' cases can be justified only on the grounds of explicit
moral commitments as to what moral purposes are to be sought,
and in what general ideological framework these purposes are to
be located. To freeze in a posture of objectivity, when objectivity
has been evidently abandoned, cramps the total and personal
'apostolic function' of the practitioner and conceals the true nature
of the influence which the counsellors have been shown to
advocate.

The second area of training activity which I selected to show
the serious practicality of these concerns is the one in which
training proceeds in a group of non-medical administrative, managerial, or academic trainees. In a 'Residential Conference' held for
these at the University of Leicester in 1959,[17] a careful attempt
was made to advance the social understanding of some experienced and mature people of this kind. The occasion was to be
used for 'further training and practice in looking for, and at, what
is normally overlooked or taken for granted; *deeper understanding
of the meaning of behaviour*; and greater familiarity with universal components of social situations'.[18] (Italics added.) The theoretical basis of the whole operation was clearly psychoanalytical,
although micro-sociology and group dynamics, so long as they
were in harmony with psychoanalytic thinking, obviously contributed. It is, of course, not possible to give a numerical index, or
some other indicator of level, when the phrase 'deeper understanding' is used. The authors of the Report certainly qualify this
'deeper understanding' when they say: 'the method was to
develop insight during the course of working through existing
problems. One could not assault people with specialist techniques
which they had not given one permission to use.'[19] But those who
participated were new to this experience and were not aware of

[17] *Op. cit.*, by Trist and Sofer.
[18] *Op. cit.*, pp. 53–54.
[19] *Op. cit.*, p. 47.

having given their permission for anything even mildly hazardous. I have already shown that this appeal to the 'mandate' or 'permission' of the client or trainee is not to be allowed. The phrase 'could not assault' is certainly a guarantee of the organisers' sensitivity and understanding of the hazards; but this could not be more than an intuitively working guide, an attentive holding of the finger on the pulse. In fact, it must be a sympathetic and concernedly watchful care, enriched by experience, and by a sensitive knowledge of human motivation. There are no simple feed-back controls, comparable to thermostatic or similar machines. A painstakingly sustained care cannot be dispensed with for the confessed aims are 'deeper understanding' and 'working through existing problems'. We have already come across the gambit of 'professional and non-professional sectors' of the trainee's personality. Now we have here an analogous and theoretically equally shaky concept of 'present problems' as presumably distinct from 'past problems'. Certainly, the harsh sound of the word 'assault' may prevent us from using it to describe what was in fact going on when the consolidated defence systems of the participants —and these were *not* clinical patients—were being nibbled away. That I am not being querulously suspicious may be more credible in the light of the following passage : 'A member summarised much of the discussion with a comment that many had come out of Study Groups with too much enthusiasm for the "new learning", had made a direct frontal attack on old ways of doing things and failed. They had not appreciated that an oblique approach in the introduction of change and the improvement of relations was often the only one possible. It was valuable to have a brake put on their enthusiasm.'[20] Assuming a certain measure of identification and over-identification of participants with staff members of this enterprise, the enthusiasm is understandable. But whatever the causes : the psychoanalytic ideology underlying this experiment does not allow for the possibility of rearranging a person's system of defences in this rapid and, therefore, casual way. I focus attention on this discrepancy not because I am sceptical of the effectiveness of the enterprise—on the contrary, I think it is probably an effective and valuable enterprise—but because I do not think that 'insight-giving' and 'ego-reinforcement' are adequate theoretical concepts to describe what is happening on these occasions. The

[20] *Op. cit.*, p. 48.

very assumption that a fortnight's residential course may bring about a radical enough change in, say, the discharge of managerial function, to matter to those concerned, is one that is not justified on the strength of psychoanalytical interpretations alone.

My study of the counselling literature leaves me with the impression that in making progress with these groups the psychoanalytic theory has a 'sleeping partner', who provides much of the capital and possibly lacks the acumen and skill necessary both for the transactions and for self-advertising. The capital, in this case, is the resource of intimacy and sympathy, for a considerately and kindly maintained obliqueness of approach, for intellectual humility, scrupulousness, and for a conscientious denial of personal involvement. Those who acted as trainers had the acumen and skill, but these would not have been sufficient had the trainers not also drawn generously on 'capital'. The reappraisal of this resource, this capital, in conventional psychoanalytic terms alone may not help, for the resource, the capital, must also 'finance' the scrupulous psychoanalytical reappraisal itself!

(2) *The Expedient of 'Levels in Practising Therapy'*

The differences between levels of counselling consist largely in differences of depth to which exploration of the patient's personality is intended and attempted. All other criteria of level seem to follow from this, for example, length of treatment, intimacy of the patient's communications, standards of non-directiveness observed, and several others. Stated briefly, and in a somewhat simplified way, the existing range of levels is between the following two extremes :

Maximal exploration of depth to be carried out by counsellors who have themselves undergone training therapy, and who have been formally qualified by their respective professional associations. This exploration sets itself no time-limit for it is assumed that both counsellor and patient will remain available for as long as it is desired that they should go on.

At the other end, the range is marked by *no exploration* of depth. Here the counsellor's function consists in giving support and reassurance, coupled with suggestion, exhortation, and social or economic or administrative aid.

The expediency of the situation dictates that we use counselling techniques of almost any kind open to us. Nowadays we are faced

with a situation when the more elaborate and circumspect administration of health and welfare measures demands that we must help
people to avail themselves of the opportunities afforded to them
by an increasingly munificent society. Over and above the finan-
cial and administrative assistance, people are to be helped in the
management of their lives which are no longer entirely at the
mercy of material stresses and handicaps. It is only too obvious
that interminable and costly psychotherapies cannot be administered to millions. Yet the therapeutic ideology of counselling
originates in a theory and technique which cannot easily justify
departures from the perfectionism of these very lengthy therapies.
That this is so, and that the inconsistencies arising from the compromises and expediencies are ironed out by the counsellor's
faith in his mission, is just as true in the case of the treatment of patients as it has been in the case of the training of
counsellors.

Most counsellors—whether they admit their affiliation to
Freudian principles or not—generally act on the Freudian assumption that the infantile prejudgment of character is all but decisive.
Their theoretical commentaries, their interpretation of what they
encounter, their prognoses, and so on, confirm this in the large
majority of cases. Yet the actual counselling activity of the
majority of these counsellors could not possibly adhere to the
specification laid down by the psychoanalytic principles of 'maximal exploration'. Most counsellors are not trained to do this, and
even if they were, they could not devote three or four hundred
hours—a modest enough estimate—to each patient in need. It is
well-known that most counselling is episodic, brief, and of necessity also desultory. Admittedly, in some cases, certain accretions
of insight may occur, but these would hardly relate to infantile
origins, and will not affect the patient's basic personality structure.
If there are therapeutic effects in this work—and far be it from
me to want to appear certain that there aren't—they do not
follow from new insight into basic and infantile structures. The
accretions of insight will relate to the present and the recent past
with the counsellor having to decide the level at which the exploration must stop. Here too, the expediency has moral justifications
but it has not received these from the psychological theory which
guides the counsellor's work.

Whilst the prolonged reductive treatments by fully trained

therapists can at least credibly claim to be relatively free from the presumption of moral tutelage, of admonitory and suggestive influences, the abbreviated methods cannot. This does not automatically condemn the abbreviated methods so long as these interferences are not explicitly disclaimed. As it is, the nature of these influences is not fully understood, and there is a certain amount of regrettably complacent unawareness of the need for confessing to arbitrary departures from objective analysis to subjective syntheses. At a time in our history when the 'welfare state' is rapidly being converted into a 'personal service state' the importance of the moral issues involved in unconscious concealment and prevarication is probably great. At any rate, the anomaly created by the nebulousness surrounding this moral issue can be documented : 'Casework cannot alter the client's basic personality structure', we read in a recently published report, 'but works with that part of the personality which is able to learn from experience and to gain insight'.[21] The argument here is analogous to that used when the trainee's personality was divided into a 'professional' and 'private' sector. Here too, the argument is to expect personality changes in almost watertight compartments of the personality, an argument which does not follow from the counsellor's psychological theory.

There is nothing very wrong with the expediencies in the levels of administering aid, *so long as decisions on the choice of levels are not pretended to be mere technical decisions,* and so long as the directive and exhortative meaning of these levels is made known well enough to all concerned, especially to the architects, administrators, and counsellors of the 'personal service state', as well as to the political advocates of social betterment along psychiatric and mental hygienist lines.

Summary of the argument in this section. The central piece of the argument is that those who have a sense of urgency to give help because their psychological knowledge discloses to them the nature of people's *malaise,* eagerly proceed to help in ways which that same psychological knowledge would not warrant. These ways are the ways of compromise; and compromises have been shown to occur both in the selection and training of counsellors on the one hand, and in the treatment of patients or clients. The four

[21] *Monograph No. 6 of the Sociological Review,* December 1962, p. 159 (from Chapter IX by I. Spackman and M. Power).

parts under the heading of 'Expediencies in Training of Counsellors' began with a critical examination of some of the anomalies
of the selection process, and the striking paradoxes inherent in
certain conditions of suitability. Nor does the situation improve
when training takes over the accepted candidate. Publilius Syrus
believed that 'unless you grow wise of yourself you will listen in
vain to the wise'. The psychoanalytic trainers of counsellors accept
this principle for themselves : if they claim any 'wisdom', they
would credit their training analyses with providing them the
experience of 'growing wise'. They would not credit their didactic
experiences, the lectures, the seminars, and the books, though, of
course, these too will be valued ponderously and respectfully. The
first sign of inconsistency between what they regard as essential in
their own training and what they stipulate for other counsellors is
that instruction, straight teaching, will be a much more central
feature of the training of others than it was allowed to be in their
own training. This concession is not warranted by their psychological principles according to which a little training is *not* necessarily
conducive to more insight than no training at all. The *second*
illustration of this same inconsistency concerned the shortcut of
supervision. Here I showed that various rationalisations were introduced to warrant serious talk about the 'professional self' which
can be treated in this setting, whilst the private self would remain
relatively undisturbed. *Thirdly,* the area of training activity where
manifestations of similar anomalies appeared was the group-
methods of training counsellors. Here too compromises were shown
to be made on grounds external to the psychoanalytic principles
which continued to be the basis of thinking about counselling. Here
I detected an inarticulate, unspecific assistance to the helping and
training process, the personal presence and concern of the guide
and teacher, the model offered for identification in this and in
the sharing of experience with group members. In fact, the teachers
of counsellors themselves have of late given ample testimony of their
trust in the value of this 'unspecific assistance', even when they have
made these many compromises out of the sheer urgency of helping
others. The dissension in their theoretical thought has not stopped
their widespread, single-minded influence, and their eager, though
often hasty, therapeutic help to the patient. And so their faith
continues to be eloquently displayed in their works.

Counselling: an End or Means?
The Mirage of 'Results'

The counsellor must evenly balance therapeutic optimism and scepticism. He must be casually confident about his effectiveness and stoically serene about his failures. Coupled with his own assurance that he does not meddle or gratuitously interfere with the personal integrity of the client, is his confidence that his ministrations will affect the client beneficially. But has he any evidence that he can do this in any degree that could be shown worthwhile? The opponents of psychoanalysis, of some other forms of psychotherapy, of social casework, in fact, of counselling of any kind, have thoroughly exhausted this field : they feel satisfied that there is no proof whatever that these procedures are successful in achieving what they purport to achieve.[1] Recently A. E. Bergin convincingly argued[2] that the cause of this 'unproven' verdict is that when 'treated' and 'untreated' patients are followed up the so-called 'untreated' ones are really treated by physicians, friends, relations, and so on, and that the professionally 'treated' do not fare distinguishably better because so many counsellors (psychotherapists) do worse than those non-counsellors who help the 'untreated' control group! Using the therapist's criteria of 'empathy, unconditional positive regard, and mature, genuine, and integrated behaviour' defined by C. B. Truax,[3] Bergin concludes that therapists who score high on these do produce positive results whilst therapists relying only on a 'well-trained armamentarium of techniques', and scoring low on the essential criteria, do not.

But this discriminating and selective use of counsellors in

[1] The two best-known philippics are H. J. Eysenck's *Uses and Abuses of Psychology*, London, 1953, and Barbara Wootton's *Social Science and Social Pathology*, London, 1959. Another attack from an interesting but very different quarter was delivered by O. H. Mowrer in *The Crisis in Psychiatry and Religion*, New York, 1961. Also Cf. *Measuring Results in Social Casework: A Manual of Judging Movement*, New York, 1950, by Hunt, J. McV. and Kogan, D. S. and 'Assessing the Results in Social Work', by G. Rose, *Sociological Review*, December 1957, Vol. V, No. 2, pp. 225–237.

[2] 'The Effects of Psychotherapy: Negative Results Revisited', *Journal of Counselling Psychology*, 1963, Vol. X, No. 3, pp. 244–250.

[3] 'Effective Ingredients in Psychotherapy: An Approach to Unravelling the Patient-Therapist Interaction', *Ibid.*, pp. 256–263.

research on 'results' has not yet been tried often enough on a systematic basis, and, for the time being, the counsellors continue to work in the face of criticism which they almost invariably regard as unfeeling and narrow.

What is so odd is that psychoanalysts and other counsellors themselves—whilst deploring the insensitivity of these critics—sometimes come dangerously near the critical views which they so strongly resent. Helene Deutsch, a psychoanalyst of considerable standing, recently observed : 'We do not eliminate the original source of neurosis; we only help to achieve better ability to change neurotic frustrations into valid compensations.'[4] Of course, there is at least some claim to progress here, though it would be desperately difficult to determine why certain compensations are valid and others not. This apprehension is unequivocally shared by another leading psychoanalyst, Thomas S. Szász, whose testimony gravely imperils his own profession's claim for objectivity. 'The lack of publicly stated and generally agreed upon criteria leaves open the opportunity to interpret observation in accord with one's unspecified personal biases. The psychiatrist's moral preferences may thus be enunciated in the disguise of scientific descriptions of "facts".'[5] What credit, if any, would Helene Deutsch's testimony about 'valid compensations' retain after it has been matched with this 'enunciation' of her prominent colleague? Then consider, for example, the following epitaph : 'I cannot count many completed analyses in a practice of some twenty years.'[6] Freud's own definitive essay, 'Analysis Terminable and Interminable',[7] the *locus classicus* of this theme, is not very much more optimistic. 'Every analyst ought periodically himself to enter analysis once more, at intervals of, say, five years, and without any feeling of shame in so doing. So not only the patient's analysis but that of the analyst himself has ceased to be a terminable and become an interminable task.' Freud, in the next paragraph, tries to mitigate the disillusionment by warning us against the misconception that, in his view, 'analysis in general is an endless business'. But apart from the occasional dramatic cure of the traumatic neuroses there is little

[4] 'Psychoanalytic Therapy in the Light of Follow-up', *Journal of the American Psychoanalytical Association*, 1959, Vol. VII, p. 445.
[5] *The Myth of Mental Illness*, London, 1962, p. 105.
[6] 'Contributions to the Problem of Terminating Psychoanalysis', by E. Weigerth, *The Psychoanalytic Quarterly*, 1952, Vol. XXI, pp. 465–480.
[7] *Collected Papers*, London, 1957, Vol. V, pp. 316–357.

more he can promise. 'The business of analysis is to secure the best possible psychological conditions for the functioning of the ego; when this has been done, analysis has accomplished its task.' There are too many assumptions here we are expected to take on trust: that the ego is a lasting enough core of the self throughout counselling, that reinforcing it in counselling doesn't amount to changing it according to the aspirations of the counsellor, that we have already agreed on what is a 'best functioning' for this or that ego and that there is such a thing as one best functioning for it. Yet, after all these assumptions about the best functioning, we are also told that there is no such thing after all.

By now the whole counselling profession echoes the warnings against therapeutic utopianism or messianism. We are now told time and again that there can be nothing conclusively rounded-off in the counselling process. Following Freud's differential prognosis for the traumatic neuroses and character neuroses, the psychoanalyst Nunberg reiterates that, in the latter, the patients' resistances and relapses are very stubborn indeed, and that the analysis of these may consequently last *'for years, endlessly!'*[8] But there is a component of character-neurosis in perhaps all the neuroses, no matter how dramatically traumatic some of them may appear to be! So, in principle, all therapies would have to be regarded as interminable and all therapeutic bonds as preferably permanent. Of course, the validity of psychoanalytic principles will not be decided by current therapeutic success or failure. 'Therapeutic efficacy cannot be the real measure of the value of psychoanalytic postulates',[9] observes one writer in *The International Journal of Psychoanalysis,* a familiar plea, also put forward by several others, putting the responsibility for theoretical postulates before responsibility for therapeutic achievements. Recently Allen Wheelis drew attention to the practice of analysts to speak much less of 'cure' and more frequently of 'progress'[10] and suggested one explanation for the persistence of trust not very much sustained by tangible results : 'The failure of prayer to bring about what was prayed for does not revise the belief in the power of prayer. The evidence is simply ignored.'[11] An unexpected plea

[8] *Practice and Theory of Psychoanalysis*, by H. Nunberg, New York, 1948, p. 204.
[9] 'Some Considerations for the Further Development of Psychoanalysis', by F. McLaughlin, *Loc. cit.*, October 1963, Vol. XLIV, Part 4.
[10] *The Quest for Identity*, London, 1959, p. 42.
[11] *Ibid.*, p. 159.

from a counsellor and a telling testimony in support of this chapter. It is now also being recalled that the proper meaning of the word 'cure' is what the Romans thought it meant: *cura* stood for 'care' which is not a finite activity in response to finite needs!

In addition to the psychoanalytic confessions about interminable treatments, now social workers too, the core of the rank and file of the counselling professions, are donning the same garb of humility about 'end-results' and 'completions'. Miss F. E. Waldron, a psychiatric social worker of considerable experience and sensibility, expresses her belief '. . . in the value of the potential interminable-ness of social work help . . . It is in contrast to the widely held idea that to choose the casework method of helping implies that it has a foreseeable end!'[12] One cannot help remembering that this open-endedness, this inconclusiveness, is not peculiar to secular counselling, and that pastoral ministration too has always been ideally an ongoing and perpetual service. I should like to stress here, that it is the counsellors themselves who draw attention to this similarity; it is the counselling ideology which elicits the sociological observation and not this writer's peculiar inclination to a mystical interpretation of counselling! The counsellor's relative inability to prove his usefulness in what is being done, leaves his enterprise relatively unhampered; as if nothing could disqualify the moral concern expressed in the extensive professional operations. To show that I am not taking liberties with the appraisal of this modern social phenomenon, I should commend the following passage from a recently published book, *Portrait of Social Work*, whose authors, presumably experienced social workers, have this to say: 'The understanding and tolerance and sense of vocation of the natural social worker give self-assurance and self-confidence. Convinced of the need to help people—perhaps on emotional rather than intellectual grounds—they feel social work is worthwhile whatever the chances of "success" or "improvement". *Not depending for its justification on its results, no failure can therefore discredit it.*'[13] (Italics mine.) On the face of it, the position of medical practice might be thought to be similar : the mortality of man, the ultimate failure of all medicine, as well as all its intermediate failures, could not detract from the value of trying to heal and comfort. In medicine too there is no *scientific* rationale for

[12] 'The Choice of Goals in Casework Treatment: A Case Study', *The British Journal of Psychiatric Social Work*, Vol. VI, No. 2, 1961.
[13] By B. N. Rodgers and J. Dixon, O.U.P., 1960, p. 155.

trying in the face of known hopeless odds; nor is there in coun-selling. It seems to me that the lurking and undeclared faith of the counsellor is that the concern which prompts him to act will overflow into the act, and will never *completely* fail if it is sufficiently steeped in a person-to-person relationship between worker and helped. Neither failure nor success need be recog-nisable by third parties if the counsellor knows that he can throw himself open to this kind of relationship, and if the client knows that he can partake in that relationship. The service must be rendered even in the face of hopeless odds and there is something inherently proper in the rendering of it irrespective of what differ-ence it could demonstrably make. J. H. Wallis explains, 'Whether or not we as counsellor or friend or relative "do anything" is beside the point. Sometimes a spontaneous action becomes a kind of sym-bol, a recognition of the other person's need for help and our own willingness to try to give it.'[14] Presumably this demonstration of goodwill is good in itself and also, hopefully, it may be good because the demonstration may make its mark on others, after all. But we mustn't worry our heads about evidence in respect of such results. The certainty of value is not rooted in empirically verified results; it is rather the assurance derived from an unanalysable moral imperative. That this is so, will become more apparent in the light of what follows.

The counsellor's offer to be a 'leaning post' to people who are weighed down under anxiety or pain does not carry with it an explicit promise of lightening the burden, even after the post is removed. This lack of results—results, that is, which continue even after contact with the counsellor has ceased—is not openly admitted and stress is laid on the relief which the counsellor can and does supply whilst engaged in counselling and whilst physically present. This is vividly brought home to us in some studies of geriatric cases and in cases of mortal illness. Here the medical social worker's reassurances about the help she could afford the patient with home, family, and so on, as well as with the patient's own personal needs, are important, but not more so than her sheer physical and warmly sympathetic presence. Understandably, social workers will record 'results' even in cases of this kind, but these could no more be described as 'therapeutic results' than could the relief from pain upon the administration of drugs. For example, in

[14] *Counselling and Social Welfare*, London, 1960, p. 30.

one case study we read that a cancer patient with *metastases* was 'reassured' by a social worker by the social worker's frank recognition of the patient's serious condition, as far as this was known and understood by the patient. The patient was also 'reassured' that there was a reasonable possibility that she might respond to the treatment she was getting. 'After a while,' runs the sombre case report, 'she was able to talk about cancer in the same way as another patient might talk of asthma, without the all-pervading fear which the diagnosis usually evokes.'[15] Surely, the anxiety experienced in such a condition as this is entirely realistic, and the very insinuation that it is a condition to be 'cured' would be objectionable.[16] Nonetheless it is a condition in which compassion of others and their attempt at helping or reassuring the dying is entirely to be expected. But the help no more envisages 'results' in terms of the patient's lasting condition than the administration of an anaesthetic would, at one end, and the administration of extreme unction would, at the other. Indeed, the descriptive titles, 'psychotherapy of the dying' or 'social casework with the dying' very much appear to be inverted euphemisms for the age-old pastoral care of the dying. In a way, one cannot help blinking at the thought of this kind of ministration being described as 'casework'. The severe matter-of-factness of this term conceals a labour of love, a communion of sharing comfort and peace in the immediate present, and not a technical operation to achieve some specifiable goal. And though it almost seems to be a secularised sacrament, a devout watch, the worker is on the constant alert against uncritical submerging in devoutness.

It is interesting that in the few studies which have been carried out to check the effectiveness of psychotherapy or counselling, the follow-up categories have often been terms such as 'improved' or 'much improved' and, of course, 'no change', but rarely 'cured', 'partly cured', 'not cured', or some such terms. Clearly no one ever expects complete restitution to some mythical state of unspoilt mental health. What matters is the noticeable (because manifest) attitude of the counsellor which seems to convey itself to the client saying: 'Take your time; don't be anxious. I will be with you as long as you need me.' In other words, even the anticipation of

---

[15] *Patients are People. A Medical-Social Approach to Prolonged Illness*, by M. Field, New York, 1953, p. 75.
[16] There was no such insinuation in this report.

interminableness may be instrumental, for it may inspire the counsellor's patience, and add to the client's feeling of security. In principle, there is no obvious stopping-point. The healer does not finish the job, and cannot retire; in fact 'healing' is an inappropriate descriptive term of the activity because healing is a finite activity. The connotation of the term is inescapably medical, and we cannot deny that the victim of an illness, injury, problem, or breakdown, invariably seeks an *in integrum restitutio*, a cure, and certainly imagines or hopes that he will be utterly delivered from the actual predicament. Indeed, in medicine, in a hearteningly increasing number of instances, he is so delivered. The model of counselling is obtained from medicine, where a good deal of help administered is strictly episodic, terminable, and completed. Physical restitution can be aimed at and, in fact, accomplished for there is a relatively accurate knowledge of the condition which must be restituted and of the techniques with which it can be restituted. Counselling, on the other hand, is not restitution. There is no *original* integrity to which one can return. It is perhaps partly for this reason that counselling is a regimen which one always breaks off 'in the middle'. The counsellor will hope that the client will continue the dialogue, in his solitariness, with an internalised image of the partner-counsellor. Or, indeed, he will encourage us to believe that 'results' or 'success' in counselling will, to some extent, consist in the client's ability to re-establish himself in some sort of close enough relationship with others. A smooth enough and effective weaning of the client from the counsellor on to others, a process sometimes described as 'resocialisation', is one thing, but when this is couched in theological terms, and 'success' is described as weaning on to a communion, or on to God, the psychoanalytically oriented theoretician is taking an entirely unexpected model to convey an agnostic meaning. Dr. L. S. Saul, a training analyst, feelingly concludes his notes on the goals of psychoanalytic therapy by quoting a 'summing-up' from a grateful letter of a patient of his, 'a hard-bitten man of the world in his early fifties', who testifies to his analyst's success by writing to him sometime later and informing him : 'Now I can pray again !'[17] It is important to note that this is offered as evidence of a successful therapy. One of Dr. Balint's students, Dr. E. J. R. Primrose, who, having applied what he had learnt in Balint's psychoanalytic

[17] *Technique and Practice of Psychoanalysis*, Philadelphia, 1958, p. 8.

seminars for general practitioners, recorded his findings in a book published in a series which was edited by Balint, a training analyst himself. The concluding paragraph of this book, as it were its epigraph, reads: 'The overlap between the fields of neurotic alienation and separation from the love of God of the irreligious is increasingly recognised (Tillich, P., *The Courage To Be*, London, 1955), and the extent to which religious pastoral counselling resembles simple psychotherapy has been shown by Oates (*Anxiety in Christian Experience*, London, 1958). It is the author's belief (i.e. Primrose's) that future development of this pastoral trend in general medical practice and in the churches will be of major benefit both to these professions and to our western civilization.'[18] This book, which was published in the Mind and Medicine Monographs, could not contain such a momentous conclusion as this, had it not been in some important way inspired, influenced, and led by the psychoanalytic tuition which preceded it and the psychoanalytic editorial control which followed its writing, or had it not been at least tacitly approved in the fashion of *nihil obstat*. A teacher and an editor can, of course, dissociate himself from the views of pupil or writer, but it is forever a reflection on the work of the preceptor when his principles are either flagrantly ignored or lend themselves to gross reinterpretations. My own hypothesis is —and in this chapter I have tried to corroborate this from Balint's own writings—that those principles do readily allow and indeed encourage the conclusions reached by Dr. Primrose.

Another work, also issuing from the Tavistock Institute, and also produced by psychoanalytically trained and psychoanalytically supervised workers, quietly makes a claim for success on the grounds of a client's revival of religious interest. One case study in this work ends with the following report: 'Mrs. Robinson reported that things were going well and that both she and her husband were feeling much helped by their membership of the religious group.'[19] No explanation is offered why this should be taken to be a 'proof' of the success of the caseworker.

Carl R. Rogers, whose influence on contemporary counselling practices has been considerable, tells us in a reflective and retrospective work[20] at the height of his career, that the end of coun-

---

[18] *Psychological Illness, A Community Study*, London, 1962.
[19] *Marriage: Studies in Emotional Conflict and Growth*, Ed. by L. Pincus, London, 1960, p. 117.
[20] *On Becoming a Person*, London, 1961.

selling is what he calls 'the process' and the end is not to be sought anywhere beyond the process. 'The good life is a process, not a state of being' he says later vaguely, evidently groping towards a conclusion which he reaches in the following frank and certainly not vague lines: 'A sort of trance-like feeling in the relationship from which both client and I emerge at the end of the hour, as if from a deep well or tunnel. In these moments there is, to borrow Buber's phrase, a real "I-Thou" relationship, a timeless living in the experience which is *between* the client and me. It is at the opposite pole from seeing the client, or myself, as an object. It is the height of personal subjectivity.'[21] It would be unnecessary to labour the point: the faith of this counsellor is untarnished by pedestrian notions about separable means and ends, for the means are here shown to be integral parts of the end and, in fact, the end fails to transcend the means at all, and consists in them.

In these circumstances it is not so remarkable, after all, that only few of the published psychoanalytical and casework studies are put forward as therapeutic success stories. The counselling literature is full of disclaimers, of guarded and qualified claims. The analyst does not promise cure. He only promises help, says one paper in *The International Journal of Psychoanalysis*,[22] or as Philip Rieff recently put this, 'Psychoanalysis does not cure, it merely reconciles'.[23] But this 'helping' and 'reconciling' activity has no obvious duration or end. 'Even if the patient doesn't get better, you know you're doing the right thing', Jerome D. Frank quotes a young psychiatrist in training[24] and seems to approve that we should regard the private and subjective testimony as some sort of evidence for the value of what this young counsellor was doing. The existentialist counsellors express similar ideas even more forcibly and, nowadays, their metaphysical ideas often colour the mainly psychoanalytical and clinical notions of the counsellors. Karl Jaspers, for example, observes that both patient and doctor are 'thus and no other', they are in their ultimate and lasting essence unchangeable. And he adds, 'Either the unchangeable element is obscured since therapy aims at reassuring and deceiving,

21 *On Becoming a Person*, pp. 75, 186, 202.
22 'Some Typical Complications Mobilized by the Psychoanalytical Procedure', Gottschalk, L. A. and Whitman, R. M., March-June 1962, Vol. XLIII, Parts 2–3, pp. 140–150.
23 'The Analytic Attitude', *Encounter*, June 1962, 105, pp. 22–28.
24 *Persuasion and Healing*, O.U.P., 1961, p. 125.

measures are adopted *ut aliquid fiat* and the aim becomes not so much the cure of an illness as the creation of an atmosphere of friendly help.'[25] Presumably, if help need not aim at cure, its purpose is itself. Elsewhere, Jaspers explains, 'If science fails one, then there is faith in one's art and good fortune; at any rate one will contrive an atmosphere of cure, even if this is only some therapeutic establishment that ticks over idly!'[26] The 'caring' and 'hand-holding' component of the counselling operation has been self-evidently proper unless, of course, through fostering over-dependency or because of some other error it must be criticised. But apart from these cases, it might be said that to demand proof of the effectiveness of counselling is no less preposterous than to demand proof of the effectiveness of the command, 'Thou shalt love thy neighbour'.

As a sociologist, studying the texture of the ideology of counselling, I have no complaint to make if a counsellor uses a theological imagery to describe what he is doing. I find nothing wrong with a therapist-counsellor citing the patient's renewed ability of finding solace in prayer as a sign of success or another one describing the process of counselling as a Buberian communion. What I must show up as an ideological construction is the presentation of these concepts and images in a context which is fully and energetically claimed to be scientific and technical. The very neglect of research into the effectiveness of counselling activities—bearing in mind the great and still increasing social investment into these services as well as expensive private practices—is itself suggestive that strong convictions must be at work to sustain a perseverance not sustained by conclusive evidence.

The spirit of this conviction is beautifully called forth in T. S. Eliot's *Family Reunion*,

> 'Not for the good that it will do
> But that nothing may be left undone
> On the margin of the impossible.'

And also in the *Talmud*,

> 'It is not thy duty to complete the work,
> but neither art thou free to desist from it.'
> (Ethics of the Fathers, II, 21)

[25] *General Psychopathology*, Manchester University Press, 1963, p. 804.
[26] *Loc. cit.*, p. 791.

Perhaps those who work 'on the margin of the impossible' may be forgiven for juggling with the notions of 'helping' and 'reconciling', and also for their hope of accomplishing these things by merging the means with the ends.

Summary of the argument in this section. To this day the counsellors labour on without the assurance that their work is rewarded by, at least some, success. In fact, psychoanalysts and social caseworkers frequently confess that there is no definable end to the process of counselling, and that to all intents and purposes the counselling relationship is not terminable. Following from this emerges the notion that the counselling process is its own justification and that it need not be vindicated by achievements. Yet a curious attempt at vindication is made in religious terms which brings to light one of the most blatant ways in which the faith of the counsellors is professed. Counselling is an 'I-and-Thou' relationship; counselling is communion, the end of which is itself. Man's undying filial dependency is not an abnormality but an essential part of his humanity. It becomes an anomalous quality only when there is nothing to depend on. The counselling theoreticians do not openly advocate dependence on God but their poetic-theological language suggests at times that they would like to.

The counsellors are markedly reluctant to attend to the issue of evidence for 'success'. The picture we are forced to form, for the time being at least, is that counselling is to be justified by the moral sustenance it gives to both counsellor and counsellee, and by the moral affirmation of concern which the widespread practice publicly and visibly makes. It is justified because in its absence we would have to take up the callous and inhuman position of 'not even trying'. Let no one underestimate the causal significance of the large-scale organised gesture of desperately-wanting-to-help! The spectacle of professionalised benevolence is a source of moral renewal for this age, whilst the spectacle of rationalist criticism might not be as readily credited so much with a clear conscience.

The Pattern Shared by These Elements: a Summing up

I have attributed a 'faith' to the counsellors, a faith, which, on the one hand, has included the unconfessed belief that counselling has justifications of a moral and metaphysical kind, and which, on the other hand, included the belief that these moral and metaphysical elements permeate the technical procedures and become themselves an essential part of the counselling process. This is not a summing-up of what *I* think the core-experience of counselling ought to be, but what the *counsellors themselves* implicitly, and sometimes explicitly, affirm as the essential quality of their work. The point is that direct affirmations are rare, and from these an inference in respect of the mysticism of the modern counselling ideology could not be fully justified. I base my inference on a characteristic, strangely ubiquitous, which, in my opinion, relegates this ideology into the category of creeds. This characteristic, the hallmark of the counsellor's faith, is his refrainlike acceptance of contradictory propositions, and incompatible canons of technique. I propose to list the antinomies, in the order as they appear in the major 'elements', which I discussed in the six previous sections of this long chapter. The pattern of contradictions shared by all these elements is what I aim to trace in this section. In anticipation of a more detailed study of this pattern, and by way of introducing the following paragraphs, I should like to say that the pattern is rather like the *credo quia absurdum*, the archetype of all faith. The list of antinomial assertions which now follows is certainly not complete but it is adequate to show the richness of this faith, and the consistency of its balanced dividedness.

A. The counsellors have come to realise that their personal intervention is so much more effective when it is carried out with spontaneous warmth and affection, than when they just go through the motions of interest and concern. The insincerity of professionally pretending cannot be concealed for long, and even when the 'role-playing of love' is diligently sustained by experienced and well-practised counsellors, it is still insufficiently convincing. There are several irreconcilable precepts professed here: both spontaneous lovingness and scrupulously thought-out strategy of technique are necessary, yet it is hard to see how the two can be had by the same person devoted to both, and identified with the roles required by both. Then there is the difficulty of 'prescribing' lovingness for the use of the counsellor: the act of prescribing cancels out the requirement of spontaneity and sincerity. For a similar reason, nor can the gestures of spontaneous sympathy be the subject of a didactic imparting of skills to counsellors by trainers of counsellors. In his recent book[1] H. Fingarette relates this to the context to which it belongs, 'Time and again in the literature of both East and West, we meet the ideal person as one who offers love and sympathy and selfless devotion while remaining in some sense "disinterested", "detached", "uninvolved", "ruthless". Compassionate objectivity, human-hearted but disinterested understanding: *the paradox in these phrases is evident.*'[2] (Italics mine.) Unexpectedly, the psychoanalytically-minded writer falls in line with an ancient discipline and he is followed by the rank and file of the counselling professions.

B. The counsellor believes in the all-pervasiveness of the impulsive, the emotional, and of the so-called *Id* forces of life yet he is a firm believer too in the supreme rationality and intelligence of life. We are initially ruled from 'below' yet the very stuff of this low instinctiveness has the inherent potential of generating from itself the rational and intelligent knower and controller of itself. In addition to this, the basic instinctiveness of life is both loving and hating, and the counsellor takes the fundamental ambivalence of life as a cornerstone of his psychology. And though with one assertion he tells us of ambivalence as an equilibrium—disturbed or not—of originally equal forces, in another assertion he takes it as no less fundamental that love is always to prevail: the fact of his profession, his dedication to healing of a certain kind proves that he believes in the eventual triumph of positive forces. In the race between love and hate, he backs love *as well as* the stoical acceptance of death.

It is strange that the modern doctrines of counselling, which have done so much to disillusion us of the eighteenth-century fiction that man is a fundamentally rational creature, should be the very doctrines which enunciate that rationality of insight into our own motives is the condition of our freedom from neurotic suffering. The counsellor seems to believe in the ultimate rationality and ultimate irrationality of those whom he helps, and of the helping process itself. This belief is shown by his attitude to the problem of the counsellor's personal involvement in the client. In applying himself to the task of helping he must, on no account, get himself involved in what he is doing. But this prescription of detachment and complete impersonal objectivity will not work.

[1] *The Self in Transformation*, New York-London, 1963.
[2] *The Self in Transformation*, p. 245.

Firstly, it will not work, because it sets an ideal which is impossible to achieve, and secondly, because were it achieved—the counsellors seem to believe—the healing enterprise would fail. With no involvement at all, the client would be 'frozen out' and with total involvement the client would be 'burnt up'. Therefore, the counsellor must do both, antinomially, contradictorily, *and* complementarily, in the manner of T. S. Eliot's 'Teach us to care and not to care', with much the same sentiment of awe and humility which informed the poetic phrasing.

The paradox of incentives for doing counselling work remains unresolved in the face of all the critical reappraisals. Whatever personal motives we may allow the counsellor, with which to sustain his efforts and warm his concerns, he is expected to continue to maintain vigilance over his compassion for the patient, using as a source of energy—necessary for maintaining this vigilance—the very compassion he is supposed to keep in check. That this feeling for the patient involves the counsellor in a relationship of reciprocity and mutuality is obscured by the professional status and presumed superior strength of the healer over the other. In private practice the patient pays the counsellor; the oath of secrecy binds the counsellor but not the patient; in public service the counsellor retains vestiges of the 'official' in him; and there are other features in the relationship which help to conceal this mutuality. Yet in fact, the professional status of the counsellor tends to be used as a defence against admitting that he does enter into a personal and non-professional mutuality of relationship, whilst paradoxically trying to maintain side-by-side with this a non-personal and professional relationship. We regularly encounter frank disclosures to the effect that mutuality is vividly experienced by the counsellor, and that it is essential for therapeutic success, and equally that its detached viewing and control are also essential.

It is interesting to observe that even in the philosophical-psychological theory of this mutuality we have a paradoxical structure perpetuated : some counsellors describe mutuality as a regression (e.g. 'return to the womb') taking the term in the psycho-analytic sense; others will represent it as an 'emergent', a product of ascending progress, ascending that is from the primitive instinctive beginnings. What is paradoxical is this : the careful reading of the texts as well as the implications of these contradictions suggests that, in fact, the counsellors believe both these interpretations. Here too there is a quietistic fusion of incompatible theoretical models.

C. In affording his help to others the counsellor must respect the personal integrity of others and must not impose his own personal preferences. In brief he must be ideally non-directive and non-judgmental. Yet, in fact, by his very efforts to be non-directive he cannot but feel called upon, implicitly and explicitly, to enjoin others and to direct others to assimilate *at least* his non-directive morality and *at most* the implicit morality of his own professional interests and commitments. Karl Menninger quoted a most illuminating testimony to the effect that the counsellors were aware of this paradox. 'One of the difficulties in teaching analytic techniques stems from the series of dilemmas in which the would-be psychoanalyst is placed. *These represent paradoxes, or as I prefer to think about them, "dialectics", the synthesis of which must be accomplished individually by each psychoanalyst.* For example you state ... that the physician is "in charge" and yet, of course, his purpose is to demonstrate to the patient that he (the latter) is really in charge not just of the treatment but of his life.'[3] (Italics mine.) This is a welcome support for the thesis of this chapter-section which is that the affirmation of the paradox is a central feature of the counsellor's faith. 'Elsewhere it was implied that the physician must sincerely want to get the patient "well". Yet to accomplish this, he must achieve an attitude of "desirelessness". 'There are I believe,' the writer of this testimony, Dr. Herbert J. Schlesinger, continues, 'a number of such paradoxes, the continuous effort at resolution of which leaves its mark on the self-concept of the psychoanalyst.'[4]

The paradoxicality of the counsellor's attitude to the issue of directiveness was well brought out by a recent study of mine in which a questionnaire was circulated among social workers, mainly probation officers, children's officers, and almoners, and in which the following two questions occurred at some distance from each other so that the response to one of them should have the least influence on the response to the other. The two questions were:

Question one. ('Students of social work should be taught that people should be accepted as responsible agents who by and large *mean what they say* and have the right to be treated as if they did.')

[3] *The Theory of Psychoanalytic Technique*, London, 1958, pp. 27–28.
[4] *Ibid.*

Question two. ('Students of social work should be taught that people often seek help with some material problem, e.g. housing, employment, physical illness, and so on, though this so-called "presenting problem" is *not always* that in respect of which they need immediate help. Students of social work should be instructed in the art of finding out about personal and emotional difficulties which may be underlying the so-called "presenting problem".')

Certainly, there could be many valid criticisms levelled against this kind of data-gathering. There were over 800 questionnaires circulated and only 427 replies received; the questionnaires were circulated through the post; the questions were involved and long; and perhaps some other weaknesses too could be found. Yet the overwhelming consistency and unequivocalness of the results must be explained in ways other than 'fortuitous outcome'. The answers were given on the questionnaire as 'agree', 'undecided', 'disagree' and one of these was to be underlined by the subjects. These were :

Question one	agree 84·4%	undecided 6·4%	disagree 8·8%
Question two	agree 94·8%	undecided 3·1%	disagree 2·1%
Both questions:	agree 78·7%(!)		

More than three-quarters of the subjects found it possible to express agreement with both of these recommendations! The moral ideal of respecting the responsibility and honesty of others, and the moral ideal of helping those who deceive themselves and also deceive others, are paradoxically fused and simultaneously—or dialectically—pursued. A similar merger of opposites is noted by a prominent social-work writer. 'On the one hand,' observes Noel Timms, 'caseworkers have asserted a faith in the potentiality of the human being to change himself and his society, whilst on the other hand, espousing a group of psychological theories which would appear to place severe limitations on the capacity of individuals to change.'[5] Here too, the counsellors suffer from—or enjoy —a condition of 'double vision', or perhaps 'stereoscopic vision' enabling them to comprehend a more plastic reality, a reality with a depth; at least this is the hypothesis which one might conjecture, when looking at the results of my questionnaire-survey. I will try to be more specific about this hypothesis further on.

D. The brand of honesty of the counsellor's era is a scientific

[5] *Social Casework, Principles and Practice,* London, 1964, p. 61.

honesty. 'Intellectual honesty' is not very surprisingly equated with scientific scrupulousness and methodicalness, or simply with an adherence to the canons of logic. The counsellor would feel insecure without some claim to his being an 'applier of science'. Yet, the crucial act of applying science in counselling is not just a cognitive act of ratiocination, or a discursive formulation, but also a deliberate expressive act of caring and helping. Were it not that too, counselling would not be effective. Many of the counsellors themselves testify that the process would fail, were it only a process of 'applying science'. In fact, the applier of science is warned not to apply science to his own total personal participation in the counselling process for this might fatally impair the effective use of his own personality. Thus, the paradoxical conclusion is reached that the counsellor must apply science, and that he must not. Nor may we easily get out of this by suggesting that there is no contradiction or paradox here—or, for that matter none in any of the other instances—but rather a skilful dialectic, a rhythmic see-saw, a reasonable 'taking turns', for often enough a simultaneity of the incompatible requirements is prescribed as essential to performance. It is suggested, at times, that there is a skill to be learnt here, that the process consists of identifiable phases and motions, which can be made the subject of training and instruction. I doubt that even with a greatly increased analytic control over the use of personality we could avoid the central paradox, which is that cerebration about technicalities depersonalises and sterilises the vital and spontaneous core of skill-using. The paradox is not unlike the well-known 'paradox of hedonism', according to which the thesis, 'all things are done for pleasure and against pain', whether true or not, will certainly make pleasure elude those who would consciously and deliberately pursue what is said to be their nature to pursue! Similarly, a perfect premeditation of technicalities in counselling will almost inexorably lead to the wrong technicalities. An overthinking of counselling is likely to modify it, weaken it, if not paralyse it altogether. It is not an accident that in counselling too the thesis : 'those who can, do, and those who cannot, write', has a certain unmistakable applicability. Articulate, sharply discursive and critical thinking is not the best, and certainly not often an essential, instrument of the work of the counsellor, if one is to judge from the counsellor's own testimony. The counsellor seems to believe that, at least in human affairs, the buoyancy of truthfulness could be maintained only when its vessel floated on 'oceanic' concerns and sympathies for man.

E. It seems to me that psychoanalytically trained and committed counsellors observe the expedient of shortcuts in selecting and training counsellors, in spite of the theoretical contradiction in which the expedient will land them. Their favourable reception of these expedients is not accountable in terms of their theoretical premises, for in those terms a little training is *not* preferable to no training at all. The analyst will countenance the abbreviated methods of training and treatment, and, on the showing of his own theory and findings, he also admits to the arbitrary directiveness and ineffectiveness of these shortcuts.

The paradox in selection is well known : we want sane counsellors, but we want them to be also a little neurotic; we want them to be sensitive yet impervious to the emotional provocations of the job; we want them to be intelligent but we don't want them to be intellectuals who tend to be, and can be, artistically or scientifically rebellious, or just searchingly critical.

The paradox of training arises from the indecision about the way one gets 'insight'. The counsellor is supposed to impart insight or evoke insight through the relationship of the counselling bond and *not* by *telling* people, by *teaching* them, by *informing* them. The counsellors' basic principle is that insight can be gained *only* because the counselling intimacy re-creates the intimacy and dependence of earlier filial situations. Only by reliving those can one understand the meaning of man's desires and aversions. The so-called 'intellectual insight', the intellectual comprehension of what these desires *might* mean, is insufficient and, even when warmly accepted, is a counterfeit of the genuine insight. These views are held by the counsellors. And yet—as the insight-givers are very few in number, and as they strive to increase the number of beneficiaries—the counsellors, the ideologists of insight-giving, can be seen *telling*, *teaching*, and *informing* candidates in courses of training of a didactic nature. They don't really believe in the training potential of didactic methods, yet they feel they must use didactic methods. They know that self-knowledge cannot be got through being taught, yet they advocate training methods as if they believed otherwise.

F. At the back of his mind the counsellor cannot help retaining the notion that what he is doing is analogous to what the physician is doing with his patient. As if there was an analogy between the physical treatment of illness and the counselling service rendered. We even speak of 'psychological illness', and think of the sequence diagnosis-treatment-recovery as the normal sequence of professional activity in the counsellor's work. This sequence is often enough completely and genuinely terminated in the practice of physical medicine. To preserve his image of instrumentality, of usefulness, and therefore his sense of worth, the counsellor tries to emulate the physician and imagines that he is a 'healer', a 'curer' of ills, that he is an applier of skills and an achiever of tangible 'results'. *At the same time*, he is also obliged to admit that his ministrations have no temporal shape or natural end to them. In fact, he is forced to confess that his help-giving is interminable, and that therapy is no more finite than brotherly compassion. Although in some traumatic neuroses the counsellor might claim to have dramatically 'completed' the 'cure', in most cases the counsellor is unable to show conclusively and objectively that a major change has, in fact, been effected. It is openly admitted that ideally the counsellor must come back to 'cure' the same 'illness' again and again. The conception of terminating the interminable is the last of the paradoxes I propose to list here before I proceed to an examination of the structure of these paradoxes, and of their affinity to the paradoxes of other and earlier creeds.

I must ask the reader to bear in mind that these antinomial and contradictory elements are listed not in an attempt at revealing muddle-headedness or indeed some deliberate deception or dishonesty. I suspect that human service is inevitably paradoxical when treated in terms of scientific objectivity. The counsellor need feel no shame about his single-minded and united self-division. But he ought to have the courage to face the fact of his own ambiguities, and recognise that the attitude—the orientation, and the affirmation—which helps him to shepherd and direct the 'twins' of these several paradoxes in one direction amounts to a basic vision and constitutes a *faith*. The use of the term 'faith' in this context is not as arbitrary as it might seem at first. In the following argument I will try to justify my usage.

For the Christian, 'faith' is a condition in which simultaneous affirmation of doctrine and of everyday empirical reality is made possible by a surrender to a beatific vision in which the antinomies are fused in a state of grace. Believing that Mary was virgin and believing that she couldn't have been, and believing that Christ rose from the dead and believing that he couldn't have, are affirmations which, though contradictory, fuse in an elation of largeness, of generosity. The contradictions become complementary to produce an awareness in which 'the law of the excluded middle' is no longer binding. The mystic often tells us of a more vivid reality to which he gains access by accepting this licence with humility and patience. The notion of a dazzling armistice between warring incompatibles is one of the most frequent in mystical literature. 'Let us delight to find Thee,' writes St. Augustine, 'by failing to find Thee rather than by finding Thee to fail to find Thee.'[6] The modern linguistic philosopher might argue that had the terms of this sentence been defined accurately the sentence would have collapsed into nonsense. In fact, one could say this of every paradox. Yet the Christian—and the counsellor—implies that this is by no means a secure position to adopt because it may be that a categorical system, yet unknown to us, would accommodate the opposing assertions. This is the underlying conception in the *Coincidentia Oppositorum*, a construct of some importance in the writings of Meister Eckhart and Nicolaus Cusanus, among others. This is a merger of dissensions which is supposed to heighten our sense of peace and confirm our hope of unity. Among some existentialists the blending of affirmation and denial is a master concept of liberation. From the tender-hearted Kierkegaard to the tough-minded Sartre, existentialist thinkers often seek rebirth and strength from the armistice of contending opposites.[7] The conception has an unebbing vitality and reappears even in the age of science : 'It is only possible to grasp this mystery', writes Simone Weil in her *Letter to a Priest*, 'by employing at the same time, like two pincers... two contrary notions, incompatible here on earth, compatible only in God', and she adds, 'The same applies to many other pairs of contraries as the Pythagoreans had realised'.[8] The point is, of course, not only that the acceptance of opposites is allowed to evoke an exhilarating feeling but also that in this acceptance a transcendental content and quality is implied about the universe which makes this tolerance and this acceptance not

[6] *Confessions*, 1, I, 6.
[7] For example, cf. *Fear and Trembling*, by S. Kierkegaard, Princeton, 1945, pp. 78, 92f., 186f.
[8] London, 1953, pp. 34–35. According to the Pythagoreans, the good consists in the union of opposites !

only possible but also proper and true.[9] In the religions of the world usually an explicit and elaborate claim is made for a transcendental content and quality, in the faith of the counsellors and certainly in existential philosophy this claim is implicit. Bowing before the paradox is a standard exercise in all mysticism, Christian or otherwise. In the *Hindu Scriptures*[10] we come across the following vivid description of the exercise :

'That One, though never stirring, is swifter than thought...
Though standing still, it overtakes those who are running...
It stirs and it stirs not.
It is far, and likewise near.
It is inside all this, and outside all this.'

Eastern mystical writing abounds in examples of this kind, and the above from the *Isa Upanishad* is no more than an average specimen of this. The Zen Master, trying to bring about enlightenment in his pupil, deliberately uses the 'double bind'[11] of mutually exclusive commands, so that stretched taut by them the pupil can renounce the logical categories of everyday thinking and be lifted to an incommunicable and ineffable state of freedom from them. 'One of the things he—the Zen Master—does is to hold a stick over the pupil's head and say fiercely, "If you say this stick is real, I will strike you with it. If you stay this stick is not real, I will strike you with it. If you don't say anything, I will strike you with it".'[12] G. Bateson *et al.* consider the 'double bind' kind of experience as part of the etiology of schizophrenia but they seem to think that those who transcend the 'double bind', like the successful Zen pupil, transcend it creatively.

The irresistible attraction of liberation from the shackles of logical discipline, the serenity of the self-abandon one can contrive to experience in equilibrating between contradictories, the happiness of the poise and largess of letting this all happen, have also affected philosophical thinking. The dualistic cosmologies, from Ormuzd and Ariman to Eros and Thanatos, have seen man as a

---

[9] Cf. *Existentialism, for and against*, by Paul Roubiczek, Cambridge, 1964, p. 119.
[10] New York, Everyman, 1943, p. 207.
[11] 'Toward a Theory of Schizophrenia', by G. Bateson, D. D. Jackson, J. Haley and J. Weakland, *Behavioral Science*, October 1956, Vol. I, No. 4, pp. 251–264.
[12] *Ibid.*, p. 254. Also cf. *Psychotherapy, East and West*, by A. W. Watts, New York, 1961, Chapter V.

creature who must find his peace in obeying the commands of irreconcilable overlords. Today, a good deal of philosophical formulation uses this dualistic mode of thinking to justify the modern, agnostic, secular, and rationalistic impartiality which is intended to be the successor to the paradoxical 'impartiality' of mystical beliefs. Jung, for example, condemns the *hybris* of modern man, whom he accuses of pretending that· 'the intellect has got hold of the transcendent mystery by a cognitive act and has "grasped" it. The paradox', he continues, 'reflects a higher level of intellect and, by not forcibly representing the unknowable as known, gives a more faithful picture of the real state of affairs.'[13] According to Jung the paradox 'does more justice to the *unknowable* than clarity can do . . .'[14] Elsewhere he declares, 'There are sound philosophical reasons why our arguments should end in paradox and why a paradoxical statement is the better witness to truth than a one-sided, so-called "positive" statement.'[15] P. Rieff in an article 'C. G. Jung's Confession'—significantly subtitled 'Psychology as a Language of Faith'—is inspired by Jung when he says that 'imbalances are corrected by fusion', and that 'one does not decide between two contradictory propositions but by the appearance of a new insight which transcends and in a way includes both sides'.[16] This is a refrain of contemporary philosophical psychology, almost compulsively recited by modern agnostic men at bay. At worst, it is an incantation which—though soothing—leads nowhere; at best it is the foundation of a perennial philosophy. Other philosophical psychologists, such as, for example, A. Angyal, tell us that 'the total function of personality is patterned according to a double orientation of self-determination (and) self-surrender . . .'[17] The constant armistice of the incompatibles is the full realisation of this personality. I proposed a similar scheme of interpretation in my previous book[18] in which the basic dualism of life was said to consist in the forces of *growth* and *cohesion* and these were made out as both antithetical and complementary.

It is interesting to observe how the absorption in the awesome spectacle of these relentless antinomies catches on in areas of think-

[13] *The Collected Works of C. G. Jung,* London, 1958, Vol. XI, p. 275.
[14] *Op. cit., Loc. cit.*
[15] *Op. cit.,* London, 1954, Vol. XVI, p. 34.
[16] *Encounter,* 1964.
[17] 'A Theoretical Model for Personality Studies', *Journal of Personality,* 1951, Vol. XX, pp. 131–142.
[18] *Towards a Measure of Man,* London, 1957, Chapter I.

ing and practice where one would expect a tough-minded scepticism. Mao Tse-tung—with whom one would not have expected to associate these concerns—quotes Lenin's definition of dialectics as 'the study of the contradiction within the very essence of things'.[19] In his own view, 'The law of contradiction, that is, the law of the unity of opposites in things, is the basic law in materialist dialectics'.[20] Mao often describes contradictions as 'interdependent' and cites the authorities of Marx and Engels in support of this view. One can and must move dialectically because the real is a union of opposites,[21] which can unfold and evolve only by giving them rein in turns. It is certainly instructive to see that the psychological exercise of fusing, and yet retaining, contradictions has not only been open to the Marxists, but that they see nothing extraordinary in their deriving serenity and solace from it.

The cultivation of the paradox overflows not only into theory (Marxist) but also into practice (medical). In an article by J. Layard in *The British Journal of Homoeopathic Medicine*[22] we find an excellent documentation of this. Layard explains that 'medical' derives from *medius*, a kind of 'middle thing' from which it would seem that the *medicus* is the physician who knows how to unite opposites! G. Stewart Prince, to whom I am indebted for the information about Layard's article, explains that the very emblem of medicine, the snake-and-staff emblem, symbolises a fundamental antithesis, the physician placed between the spectacle of life at the threshold of death (snake) and also 'a hidden force, dark and cold, but at the same time warm and radiant, that stirs beneath the surface of the waking world and accomplishes the miracle of cure'.[23] Asklepios, the arch-physician, is supposed to 'reconcile' the forces of darkness and light. Now whatever fancies the Jungian mythologiser may take himself to, there is no doubt of the 'mediating' connotation of the physician's function. And this, in view of the medical echoes in counselling, is certainly of no small interest to us in the present context.

That all paradigmatic experiences are to be found at the crossroads of the paradox is suggested by both theology and philosophy.

[19] *Philosophical Notebooks*, quoted by Mao Tse-tung, in *On Contradiction*[20].
[20] *On Contradiction*, Peking, 1958.
[21] *On Dialectics*, quoted in *On Contradiction*[20].
[22] 'The Meaning of Medicine', Vol. II.
[23] 'Medical Psychology', *British Journal of Medical Psychology*, 1963, Vol. XXXVI, Part 4, pp. 299–356.

That a 'state of mind' is engendered by them is generally recognised. Writers on aesthetics are the first to recognise that the paradox-engendered state of mind tends to be more creative than one which is not stirred up by dissension. And so, the fusion of the paradox can be mystical-aesthetic and can be creative. Herbert Read, for example, puts this in a language which is familiar to the counsellors : 'In Freudian terms, the aesthetic experience depends upon the resolution of an antinomy created by the simultaneous operation of the libido (the life principle) and the destructive urges (the death principle)'.[24] To cite a concrete instance of creativity interpreted in terms of the fertilising paradox : Wordsworth's 'latent awareness of the paradoxical place of mind in the natural world', and his 'feeling for the ambiguity and the strangeness of perception, a largely unconscious perplexity in fact, was the "cause" of some of his finest poetry . . .'[25]

Unfortunately our basic categories of thinking do not furnish us with a suitable thought-model to demonstrate what is going on here. According to these the metaphor of fusion of opposites, resulting in pregnancy with novel ideas, is too naive, and also implausible. And yet the claim, that the dissonance of ideas bears fruit, is a general one and not restricted to aesthetics. W. V. Quine states this probably accurately when he commends antinomies by reminding us that they 'bring on the crises of thought'.[26] There is then a paradox even in the very psychological potentials of the paradox : they are either those of serenity and peace, or of restless innovation and rebellion. Whichever of the two, the dissonance is creative : it is creative of faith or of works and, by fusion, of both.

And this brings us back to the paradoxes of counselling. My thesis is that the elements of the faith of the counsellors have one significant structural characteristic in common : they all affirm paradoxes. I believe that this affirmation is a psychological requisite to their performance for it generates creative works and excites dedication and faith. This, *the theory of creative dissonance,* is not a new conception at all, but merely the application of an old conception to a modern kind of activity. Let us now see how this psychological interpretation could be made plausible.

[24] 'Psychoanalysis and the Problem of Aesthetic Value', *International Journal of Psychoanalysis*, 1951, Vol. XXXII, Part 2, pp. 73–82.
[25] *Romantic Paradox*, by E. E. Clarke, London, 1962, pp. 1–2.
[26] 'Paradox', *Scientific American*, April 1962.

Leon Festinger's recently expounded theory of 'cognitive dissonance' would seem to weaken what I am suggesting here. According to Festinger's theory,[27] when mind-contents are contradictory, contrary, inconsistent, incompatible, and so on, the *dissonance* thus created will act as a motive, impelling the organism to reduce dissonance, and to avoid future dissonance. Now it may be that the theory of cognitive dissonance would treat the paradoxes of counselling as instances of cognitive dissonance, and the ensuing 'faith of the counsellors' as an illusory superordinate state of consonance. According to the theory, 'dissonance-reduction' is a 'must' to the organism and, therefore, our present instance would be no exception to the rule, 'dissonance must be reduced or altogether avoided!' Yet it would seem that here we may well have an instance of dissonance, to which the theory does not apply. Instead of the organism eliminating the dissonance, and replacing it by a rationalised formula of consonance, we have here a *retention* of dissonance, a dwelling on it, an interminable savouring of it. Side by side with striving for mind-contents of a consonant kind, the dissonance is *preserved*, so that its potency is not weakened by consonance. In fact, Festinger's idea that consonance tends to triumph is not the case here : the hope for cognitive consonance of a final resolving kind is here abandoned and the awareness of strength to live in peaceful dissonance, and of the patience to wait indefinitely for a resolution, is all that the organism gets in exchange for the promise of a settlement on 'consonance-terms'. Furthermore, there are some side-effects of this, which appear to affect Festinger's theory of cognitive dissonance. Psychological evidence is accumulating in support of the notion that sanity and an *acceptance of dissonance* may correlate with each other.

Psychologists and therapists of various affiliation have often been inspired by the metaphorical and metaphysical notion that the congress of opposites may be the fountain-head of renewal. H. Fingarette, for example, writes about the 'seminal ambiguity of psychoanalysis' and discovers in this ambiguity a 'generative source of power'.[28] Whether the charm of the sexual imagery or the seminal nature of the congress of opposites is responsible for the popularity

---

[27] *A Theory of Cognitive Dissonance*, by L. Festinger, London, 1959. Also *Explorations in Cognitive Dissonance*, by J. W. Brehm and A. R. Cohen, London, 1962, as well as *Deterrents and Reinforcement*, by D. H. Lawrence and L. Festinger, London, 1962.
[28] *Op. cit.*

of this idea, it does not take away from its evidently inspiring character. In fact 'tolerance of ambiguity' is now a recognised virtue, and logically so, for it is regarded both as the fertile soil of creativity and of therapeutic talent. Already Alfred Korzybski advocated the idea that our sanity was jeopardised by the Aristotelian principle of contradiction and that we urgently required a so-called non-Aristoteleian integration of opposites.[29] A. H. Maslow, writing with sympathy about Korzybski's work explains that his own psychiatric research seems to bear out Korzybski's thesis. Maslow finds that his 'healthy' subjects were 'relatively unthreatened and unfrightened by the unknown...' and he continues, 'They not only tolerate the ambiguous and unstructured; they like it... They can be, when the total objective situation calls for it, comfortably disorderly, sloppy, anarchic, chaotic, vague, doubtful, uncertain, indefinite, inexact, or inaccurate...'[30] Maslow believes that a kind of supremely healthy condition—which he sometimes calls 'peak-experience' and compares to the oceanic experiences in religious faith as well as in aesthetic rapture—is possible only to those who are not 'rubricised, polarised, categorised, and divided by opposites' but are rather sustained by them. And then Maslow crowns his poetic pleas with a paradox of his own. The moments of the most extensive uncertainty are also to be the moments in which

'... all the powers of the person come together in their most efficient and enjoyable integration and co-ordination. Inhibition, doubt, fear, control, self-criticism, caution, all diminish toward zero-point and he becomes the spontaneous, effective, fully-functioning organism, performing like an animal without conflict, or split, without hesitation or doubt, in a great flow of power that is so peculiarly effortless that it may become like play, masterful and virtuoso-like.'[31]

So it seems that the tender and patient cultivation of doubt and ambiguity are the begetters of certainty and freedom from doubt. This is achieved *not* because the cultivation of doubt led to more conscientious enquiry, and thus to knowledge and certainty, or to an acceptable 'consonance-formula' in Festinger's sense, but be-

[29] *Science and Sanity*, by A. Korzybski, Lakeville, 1948.
[30] 'Alfred Korzybski Memorial Lecture', by A. H. Maslow, *General Semantics Bulletin*, 1957, Nos. 20–21.
[31] *Ibid.*

cause it is a humble acceptance of limitations, and a cheerful tolerance of provisional and tentative knowledge. The state of mind which the contemplation of contradictions may induce need not be mystically rapt, it may be no more than the serenity of one who is not in a hurry and who is not greedy for certainties and decisions. The intelligent inconsistency, the cultivated contradiction, the 'dichotomy transcendence',[32] and other carefully maintained tolerances of antinomies have been known by philosophers and poets as virtues. Keats' 'negative capability', for example, is an especially good instance of this. Of course, the range of 'moods' in which one may accommodate two warring notions and hold them in one's palm affectionately—as a parent would look upon his quarrelling children—the range of moods is wide indeed. But whatever the range, the important point to remember is that the state of mind thrives on dissonance, on the paradox, and that the theory of cognitive dissonance is faulted by it.

At first, it is difficult to believe that there might be a correspondence between serenity-sanity on the one hand and one's ability to cherish paradoxical notions on the other. The counsellors, of all people, may be disconcerted by this suggestion. For them, 'vision' and 'faith' are obscurantist terms which, at best, may signify extravagances in thinking; and at worst, plain psychopathology. But even the counsellor's own psychoanalytical training will disclose some inconsistencies in this sceptical picture. A careful study of psychoanalytical literature will show that these sceptical conclusions do not follow inevitably from psychoanalytical premises. To show that this is so, one must refer to a basic orientation of psychoanalysis, according to which those who polarise their views, rather sharply into 'either-or' statements, and those who dichotomise their attitudes, either to people, or to things, or to both, are merely expressing their unresolved, infantile ambivalence towards their parents. It seems that an uncompromising insistence on making decisions here and now, and on making sharp distinctions of what is 'true or not true', are included under the heading of 'unresolved ambivalence'. This interpretation was first offered in respect of dogmatic certainties and prejudices about people and causes.[33] Some children would express their love and hate in response to

[32] 'Fusion of Facts and Values', A. H. Maslow, 11th Annual Karen Horney Lecture, New York, 1963.
[33] Cf. *The Authoritarian Personality*, by T. W. Adorno, *et el.*, New York, 1949.

parental treatment by attaching unqualified love—hero-worship—to one sort of people, and equally unqualified hatred to some other sort of people. People will be perceived as black or white so as to make it possible to love and hate them without reservations. In this way much that is uncompromising and intolerant or absolutely and blindly loyal has been explained. What interests us here is that intolerance and loyalty of this uncompromising kind tends to be transferred to the 'perceptual and cognitive' areas as well.[34] 'It is apparently the great number of conflicts and confusions present in the prejudiced which leads to resorting to black-white solutions. Too much existing emotional ambiguity and ambivalence are counteracted by denial and intolerance of cognitive ambiguities. It is as if everything would go to pieces once existing discrepancies were faced.'[35] So it would seem, according to this view, that being able to accept unresolved ambiguities and to live with them is a sign of relative freedom from sharply divided ambivalence, and from the infantile experiences which are said to have caused it.

Most philosophers would hold that to utter a 'Yea' and a 'Nay' in respect of the same proposition is just mushy thinking. According to them there is no accretion of knowledge from cultivating our wonder at paradoxes. For them the paradox is the end of all argument. But for those whom Susanne Langer calls the 'more extroverted thinkers' it is the beginning.[36] It is doubtful that the Jungian dichotomy of 'extroversion-introversion' corresponds to the dichotomy of tolerance-intolerance of paradoxes; but Langer's suggestion that this tolerance-intolerance is a function of personality is probably correct.

And so one could say that the faith of the counsellors is requisite to their practice for the even-tempered acceptance of contradictions, the calm tolerance of uncertainty and dissension are essential to it; and, one could say, that the absence of a rigid and compulsive insistence on choosing and on deciding are important characteristics of a sane personality; and, finally, one could say that the selection and training of counsellors was, in fact, vaguely guided by these considerations, by the consolidated faith of those who select and train. The counsellors behave as if they believed

[34] 'Intolerance of Ambiguity as an Emotional and Perceptual Personality Variable', by E. Frenkel-Brunswick, *Journal of Personality*, 1949–1950, Vol. XVIII, pp. 108–145.
[35] *Ibid.*
[36] *Philosophical Sketches*, London, 1962, p. 176.

that, when two propositions are at loggerheads, they may still be true and their prelogical truth is somehow the dictate of our elementary nature in the unfathomable depths of which no light is cast by a mind buoyant far away on the surface. The documentation of this in the recent paragraphs is marginal to my present task : which is to present an analysis of the beliefs and principles underlying counselling work and not to plead for this or that particular world-view, whether it is good for counselling or not.

I should like to point out that, irrespective of its rationality or irrationality, the response-system called 'faith' is a socio-psychological reality and one of considerable interest to sociology. The reason for this lies in the institutionalisation of the paradoxical and doctrinal principles, in training bodies, in professional organisations, in codes of practice, and so on. The social reality which the new recruit finds around himself, thereafter becomes a determiner of viewpoints which collect into an ideological system. In this sense we may speak about the counselling ideology.[37] The social ramifications of this ideology are complex and I have touched upon one major factor, which helped in evolving it, when I considered the discrediting of political solutions in the first chapter. Naturally, the emergence of this ideology calls for a more systematic enquiry. My task has been to show that a set of doctrinal affirmations, deeply felt human dedications, as well as an ideological system potently dominate the professional activities of the counsellors. In the next and final chapter I will endeavour to show that this ideological system exerts a specific influence on society, so that we should be in a position to round off the analysis of the counsellor's faith with an analysis of its impact on our times.

Summary of the argument in this section. In each of the previous sections an element of the counsellor's faith was sketched; and, in this section, each one of these major elements was shown to comprise a core of contradiction. I tried to show that the paradoxicality of this core is itself the creative agent in the counselling function. Christian and other mystical literature was cited to illustrate the point that the paradox is the germ of faith, and that an acceptance of the antithetical assertions, as well as their continued existence, are characteristic of mystical ideas, and experience. The overspill of this into philosophical and aesthetic theory,

[37] Cf. *Ideology and Utopia*, by Karl Mannheim, London, 1946, pp. 238–239.

as well as into medical professional orientation, was also mentioned so that its presence in the counsellors' attitudes be seen as it ought to be seen : inevitable and entirely natural. Finally, I argued that the counsellor's attempt to link tolerance of contradiction with sanity and suitability for the counselling vocation is consistent with psychoanalytic psychology as well as with theology. The theory of creative dissonance is offered to complement Festinger's theory of cognitive dissonance in the realm of human creativity, and especially in the area of professional devotions and activities.

Most counsellors will deny that their *actus fidei* plays an important role in their day-to-day practice. They are likely to continue to believe that they are appliers of socio-psychological knowledge and skill, much as medical men are appliers of biological and physiological knowledge, of diagnostic, surgical, or some other skill. It may be better for their practice for them to think in these pedestrian terms about their practice whilst continuing to affirm their faith in their work silently and implicitly. The counsellor would, with much justification, restrain his colleagues and others from thinking piously about their 'spirituality', for this sort of indulgence would breed complacency and obscurantism, and obstruct the development of a workable social science. Happily, the counsellor has not abandoned the ideal of mastery through verified scientific knowledge and, though he implicitly admits that there is no prospect of a social scientific 'mastery', he continues to seek more and more reliable information about human nature and nurture. The counsellor would discourage much preoccupation with the ultimate sources of his own moral inspiration, and to achieve this, he would deliberately underestimate the clinical significance of these ultimate sources. In writing about the faith of the counsellors, I have no desire to make things difficult for him by encouraging sentimental self-indulgence and conceited intuitions, for I know, of course, that uncritical lovingness and kindliness are not enough; indeed faith is not enough unless it includes the faith in our capacity to find out and learn. My consolation is that most counsellors don't need the smug glow of virtuousness, and will cheerfully deny every word I have said about them. I shall, of course, note their abstinence as yet another proof of the validity of my thesis that they profess faith.

CHAPTER FOUR

The Counsellor and Western Morals

✳

The seeming complexity of the counselling ideology may make us think that it is the mere mentality of a marginal professional expertise, of little importance to the culture of the society in which it occurs. Were we to think that this is so, we would grossly underestimate the social influence of this ideology. The counselling literature as well as its popularised casuistry and prescriptions, printed and broadcast, have an immediate impact on the rank and file of society. The critical and interpretive work of the professional literature has been reaching and influencing the cultural and moral leadership in society, and it is a trite observation to make that our philosophy, science, and art, have been profoundly affected by most things that have been written on counselling, ever since the time of Sigmund Freud.

But now, through the very counselling activities of the counsellors, through the growth of the practising profession itself, the socio-cultural and moral influence of this ideology gains strength. It is not generally recognised, for example, how extensively counsellors concern themselves with the 'handling' of officials, staffs of schools and other educational as well as health authorities or private organisations. The psychiatric social worker of a child guidance clinic will do some unobtrusive casework on a local headmistress, and a hospital almoner, at her best, will act as a staff consultant to a whole hospital. It is not only that these counsellors will do therapeutic or 'readaptive' work on colleagues and associates, but they will also go some way towards indoctrinating them with the moral principles characteristic of the counsellor's own professional work. 'The quality of a good clinician (clinical psychologist) is the ability to exert an influence through his ideas and skills on the community in which he works', write N. D. Sundberg

and L. E. Tyler in their book, *Clinical Psychology*,[1] and they go
on to recommend an even more deliberate, and almost grey-
eminence-like, role when they explain that 'the psychologist may
attend meetings of community groups concerned with psychological
and social matters. With his eyes open, but not saying much at the
start, he will soon learn to identify the major community problems
and local power groups.'[2] In addition to the administrative and
organisational activities, the counsellor will exert a considerable
influence through the therapeutic work itself : but this is an outcome which I have considered already in Section C of the previous
chapter which concerned itself mainly with the counsellor's directive influence on the client. Naturally, when the client-patient is a
cultural, political, or moral leader, the influence exerted on him
is writ large through the subsequent leadership acts of the client-
patient.

Certainly the counsellor's influence on the ideological fabric of
society will be subtle and slow when it passes through these
channels, but it will be no less thorough for that. In this way they
are potentially also political agents. It is the counsellor's vocation
to change people's opinion about themselves and about the world.
The circumstance that their technique is personal, piecemeal,
and private, merely conceals the fact of their great and lasting
effectiveness with which no advertiser or propagandist can hope
to compete successfully.

Nor would it be entirely true to say that this moral influence
must always be rather feeble because its essence is a dignified indecision, and because it is inexplicit politically. Though I have
shown in Chapter One that the counsellor is the product of a politically disillusioned century, the counsellor may not be forever trying
to find private solutions for public evils or persuading others of the
futility of political solutions.[3] After all, the counsellor is a 'betterer',
and, as such, he will have to become alert to the political avenues
of betterment, as soon as he can come round to thinking that in a
'personal service society' there will be more scope for counselling
activities. No doubt, he will remain mainly an observer, and rarely
more than a lobbyist, but he will not be a political cynic or a
political nihilist. After all, he well realises that certain specific

[1] London, 1963, p. 467.
[2] *Loc. cit.*
[3] Cf. *Out of Apathy*, Ed. by E. P. Thompson, London, 1960, p. 5.

failures in parents and others around the infant and the small child, make it imperative that we should constantly review the social norms of family life, the social and economic circumstances which regulate it, and the social institutions which serve it. Doing this may eventually amount to a full-scale criticism of the social order and structure. In fact, a good few social workers have re-defined their role in political terms and assigned to themselves political tasks at the expense of counselling ones. The problems which this attempt at redefinition creates are complex and I felt it necessary to devote a whole book, *The Personal and the Political*, to their examination. But even if social workers do not politicise their roles they have certain sobered suggestions to make about the provision of mental health services, about educational methods, about opportunities for mothers and wives to go out to work, about illegitimacy, divorce laws, children in hospitals, foster-homes, courts and prisons, the mass media of communications, housing, and about scores of other matters which impinge upon their daily professional care of clients. No simple political-ideological formula will attract the counsellor *qua* counsellor as a most appropriate, congenial and relevant system of doctrines to bring him his counselling goals; and perhaps, in an important sense, he is predestined to remain politically reserved or wholly uncommitted. Yet he is certainly not committed to be politically indifferent: he will be in favour of the kind of society whose arrangements will tend to reduce people's needs for his services—an aspiration no more paradoxical than that of the doctors.[4] Just the same, the counsellor will try to refrain from knitting his approvals and disapprovals into a coherent politico-ideological system because he knows that people are likely to go on needing some extension of parental care in their lives, and because he is eminently a private person, a solitarily and discreetly operating practitioner, whose primary interest in sweeping proposals is a clinical interest in the kind of personality which would be disposed towards making them.

In a world which may at any moment relapse into the extremes of political violence, the cultivation of private re-ordering of lives in publicly disordered circumstances may provoke our animosity.

[4] An example of this is Erich Fromm who in *The Sane Society* (New York, 1955) advocates specific social reforms so as to enhance mental health by creating a social order which is favourable to it.

Those who are whole-heartedly engaged in proselytising and pleading for the public causes look upon the private practitioners as frivolous and irresponsible distracters of attention from the only thing that matters; a change in the general design of social living. And yet the counsellor's starting point, focusing attention on the concrete case, in the here and now, and not in a better society to come, fosters certain moral efforts which may be held commendable in any circumstances. The counsellor will reflect, 'Whatever I may advocate, I must make it my duty to be truthful and honest to myself, to clear away the obstacles to liking people, and to wanting to help them personally, privately, intimately, and not only politically'. No political order can relegate this kind of moral inspiration to second place.

Let us then turn to this moral inspiration and discover, identify, and describe the specific values which the counselling ideology does, in fact, advance. To do this objectively we must begin with questioning the claim of moral inspiration altogether. It would be foolish to think that the literature of the counsellors actually strives to be 'inspirational'. One could hardly regard Freud's or his followers' writings as obvious 'uplift' literature about the nature of man and society. Indeed, there are some explicit repudiations of moral inspiration and responsibility in these writings yet, paradoxically, the asceticism of these is so impressive, that they fail to sound amoral : 'To the extent to which we know ourselves we shall not need to concern ourselves with the morality of others', writes a contributor to *The International Journal of Psychoanalysis*.[5] And the writer concludes, 'This is the ultimate and original ethic—freedom from morality.' The paradox in the conclusion betrays that even when the psychoanalytical mentors of counsellors, like this one, don the garb of the sceptic, the moral underwear shows. The influence of this kind of teaching on the moral climate of the age in which it is proclaimed is twofold, and not dissonantly so. *Firstly*, not concerning ourselves with the morality of others strips us of moral indignation and of malicious righteousness. Cultivated reserve in judgmentalness will certainly limit the pretexts of guilt-free aggression—though it may also encourage indifference and alienation. Yet it does not because, *secondly*, the counselling theories postulate man's social needs, and man's need for mutuality

[5] 'The Ethic of Freud's Psychoanalysis', by J. Shor, 1961, Vol. XLII, Parts 1-2, pp. 116-122.

in relationships, his need for sympathetic identification with his fellows. Thus, to the extent that we know ourselves, we cannot but realise and accept our native concern for others! Self-knowledge will not make us more callous, on the contrary, it will make us more forgiving and accepting. The paradox of this position is that the counsellor aims at both objectivity and compassion and that he aims at a maximal non-judgmentalness so that he should be able to judge better than others.

And not only judgmentalness was to be purged in this way but sympathy too : the counsellors have made it extremely difficult to practise exploitive and dominative charity and have cleansed sympathy of much of its self-seeking dross. I have tried to show that the theoretical premises of the counsellor's profession do not allow him much scope to indulge in the pride of virtuousness. At most he will disillusioningly speak of the therapist's increase in 'egosyntonia', a gentle glow of contentment with self, which is a term possessing no spiritual glamour.

These contributions to contemporary sentiments and values have greatly assisted the growth of psychological, sociological, and philosophical sobriety and fair-mindedness in our times. They have constituted a reaction to the facile, idealistic self-deceptions of the past and, therefore, they have inevitably appeared anti-idealistic. And yet a charge of anti-idealism would be entirely wrong-headed. The counsellors have merely given idealism a new look by insisting on the supreme authority of intellectual correctness and frankness. Though sometimes they appear to be, they are not specialists in self-mortification or masochistic self-denigration; on the contrary, their campaign against joy-killing, shame, and guilt is well known. Above all, the counsellor's concern with the alleviation of human misery is a categorical moral gesture of the right hand, which no amount of neutral, sceptical, and intellectualising beckonings with the left can cancel out.

To continue to obtain an impartial assessment of the counsellor's moral influence on society we must once again turn to those who criticise this influence, so that both praise and blame are given their share of our attention. There are some critics who say that there is little cause for jubilation on account of the counsellor's influence on society. Not surprisingly, some critics' ire is provoked by the knowing air of some counsellors and by their meddlesome activities; their protests are salutary even if their motives cannot often be identified. Our recurrent criticism is that the counsellors encourage an oversolicitous and overprotective counselling mentality, making people indolent, fatalistic, and undermining their moral stamina. Richard T. Lapière, for example, complains that '*the tender concern* of a host of modern writers with the psychological welfare of the working man is inexplicable except as a reflection of the wide acceptance of the Freudian view of man',[6] (my italics) a view which according to Lapière is contributing to the moral corruption and emasculation of modern man. He cites some of Freud's deeply unflattering comments on man's nature and brands the Freudians as the principal source of this odious influence. But if there are no saving qualities, how are we to explain the literal and *not* ironical '*tender concerns*'? Lapière's opinion that 'Freudianism is a doctrine of social irresponsibility and personal despair'[7] is massively contradicted by the emergence—largely on Freudian instigation—of the modern counselling professions.

The plaint against the counselling pamperers of man is a frequently adopted form criticism takes. Little do these critics realise that much of their apprehensions about a psychoanalytic corruption of moral responsibility ought to be equally strongly aroused by any scientific, and therefore deterministic, psychology.[8] Those who are familiar with the quality of the counsellor's professional attitudes cannot but smile at Lapière's bitter denunciations against the personality theory which has, in fact, done so much to inspire kindliness, tolerance, and sympathy, and which has discredited a great deal of cant, vicious righteousness, and malice. 'Translate a therapeutic proposition', says L. S. Feuer, 'and it says something like this : "We have faith in you. Do what you wish, discover your desires, we shall not condemn you." The person aided by the affection of others, is aided to cultivate the emotional resources which can overcome resistances...'[9] Does this sound like subversion of morals? The one who treats, by the act of treating avers that the recipient is worthy of being treated, and thus induces in the recipient a desire to live up to what is expected of him. But, above all, the willingness to persevere unendingly with the same person for years, in face of the obvious social uselessness of it all,

---

[6] *The Freudian Ethic*, London, 1960, p. 72.
[7] *Loc. cit.*
[8] Cf. *Psychiatry and Responsibility*, Ed. by H. Shoeck and J. W. Wiggins, New York, 1962.
[9] *Psychoanalysis and Ethics*, Springfield, 1955, p. 40.

amounts to a credo in the incalculable worth of the human person.[10] Lapière and other critics might well remember that neither righteous indignation nor guilt-mongering, through the responsibility-and-blaming-game, have fared all that well throughout the centuries. On the whole, the attack on the ethics of counselling can probably not be sustained by Christian justifications for the works of counselling are more Christian than most practices of our times, even if the counsellor's puritanism forbids him the easy solace of naive and pious fantasies.

Earlier on, when writing about the 'fiction of non-directiveness', I was concerned to show that it was not possible to direct the patient-client to health, and refrain from directing him at all. Be that as it may, the reverence for the personal integrity of the client-patient as expressed in the preservation of this 'fiction' is an important contribution to the moral climate of this age. Non-direction as a clinical standard may not be possible to realise in the clinical practice itself, but the advertising of the ideal will inspire others, in or outside the clinics, to try to live up to it. 'There is something old-fashioned about the psychoanalytic movement', writes Philip Rieff; 'it is, in fact, although more subtly than ever before, a movement of self-help. For all the analyst can do is teach another how to become his own therapist, strong in the knowledge of his particular weakness.' The paradox again! There is no pampering tutelage of the weak but the age-old challenge to the weak, according to which God helps those who help themselves. Of course, the counsellors make no mention of God, but the sentiments about making the weak strong and responsible by making him help himself are nevertheless familiar.

In case some severely psychoanalytical readers may think that I idealise the facts and am guilty of a superficial and naively mystical blurring of the counsellor's matter-of-fact, clinical position : they should reflect on how some of their colleagues define— for all the world to see and be edified by it—the ideally well-trained psychoanalyst. 'Above all', begins one such definition, 'we can imagine him (the analyst) with a rounded-out personality enabling him to combine his knowledge with creative intuition, making him capable of empathy and of identifying himself easily with his patients, of being kindly without expecting anything in

10 This is especially well argued by Erich Fromm in *Zen Buddhism and Psychoanalysis*, London, 1960, pp. 83–84.

return, and of never feeling narcissistically wounded by certain developments in the treatment of his patients...'[11] Surely this profile, strongly reminiscent of the profile of a Buddha or Christian saint, is not a list of assessable entrance qualifications to the profession, but an idealised hero-image, which held up high and exhibited to all, cannot fail to make its mark on those who look at it. The same holy pictures are offered for inspection throughout the counselling profession, and not only in psychoanalysis. The distinguished social work educator, Charlotte Towle, who so admirably speaks for all counsellors in her *Learner in Education for the Professions*,[12] concurs with the psychoanalysts, 'Social work, by its very nature, needs workers who have considerable capacity to live beyond absorption in self and who are potentially creative... The capacity is revealed in the educational process through liking and concern for people as individuals, which holds when they, in the midst of disadvantageous circumstances, are often least likeable. It is revealed in readiness, as knowledge and understanding is attained, to assume responsibility, to give understanding as well as services, to endure denial and frustration of unresponsive or hostile clients—in short, to give both mind and heart to the learning experience.'[13] This inventory of virtues is, if anything, longer, and the virtues more excellent, than the required qualifications for the ideally trained psychoanalyst in the previous example. Surely, these models of merit in the counselling professions cannot help being models of merit all round; they cannot help securing for the counselling ideology the honour of being the revitaliser of an otherwise weakening confidence and hope in the nobility of man in our time.

The portraits of the ideal counsellor are not kept secret from the outside world and the world's conception of virtuousness will be inevitably affected by them. One could usefully cite Kierkegaard's remark about Socrates to illuminate the most important common feature of these portraits, 'How rare the magnanimity of the helper who can be sufficiently concerned with the other person's self-realisation and sufficiently free of his own need to dominate that he is willing to be merely an "occasion" for the

[11] 'Training for Psychoanalysis', by S. Nacht, S. Lebovici and R. Diatkine, *The International Journal of Psychoanalysis*, January–April 1961, Vol. XLII, Parts 1–2, pp. 110–115.
[12] Chicago, 1954.
[13] *Op. cit.*, pp. 39–40.

other's achievement of his own "values"?' To recognise a professional person of this kind as the ideal—and the counsellors aspire to do just that—will in itself make the Lapière kind of attack sound grotesque. Instead of 'personal despair' the challenge of the ideal is full of confidence, and faith in the triumph of love and reason.

While aiming as high as this, another important feature of this aspiration is that the counsellor must not give himself airs about the nobility of his aspirations. This too cannot fail to be noticed by the world. The counsellor is alerted against tendencies of liking himself in his 'apostolic role'. In those cases where the counsellor has made some progress in adapting himself to his function, his mood is quietly musing and, if anything, casual. There is no forcible self-restraint about responding emotionally to those who receive his help, and there are no deliberate efforts to respond. Although once Edward Glover spoke of analysts having to do the 'analyst's toilet', a kind of psychological exercise to ensure that the self-critical equipment is in good working order, on the whole no strenuous psychological jerks are expected of him daily, so as to make sure that he will be cool-headed and calmly objective. The whole exercise of keeping in touch with one's unconscious demands is a relaxed and self-forgiving watch, no more. To have a proper view of the social influence of this standard it is necessary to remember that, to the outsider, the moral stature of this position will seem more athletic, more of a rare and expert accomplishment and a moral stand, than it is for the counsellor himself. Clearly, the publicised statements about what the counsellor is like at his best make a deeper impression on the world than on the counsellors themselves, though the nature of this impression we can only guess at, not measure. Reflect, for example, on the sort of echoes which a statement, such as the following by Carl R. Rogers, may elicit from non-counsellors, as distinct from counsellors: '(the counsellor's) attitude, at its best (is) devoid of the *quid pro quo* aspect of most of the experiences we call love'; though the words are not, the content is biblical. Rogers continues to explain, 'It is the simple outgoing human feeling, it seems to me, which is even more basic than sexual or parental feeling. It is caring enough about the person, that you do not wish to interfere with his development, nor to use him for any self-aggrandising goals of your own. Your satisfaction comes in having set him free to grow in his own fashion.'[14] Admittedly, the Freudian version of this would sound much more modest, and the love, of which Rogers spoke so well, would not be described as much else than sublimated sex or parental love. The truth is, of course, that the rigour and abstinence characteristic of the refusals to take self-flattery about man's so-called spirituality seriously have a distinguished moral quality about them, and that this quality will not be lost on the outside world, on the cultural-moral climate of society. And this is likely to be so, because side by side with disclaimers about monastic, let alone cathedral, virtues and dignities, we get entirely unapologetic idealisations, such as for example, 'Psychoanalysis demands confidence in the integrity and intelligence of the analyst, an intellectual willingness to co-operate, and a wholehearted purpose to abide by the rule of the analysis that the patient produce material freely and honestly. This in turn requires a courageous willingness to accept pain, anxiety, and deprivation, and to face unpleasant facts.'[15] Lawrence Kubie, who is the author of these lines (including the rather odd anticlimax at the end), carries the idealisation a step further by pronouncing the central paradox of the counsellor's faith, 'Psychoanalysis, however, not only does not demand blind faith, it attempts constantly to analyse it away *even when this is faith in the analysis itself*.'[16] (Italics mine.) The courage and idealistic abstinence of this credo is as impressive as the doctrines of a blind faith can ever be. How strangely and heroically scrupulous is this refusal to be lulled by strong loyalties and submissions even when it is a submission to a regimen of not submitting! To set the purpose of analysing away a faith in analysis can't succeed, for its success would guarantee its failure: once again the paradoxical core of the counsellor's truth is revealed.

So far I have been looking at the nature of the moral inspiration counsellors may convey to society. They may plead with their colleagues as well as with others that they should honour certain values of a general character, such as honesty, courage, sympathy, and so on, or they may present us with idealised models to follow and emulate. Let me now examine another related matter, which has been mysteriously neglected by both counsellors and others.

[14] In *Psychotherapy, Theory and Research*, Ed. by O. H. Mowrer, New York, 1953, p. 51.
[15] *Practical and Theoretical Aspects of Psychoanalysis*, by L. S. Kubie, Int. Univ. Press, 1950, pp. 148, 159.
[16] *Ibid.*

This matter concerns the strikingly odd convergence of a good deal of the sexual moral principles of counselling with those of historic Christianity. In examining suitability for psychiatric training we find, for example, that 'sleeping with nurses in the hospital is a contraindication to psychiatric training',[17] and that 'happy marriage with children if possible'[18] is a desirable domestic qualification for the profession of counselling. In the psychoanalytically guided services which are being made available for counselling in marital difficulties the conservative moral position of the counsellors is much in evidence. The guiding theoretical principle is, as Dr. J. D. Sutherland put it : 'that what both partners complain of in the other is a projection of an unwanted bit of themselves',[19] and that, therefore, an effective realisation of this by both partners will lead to reconciliation of their respective needs. There is no doubt that these projective systems are responsible for bitter resentments and cold alienations in marriage, but they are surely not alone responsible! For the counsellor to appreciate the importance of the reality situation that, for example, a wife may be a stupid and insensitive woman or a husband a psychopathic and callous man, is made difficult, if not impossible, by the psychoanalytic preoccupation with projective systems and other infantile reactivations in the marital setting. 'Nowhere in psychoanalysis', writes Thomas S. Szász, 'is there a sufficient allowance made for a person who acts in a self-damaging way because he is stupid or ill-informed.'[20] Of course, insight in the one make these defects in the other easier to bear, though it can certainly not correct them, and in marital counselling, for example, where it would be futile to expect the insight of the one to correct the intellectual or moral incompatibility or defect of the other, an interpretive and reductive approach by the counsellor amounts to the taking of a moral stand in favour of the *status quo*. A painstaking fostering of mutual understanding is a declaration of faith in the value of marriage. It is not good enough to plead that couples seek help because *they* believe that they need help with their marital relationship, which *they* wish to improve and therefore preserve. Surely, the psychoanalytically

---

[17] *Personality Patterns of Psychiatrists*, R. R. Holt and L. Luborsky, Imago, London, 1958, p. 270.
[18] *Ibid.*, p. 270.
[19] In the Introduction to *The Marital Relationship as a Focus for Casework*, London, 1962, p. 9.
[20] *Op. cit.*

alerted counsellor will not take the overt and presenting moral decision of a client literally and as a licence to pursue a certain line? Also, when the case arises in an agency setting specialising in, say, juvenile delinquency, and where the presenting problem is not marital, counsellors (presumably probation officers in this case) may relate the difficulty to a marital discord, and attempt reconciliation, no matter whether the facts responsible for the discord can respond to interpretive work or no. The immovables of the marital relationship are glossed over, and *marital* counselling will be used to the advantage of the juvenile client irrespective of what will be expected from the parents in terms of resignation and acceptance. Certainly, we are entitled to approve of this course, provided that we admit that our choice to pursue it is the outcome of a moral decision, and is not derived from the manipulative skills learnt in the counsellor's training and experience. Nor is it reassuringly explained to us, by the counsellors in marriage guidance, how they decide whether a so-called neurotic collusion 'works' or no. Who decides, and how is it decided, that instead of some interpretive working-through the collusion should be reinforced? We are told that the function of the Family Discussion Bureau of the Tavistock Clinic in London is 'to prevent marriage breakdown'[21]—fine, but what is the moral authority for this function? The social case-work supervisor is sometimes entirely definite in her commitment to defend the established institutions of a frugal and well-tempered family life. 'It is generally agreed', writes N. D. Levine, 'that the family agency has as its purpose the preservation and strengthening of family life.'[22] There is no doubt that the publication in which this statement appeared is one that is inspired by psycho-analytical thought and orientation, whilst its moral purposes are defined without reference to that thought and orientation. I feel that harmony of these purposes with, at least, some aspects of the morality of Christian restraints cannot very well be regarded as accidental, and that, therefore, the influence of this aspect of the counselling ideology reinforces the moral influence of Christianity.

The counsellors have certainly not been guilty of encouraging sexual licence, a charge which has so often and so ignorantly been levelled against Freud and his followers. In an age in which hell

[21] *Op. cit.*
[22] *Techniques of Student and Staff Supervision*, Family Service Association of America, 1950–1953, p. 41.

fire and brimstone have ceased to be effective deterrents against illicit sexual behaviour, the diagnosis that such behaviour is 'neurotic' or just 'sick' will exert a greater influence on people who are anxiously trying to be 'normal' and 'healthy'. According to Dr. Bowlby, 'it is emotionally disturbed men and women who produce illegitimate children . . .' and 'the girl who has an illegitimate baby often comes from an unsatisfactory home background and has developed a neurotic character, the illegitimate baby being in the nature of a symptom of her neurosis'.[23] The new stigma attaching to promiscuity may seem less dramatic and less frightening than the retributions promised by a displeased deity: nonetheless, if to be neurotic is to be not acceptable by our fellow men, the sanctions provided by the counselling ideology *in lieu* of the otherworldly deterrents—which, incidentally, had been discredited long before that ideology gained wide credence—must be viewed as reinforcers of conventional sexual morality. Leontine Young has warned about the ideological nature of this reinforcement when she wrote, 'does the girl have to be neurotic or psychotic to bear an out-of-wedlock child? . . . the large number of girls having out-of-wedlock babies are not like this. They seem to be much healthier emotionally, have usually had a more enduring love relationship with the baby's father, and are generally devoted to their children.'[24] The counsellor's distrust of this pagan and animal-like healthiness sounds like a belated echo of the Christian moralist's condemnation of sinfulness. Certainly, the clinical diagnosis of much indiscriminate promiscuity does seem to be correct but there are weighty reasons for doubting the validity of the clinical verdict when pronounced on *all* non-conforming cases.

Dollard and Miller, who could not be accused of dabbling in dynamic psychology and of getting tainted by 'mysticism', unashamedly put forth, '. . . it is better that the therapist be married than single', (echoes of Paul's *First Letter to the Corinthians*, VII, 9.!) and they go on to stipulate that it is better 'that he have a stable *normal* rather than *perverse* sexual adjustment; that he show evidence of a good conscience in dealing with his personal affairs; that he be a professionally responsible and co-operative person rather than a lone wolf or a prima donna; that he have some viable

---

[23] *Maternal Care and Mental Health*, W.H.O., 1952, pp. 95, 93.
[24] *Out of Wedlock*, 1954, pp. 114–116, quoted by Virginia Wimperis in her book, *The Unmarried Mother and Her Child*, London, 1960.

sublimations rather than an incontinent preoccupation with pro-fessional work; and that he have a sense of humour. Although therapists will invariably fall short of the ideal in some respects, that ideal should be left to beckon them.'[25] This is yet another idealistic portrait, this time including some specifications on sexual morality as well. It is incredible that psychologists, whose allegiance to a type of learning theory would oblige them to reappraise and atomise 'ideals', should go on to rely on the reverential and mysterious qualities of the connotations of 'ideals', for, of all people, the learning theorist ought to know that these reverential and mysterious qualities are essentially conditioned stimuli, and that their atomising and dissolving theory—if consistently applied—will liquidate ('decondition'?) the very potency of the ideals to which they make an appeal!

It would certainly seem then, that the moral standards of the counselling century, clearly indicated and also enjoined in a number of important instances, are far from being subversive of the earlier established standards : they actually reinforce them. Instead of undermining conventional morality, the ubiquitous admonitory clauses have given traditional morals a kind of clinical and scientific respectability.

Before I explore the signs pointing to a possible change in the nature of the counsellor's thinking and influence—a task one must not shirk at this time—I should like to deal with the suggestion that the counsellor's faith, philosophy, and ethics are a not very distinctive variation of the physician's faith, philosophy, and ethics, and that there are not really any new influences at work here, and that the counselling ideology is a derivation of the healing ideology in medical thinking.

I should like to point out that the Hippocratic Oath is not a Christian or an explicitly religious oath, and that its hold over medical consciences can be weakened by other ideologies, such as mainly religious or political ones. We have been painfully reminded of this by the experiments on human subjects carried out by Nazi doctors in the recent past. The very structure of the counsellor's creed is such as to make brutal departures from it impossible, and yet retain the pretence of practising professionally. Secondly, whilst in physical medicine the ritual of formal etiquette—anonymity on

[25] *Personality and Psychotherapy*, by J. Dollard and N. E. Miller, 1950, p. 417.

public occasions, jealous protection of confidential information, or even getting the receptionist to present the bill to the patient[26]—may be important for establishing an unspecific trust in the physician, these observances have little direct influence on the efficient performance of, say, surgical or orthopaedic treatment. In counselling, however, every phase of the counselling process is vitally affected by the quality of trust the counsellor may inspire, and by the image he may present of himself. Thirdly, the physician of the body also acquires an uncompromising decisiveness of manner, especially in the handling of cases where, as it were, 'there are no two ways about it'. When first aid is to be administered, or indeed in any emergency, he must make decisions, and having made them, he must act in precisely predetermined ways. As medicine advances, the number of situations, in which the medical man can be reasonably certain about what to do for the ailing body, increases, so the authoritarian and unhumble role-functions of the medical practitioner are extended. Precisely at this time counselling ideology—the product of counselling practice—appears to make good what has been lost in humility, patience, and respect for the patient's personality. Counselling has brought back to the healing professions much of the humanity which an advancing science has made precarious. Audacious interventions, such as those in psychosurgery, highlight this process. My belief is that the counsellor is by no means a mere receiver of a 'good name' from the physician. The counsellor has not only created a new professional ideology but has enriched the professional consciousness of general medical work. One might even conjecture that without the twentieth-century counselling philosophy medicine could easily have become somewhat dehumanised by now.

One of the most important features, if not *the* most important, of the western moral character is its faith in progress. The ideology of progress is at the heart of western man's social thinking. A very useful way of explaining how the counselling ideology has affected western morals is by contrasting its psychological teaching with the kind of teaching which inevitably follows from the application of physiological and behaviouristic psychologies of human conduct. I regard this comparison especially important and should like to conclude this book by attending to it at some length.

Ideologies of progress sprout from an inextinguishable hope that

[26] Not so much in National Health Service Britain as elsewhere.

one day things will be better. Somewhere ahead life will be more abundant and there will be less pain and fear. Somewhere ahead there will be more rationality, objectivity, and truth. Somewhere ahead there will always be more love and compassion for others.[27] Any combination of these and of other values could easily be extracted from the literature of progress. When writers begin with the thesis, 'there is progress in the realisation of values', they assume two things. *Firstly*, they put forward a sociological-historical hypothesis according to which social changes proceed in a set direction and fall into some sort of sequential pattern, and *secondly*, they contrive to find that on the whole, in this sequence, there is a linear increase in the realisation of some values which they regard as essential to humanity. A careful inspection of the second of these two assumptions discloses the belief that not only things will be getting better and better, but people too. Ideologists of progress then are committed to a coherent directionality not only in the betterment of circumstances but also in the betterment of people. In brief, social changes will be accompanied by changes in the 'modal' personality of man as well.

In spite of the great multiplicity of accounts describing the critical values which are supposed to be increasingly realised by man in the course of his social development, one critical value seems to receive more prominent mention than any of the others. It comes in various guises, for example, as 'altruism', 'sympathetic imagination', 'capacity for identification', 'fellowship', 'co-operation', 'kindness', and of course 'love'. Even when other neutral-sounding words are used, such as 'humanism', or 'wisdom', love is still implied, but it is self-consciously concealed in less sentimental seeming terms, for surely neither humanism nor wisdom could be conceived as meaningful, unless they included the orientation of loving as well. It is then hardly an oversimplification to say that the ideologies of progress arrange their account of history so that the chain of historical episodes can be shown to represent human behaviour as growing in love, and that the series of episodes could also be plausibly extrapolated into the future in which this growth can confidently be expected to continue.[28]

---

[27] *Evolution and Progress*, by M. Ginsberg, London, 1961, pp. 1–56. Also cf. 'The Myth of Progress', by Eder, M.D., *The British Journal of Medical Psychology*, 1962, Vol. XXXV, Part 1, pp. 81–88.

[28] Cf. *Towards a Measure of Man*, by P. Halmos, London, 1957, Chapter I.

We have then before us not only a sociological hypothesis about social development, but also a psychological hypothesis about the progressive development of 'modal' personality, so that it embodies more and more readiness to behave lovingly, or if you like, kindly, tolerantly, as well as imaginatively and sensitively. Or to phrase it differently, human social development is of such a kind, that it moulds man in its social behaviour to be more frequently, variedly, and effectively loving of other people.

One might say that the doctrine of progress is a doctrine of the growth of love, and my task is to examine what effect, if any, the counsellor's interpretations of the experience of love, or of 'loving behaviour', have on the growth of love in human society. The presence of a counselling psychology in the stream of an allegedly progressing culture must of necessity act on the culture of which it is a part. This is manifest enough from the way our social and moral development has been coloured by widely disseminated and popularised psychological notions and interpretations in the twentieth century. Few items of legislation or processes of administration of healing, welfare, or education have escaped the influence of psychological appraisal. One may say that there is no new issue to be resolved here and that there is no urgent diagnosis to be made. Nevertheless I am prompted by expectations of a possible major change in the nature of this psychological influence and my thoughts here concern this expected change.

As social change follows social change, the moral fibre of the period will be, at least, toned by the life-blood of ideas and images which happen to be circulating. In past centuries the religious and philosophical ideas inspired and regulated much of human conduct, loving and affectionate or otherwise. In the twentieth century, two major groups of psychological theories have joined the theological-philosophical interpreters of, and dealers in, ideas about love and hate. These two I shall call, rather uninventively, vitalistic and mechanistic psychologies. The counsellor's psychology is vitalistic, and this is what I will consider first.

During this century, and even to this day, the large-scale influencing of public opinion, of nursery practices, of institutional arrangements and procedures has been guided either by traditional ethical considerations or by the notions of a vitalistic-psychoanalytical psychology which, as I have shown, have tended to reinforce the traditional ethical regimens of love, sympathy, and reverential notions of spirituality. During these decades, the mass media of communication have profusely and almost universally advertised psychoanalytic insight as kindness, acceptance, tolerance, permissiveness, and made the moral lesson taught by this, and other related vitalistic psychologies, indistinguishable from the moral lessons of Christianity. In the meantime, mechanistic psychologies flourished too, but their key-concepts have not spread out into the various private and public sectors of life, or succeeded in making an impression on man as an experiencer of love, sympathy, and concern. Somehow, mechanistic psychology would never venture far outside the laboratory. It seems to me that since the re-emergence of Pavlovian methods in contemporary 'behaviour therapy',[29] since the more recently spreading application of learning theory to clinical treatment, and since the reappraisal of maternal love in terms of sensory stimulation, we may well be on the threshold of a period, during which the relatively peaceful, armistice-like compact between traditional ethics and psychoanalytical metaphysics may be outdated by the rude objectivity of new ideas. *My hypothesis is that to preserve its ethical impartiality in man's progress, the more objective and quantitative psychology succeeds in becoming, the more it will have to turn its attention to the psychological problems created by the impact, of its own growth, in articulation and precision, on human behaviour.*

Before considering this hypothesis, certain general observations should be made in respect of *all* psychological enquiries, be they vitalistic or mechanistic in their basic categories. It is common knowledge that an attempt at understanding is an attempt at control. When confronted with human experiences of a puzzling, and indeed mystifying, nature we cannot but have recourse to *analysis* so that we may be able to disperse our mystification by successfully fragmenting the opaque totality of an experience. Our conditioned response to uncertainty, in the face of obscure totalities, is to analyse them. The response is reinforced by the reward of mastery in terms of a self-assurance felt when proceeding through the darkness that is between two lamp-posts. While entering into the glare of the next one, we do not fully perceive the darkness beyond, and for a while the reward of illumination is therefore

[29] Cf. *Behaviour Therapy and the Neuroses*, Ed. by H. J. Eysenck, London, 1960.

great. Now from time to time the seemingly obscurantist complaint is made that, though the explainers of human experience may temporarily dispel mystification and displace metaphysical notions, through their analysis of total and personal experiences, they also bring about a disintegration of these experiences.[30] The pertinence of this to the social influences of the two psychologies is obvious.

In a psychological science, enquiry aims at discovering the minutest part of the machinery of experience, for the canons of scientific thinking are assumed to require that understanding of the whole is contingent on the disclosure of parts. Attention to detail is a matter of scientific scrupulousness and pausing to stare at a total picture will be regarded as an enquiry-stopping excuse, a self-deceiving act, or at best, an aesthetic and non-scientific indulgence. All the same, so far as psychology is analytical and anatomical, so far as it is objective and quantitative, in short, so far as it is rigorously scientific, it is also irrevocably burdened with the task of examining the function of synthesis in human experiences, the function of totalities and of undivided images. It would be less than good psychology to assume that the naive and spontaneous experience of love will remain unimpaired by analysis and self-consciousness, and that this absorbingly total experience will, therefore, need no protection against disruption. The important thing to remember is that whilst the vitalistic psychological teaching of psychoanalytically oriented counsellors has been, by definition, analytical, its moral teaching has *not* been analytical, and that its ultimate categories of Libido, Eros, Transference, Countertransference, Sublimation, and Identification, have preserved total, non-fragmental images of *personal* functioning and, thereby, underpinned and perpetuated traditional moral confidence in a humanistic and noble conception of human love. Meanwhile, the other psychology, which based itself more conscientiously and consistently on physiology, or on the simple mechanical notions of learning, has made such a mutual accommodation with traditional moral images of love impossible.

I think that the faith of the counsellors has implicitly retained the notion of an unanalysable proclivity and need to love and to be loved, and indeed, frequently and openly abandoned the claim that this asset of humanity could ever be turned into the small change of physiology or mechanics.

[30] *Ideology and Utopia*, by K. Mannheim, London, 1946, p. 79.

The chapters of this book have amply documented that the pieties and traditional respect for the notion of 'spirituality' in love are often enough perpetuated by the vitalistic philosophy of psychoanalysis and of its derivatives. In spite of *The Future of an Illusion*,[31] psychoanalytic modes of thought have often and powerfully come to the aid of Christian spirituality, and of traditional moral images. A simplified and popularised casuistry of these modes of thought has been disseminated through the mass media of communication, and this has not only continued to be entirely inoffensive to some dominant Christian ways of feeling about fellowship, but has actually strengthened these ways by the constant advocacy of tolerance, permissiveness, and turn-the-other-cheek paedagogy and penology.

Let me now turn to the other type of psychological enquiry which has been going on parallel with—though not entirely unmindful of—psychoanalytical and similar thinking. Not unlike vitalistic psychology, this second main stream of contemporary psychology has had many names and many constituent rivulets. On the whole, these originate partly from the hinterland of physiology and mechanics and nowadays much of this second stream passes between the banks of so-called learning theories. There are, perhaps, fewer swamps and misty turnings along this tributary to our present pool of psychological knowledge than there are along the other stream, though at times it is suggested that this tributary is more navigable for vessels conveying animals. To depart from the overstretched metaphor : to appreciate the influence exerted by the counselling ideology, we must remember that the mechanistic psychology of the twentieth century has a conceptual system, and a manner of formulating the paradigm experiences of man, which may exert an influence on the progress of social changes, presumably representing a kind of 'progress in love and compassion', radically different from that of the counselling psychologies.

I propose to illustrate the purport of this apprehensive thesis from recent psychological literature. I have already referred to the way in which the reverential notion of love has been reinterpreted by H. F. Harlow, and others, in terms of 'sensory stimulation', carrying with it the supposition that love can be replaced by an engineered set of sensory stimuli administered without the total

[31] S. Freud, London, 1943.

personal participation of any human being. The immediate moral implications of this are brought to the surface by H. F. Harlow himself : explaining that redivision of labour between the sexes may lead to the displacement of men by women in American industry, he concluded, 'we know that women in the working classes are not needed in the home because of their primary mammalian capacities; and it is possible that in the foreseeable future neonatal nursing will not be regarded as a necessity, but as a luxury—to use Veblen's term—a form of conspicuous consumption limited perhaps to the upper classes'.[32] This is by no means a playful extravagance which is not really seriously contemplated. On the contrary, the view expressed here is the logical extrapolation of the psychological assumptions earnestly held. Seymour Levine comes to a very similar conclusion, 'It may be', he writes, 'that the detrimental effects of the foundling home have less to do with maternal deprivation than with the simple lack of stimulation that is inevitable in most such environments.'[33] Another psychologist, L. Casler, proceeds from the same baseline to a most unequivocal challenge which could hardly be ignored by anyone interested in the future of human sociability and sympathy : 'if institutionalisation were to become an acceptable, commonplace means of child rearing', Casler writes, 'rather than serving chiefly as a last resort, what gains would accrue to women freed of the necessity of staying at home during the early months of the child's life? If child rearing—regarded by many as the ultimate justification for marriage in twentieth-century western society—is put entirely in the hands of professionals, what predictions could be made about the fate of marriage itself?'[34] And indeed, what predictions could be made about the fate of human sociability, sympathy, and love? Casler follows the theory recently formulated that when infants are said to have been deprived of maternal love, they have not in fact been deprived of more than the sum total of specifiable sensory stimulations. Casler concludes that one day these may be quantified, prepackaged, and administered, by appropriately trained personnel entirely supplanting and displacing the nursing functions of natural

[32] 'The Nature of Love', by H. F. Harlow, *American Psychologist*, 1958, Vol. XIII.
[33] 'Stimulation in Infancy', *Scientific American*, May 1960.
[34] 'Maternal Deprivation: A Critical Survey of the Literature', *Monograph of the Society for Research in Child Development*, 1961, No. 80, Vol. XXVI, No. 2.

motherhood. The counsellors will probably ask, 'is this a fantasy of an oral-sadistic child or a prediction about the development in psychology's influence on human relations?' A recent Reuter report in the *New York Times* lends strange significance to this, making it seem a prediction: 'The Majima Manufacturing Company of Tokio has begun marketing an article called "mother heart"—a breast-shaped device that gives off the sound of heartbeats. It is supposed to put crying babies to sleep.' It would appear that spare parts for rejecting mothers may now turn up in our mail-order catalogues any day, and abolish our doubts whether the mechanisation of love is only a nightmare or also a prediction.

Whilst anticipating the superannuation of all human motherhood may be somewhat premature, an examination of the social impact of this kind of psychologising is less so. It seems to me that the psychologist and the sociologist would be a good deal less than a psychologist or a sociologist if in their sanguine analytical quest they ignored the consequences of dispensing with a personalistic and total imagery altogether. So long as the large-scale influencing of public opinion, of nursery practices, of institutional arrangements and procedures, in health, education, and welfare, is guided by traditional ethical considerations or, as it has been to some extent during this century, by the theoretical systems of a counselling psychology with its moralistic concepts and personalistic categories, an atomistic account of social concern, discussed on the pages of scientific journals and books only, is not going to lead to radical changes in our experience of loving. But if, in an age in which the channels of information from psychological expert to public have been vastly extended and consolidated, we begin to re-interpret the experience of tenderness in the manner of Harlow's observations, for example, and disseminate the information and its logical consequences, in the manner of Casler's suggestions, then our psychologists and sociologists are landed with a new and momentous assignment which they cannot shirk: they will be obliged to investigate anew—and with some urgency—the psychological consequences of disseminating psychological theory and interpretation of affectional behaviour on the affectional behaviour so interpreted.

An interesting and hardly unimportant issue must be mentioned here too: what do mechanotherapy, or the practice of it, and mechanistic psychology, and the cultivation of it, do to the therapist or researcher? It would seem that counsellors and mechanotherapists consume much of their respective medicines. S. M. Jourard rightly observes, 'The "technical" therapist is striving to manipulate himself and his patient rather than respond to him...I have come to recognise that those who habitually strive to manipulate others in one way or another, do violence to their own integrity as well as to that of their victims.'[35] An awareness of the automatic quality of experience cannot but taint the experience itself, and theoretical assumptions about sentiments will qualify them in the long run. To attend to others regularly, daily, and with calculated bits of signals and tactical ruses, can become a marked quality of the practitioner's personality. To deny that such accretions might occur would take some explaining away especially when one is already committed to a theory of learning which postulates the continuous occurrence of such accretions. To deny these accretions would be to state eloquently that the psychologist's psychology is irrelevant to his existence.

Naturally, one might argue that a dissolution of the molar and personalistic images of love has occurred often, before and since the time of Pavlov, yet this has not impaired the spiritual imagery, the popular romanticisation of love, or cooled the sentimental potentials and affectional ardours of people. The psycho-physiological interpreters of love have consequently assumed that a naive and spontaneous affection can co-exist, and flourish side by side, with an exclusively neurophysiological mirror-image of it. Or at least they seem to think that any influence they may exert with their version of this paradigm of humanity will make no more mark on man's morality than the previous versions have made, or for that matter, social science has ever made, and that there is plenty of time to look at the future vicissitudes of love after we have learnt a great deal more about its molecular causes and nature.

I feel that we would be complacent to go along with this. The socio-psychological influence of psychological interpretation has considerably grown since the times of the early behaviourists. Today, the casuistry of mostly psychoanalytically inspired mental hygiene is published in the magazine and paperback press, and its psychological prescriptions have become important elements in our

[35] 'I-Thou Relationship Versus Manipulation in Counselling and Psychotherapy', *Journal of Individual Psychology*, 1959, Vol. XV, pp. 174–179.

social control. The counselling ideology has in fact permeated to every layer of society. For the time being, there are no signs of a new casuistry begotten by popularised learning theory to influence private conduct in a similar way. Although behaviouristic practices are rapidly gaining ground among social workers, there are as yet no signs of a synthetic love concept actually exerting a moral influence on either parental solicitousness or on the professional dedication of workers in either health or education. 'Love', 'compassion', and 'fellowship' still carry the accumulated reverence of past ages, and the complex notions still act as powerful stimuli to socially necessary performances. The new categories, such as for example, 'sensory stimulation', are not used widely in child guidance clinics, or in the planning and administration of children's homes yet. In fact, we find the tough-minded social scientist saying, *'the counsellors are wrong but they have a good influence on society'*. One of the most articulate critics of the vitalistic psychology of counsellors, Lady Wootton, provides me with an exceptionally good illustration of this. Having repudiated the psychoanalytical interpretations of the concept of maternal deprivation, interpretations mostly associated in Britain with the name of John Bowlby, she concludes, 'Up to the present . . . research into the effects of maternal deprivation is to be valued chiefly for its incidental exposure of the prevalence of deplorable patterns of institutional upbringing, and of the crass indifference of certain hospitals to childish sensitivities. Without doubt this research has already had excellent practical effects in stimulating many of the authorities responsible for children's homes and hospitals to change their ways for the better.'[36] Here we have an entirely unsolicited testimonial from a social scientist whose empiricist intellectual rigour would not allow support to the faith of the counsellors. The testimony says, in effect, that deprivation has not been proved to matter but how good it is that as a result of pretending that it did matter there is already less of it! Could we, either opponents or friends of the mechanistic learning theories, come to a similar conclusion in respect of the moral influence these theories exert?

If the alleged progress in love is real, presumably it must be

[36] *Social Science and Social Pathology*, B. Wootton, London, 1959, p. 156. Incidentally, the recognition of these 'childish sensitivities' and of the possibility of their being treated 'better' amounts to a declaration of faith, for surely, what else could it be after pages and pages of denials that these things mattered?

sustained by man's faith in its occurring at all. It could not unfold in the face of man's scepticism. For this reason, man's interpretation of his own experience—his psychological interpretation of his role in the social process—is an important determinant of the reality of progress. Our psychological interpretation may help or prejudge the naive and spontaneous practice of love and compassion. I have been trying to show that the so-called vitalistic-psychoanalytical mode of thought, the ideology of counselling, has been an ally of love's growth among men. And I have been trying to show that a displacement of this counselling ideology by a behaviouristic theory of helping may produce a moral climate in which the progress of the regimen of love may be halted.

If the act of tenderness can be resolved into its mechanical parts, then it should be possible to reassemble those parts into an act of tenderness. Yet, could this tenderness have developed fully without a naive belief—at least a suspicion or hope—that the act of tenderness was a total, indivisible, and personal act? Within the counselling situation and in related administrative settings, could this belief, suspicion or hope, have gone on without the energising faith of the counsellors? The question is primarily not whether the mechanistic account of love is true but how we shall continue our progress in love and, indeed, survive when everybody thinks it true? And how shall we be able to administer help to others without the Faith of the Counsellors?

BIBLIOGRAPHY

(Alphabetical List of Authors Mentioned in the Text or Footnotes)

ADORNO, T. W., FRENKEL-BRUNSWIK, E., LEVINSON, D. J., and SANFORD, R. N., *The Authoritarian Personality*, New York, 1949.

ANGYAL, A., 'A Theoretical Model for Personality Studies', *Journal of Personality*, 1951, Vol. XX.

BALES, R. F., *Interaction Process Analysis*, Cambridge, 1950.

BALINT, M., *The Doctor, His Patient and The Illness*, London, 1957.

BALINT, M. and F., *Psychotherapeutic Techniques in Medicine*, London, 1961.

BANDURA, A., 'Psychotherapy as a Learning Process', *Psychological Bulletin*, 1961, Vol. LVIII, No. 2.

BATESON, G., JACKSON, D. D., HALEY, J., and WEAKLAND, J., 'Toward a Theory of Schizophrenia', *Behavioural Science*, October 1956, Vol. I, No. 4, pp. 257–264.

BECKER, H. S., and GEER, B., 'The Fate of Idealism in the Medical School', *American Sociological Review*, February 1958.

BELL, D., *End of Ideology*, Glencoe, 1960.

BENEDEK, T., 'Dynamics of Countertransference', *Bulletin of the Menninger Clinic*, 1953, Vol. XVII, No. 6.

BERMAN, L., 'Countertransference and Attitudes of the Analyst in the Therapeutic Process', *Psychiatry*, 1949, Vol. XII, No. 2.

BERGIN, A. E., 'The Effects of Psychotherapy: Negative Results Revisited', *Journal of Counselling Psychology*, 1963, Vol. X, No. 3.

BIBRING, G. L., 'Psychiatric Principles in Casework', *Journal of Social Casework*, 1949, Vol. XXX, No. 6.

BIESTEK, F. P., *The Casework Relationship*, London, 1961.

BONNEL, J. S., *Psychology for Pastor and People*, New York, 1948.

BOWLBY, J., *Maternal Care and Mental Health*, W.H.O., 1952.

BOWLBY, J., *Maternal Care and the Growth of Love*, London, 1953.

BREHM, J. W., and COHEN, A. R., *Explorations in Cognitive Dissonance*, London, 1962.

BRODY, E. B., and REDLICH, F. C., *Psychotherapy With Schizophrenics*, New York, 1952.

BRODY, S., *Patterns of Mothering*, New York, 1956.

BURNS, C. L. C., 'Psychiatric Treatment of Children in a Residential Setting', *The British Journal of Criminology*, 1960, Vol. II, No. 1.

BURTON, A. (Ed.), *Psychotherapy of the Psychoses*, New York, 1961.

CASLER, L., 'Maternal Deprivation: a Critical Review of the Literature', *Monograph of the Society for Research in Child Development*, No. 80, Vol. XXVI, No. 2.

CLARKE, E. E., *Romantic Paradox*, London, 1962.

CLYNE, M. B., *Night Calls*, London, 1961.

COLEMAN, J. V., 'Distinguishing Between Psychotherapy and Social Casework', *Journal of Social Casework*, 1949, Vol. XXX, No. 6.

CRONBACH, L. J., 'The Two Disciplines of Scientific Psychology', *American Psychologist*, 1957, Vol. XII.

DEUTSCH, H., *The Psychology of Women*, London, 1947.

DEUTSCH, H., 'Psychoanalytic Therapy in the Light of Follow-up', *Journal of the American Psychoanalytical Association*, 1959, Vol. VII.

DOLLARD, J. and MILLER, N. E., *Personality and Psychotherapy*, New York, 1950.

EDER, M. D., 'The Myth of Progress', *The British Journal of Medical Psychology*, 1962, Vol. XXXV, Part I.

EHRLICH, D., and SABSHIN, M., 'A Study of Sociotherapeutically Oriented Psychiatrists', *American Journal of Orthopsychiatry*, April 1964, Vol. XXXIV, No. 3.

EISENDORFER, A., 'The Selection of Candidates Applying for Psychoanalytic Training', *The Psychoanalytic Quarterly*, 1959, Vol. XXVIII.

EKSTEIN, R. E., and WALLERSTEIN, R. S., *The Teaching and Learning of Psychotherapy*, London, 1958.

EYSENCK, H. J., *Uses and Abuses of Psychology*, London, 1953.

EYSENCK, H. J. (Ed.), *Behaviour Therapy and the Neuroses*, London, 1960.

FAIRBAIRN, W. R. D., 'On the Nature and Aims of Psychoanalytical Treatment', *The International Journal of Psychoanalysis*, 1958, Vol. XXXIX, Part V.

FARMER, M. E., 'Authority in Social Casework', *The Sociological Review*, 1963, Vol. XI, No. 1.

FERARD, M. L., and HUNNYBUN, N. K., *The Caseworker's Use of Relationships*, London, 1962.

FERENCZI, S., *Further Contributions to the Theory and Technique of Psychoanalysis*, London, 1950.

FERENCZI, S., *Final Contributions to the Problems and Methods of Psychoanalysis*, London, 1955.

FESTINGER, L., *A Theory of Cognitive Dissonance*, London, 1959.

FEUER, L. S., *Psychoanalysis and Ethics*, Springfield, 1955.

FIEDLER, F. E., 'The Concept of an Ideal Therapeutic Relationship', *Journal of Consulting Psychology*, 1950, Vol. XIV.

FIEDLER, F. E., 'A Comparison of Therapeutic Relationships in Psychoanalytic, Non-directive and Adlerian Therapy', *Journal of Consulting Psychology*, 1950, Vol. XIV.

FIELD, M., *Patients are People, a Medical-Social Approach to Prolonged Illness*, New York, 1953.

FINGARETTE, H., *The Self in Transformation*, New York, 1963.

FOREST, I. DE, *The Haven of Love*, London, 1954.

FOULKES, S. H., 'Psychotherapy', *The British Journal of Medical Psychology*, 1961, Vol. XXXV, Part II.

FRANK, J. D., *Persuasion and Healing*, London, 1961.

FRENCH, L. M., *Psychiatric Social Work*, New York, 1940.

FRENKEL-BRUNSWIK, E., 'Intolerance of Ambiguity as an Emotional and Perceptual Variable', *Journal of Personality*, 1949/50, Vol. XVIII.

FREUD, ANNA, *Introduction to the Technique of Child Analysis*, New York, 1928.

FREUD, S., *The Future of an Illusion*, London, 1943.

FREUD, S., *Civilisation and Its Discontents*, London, 1930.

FREUD, S., 'Analysis Terminable and Interminable', *Collected Papers*, Vol. V, London, 1950.

FREUD, S., 'Postscript to a Discussion on Lay Analysis', *Collected Papers*, Vol. V, 1950.

FROMM, E., *The Sane Society*, New York, 1955.

FROMM, E., *The Art of Loving*, London, 1957.

FROMM, E., *Sigmund Freud's Mission*, London, 1959.

FROMM, E., SUZUKI, D. T., and DE MARTINO, R., *Zen Buddhism and Psychoanalysis*, London, 1960.

FROMM-REICHMANN and MORENO, J. L., *Progress in Psychotherapy*, New York, 1956.

GARRET, A., 'Historical Survey of the Evolution of Casework', *Journal of Social Casework*, 1949, Vol. XXX, No. 6.

GINSBERG, M., *Evolution and Progress*, London, 1961.

GINSBURG, S. W., 'The Impact of the Social Worker's Cultural Structure on Social Therapy', *Social Casework*, 1951, Vol. XXXII.

GITELSON, M., 'The Emotional Position of the Analyst in the Psychoanalytic Situation', *The International Journal of Psychoanalysis*, 1952, Vol. XXXIII, Part I.

GLOVER, E., 'The Psychology of the Psychotherapist', *The British Journal of Medical Psychology*, 1962, Vol. XXXV, Part I.

GLOVER, J., 'Divergent Tendencies in Psychotherapy', *The British Journal of Medical Psychology*, 1962, Vol. XXXV.

GOTTSCHALK, L. A., and WHITMAN, R. H., 'Some Typical Complications Mobilized by the Psychoanalytical Procedure', *The International Journal of Psychoanalysis*, 1962, Vol. XLIII, Parts II–III.

GREENWOOD, E., 'Social Science and Social Work: A Theory of their Relationship', *The Social Service Review*, 1955, Vol. XXIX, No. 1.

GUNTRIP, H., *Personality Structure and Human Interaction*, London, 1961.

HALMOS, P., *Solitude and Privacy*, London, 1952.

HALMOS, P., *Towards a Measure of Man*, London, 1957.

HALMOS, P., 'Social Science and Social Change', *Ethics*, 1959, Vol. LXIX, No. 2.

HALMOS, P., *The Personal and the Political*, London, 1978.

HAMILTON, GORDON, 'Helping People—the Growth of a Profession', *Social Work as Human Relations*, New York, 1949.

HAMILTON, G., *Theory and Practice of Social Casework*, N.Y., 1951.

HAMILTON, M., 'Group Work with Girls and Under-Sevens', *The Sociological Review Monograph*, No. 6, *The Canford Families*, December 1962.

HARLOW, H. F., 'The Nature of Love', *American Psychologist*, 1958, Vol. XIII.

HARLOW, H. F., 'Love in Infant Monkeys', *Scientific American*, June 1959.

HARLOW, H. F. and M. K., 'Social Deprivation in Monkeys', *Scientific American*, November 1962.

HEIMAN, P., 'Counter-Transference', *The British Journal of Medical Psychology*, 1960, Vol. XXXIII, Part 1.

HILDUM, D. C., and BROWN, R. W., 'Verbal Reinforcement and Interview Bias', *Journal of Abnormal and Social Psychology*, 1956, Vol. LIII.

HOLT, R. R., and LUBORSKY, L., *Personality Patterns of Psychiatrists*, London, 1958.

HOMANS, G. C., *The Human Group*, London, 1951.

HUNT, MCV., and KOGAN, L. S., *Testing Results in Social Casework*, New York, 1950.

HUNT, MCV., and KOGAN, L. S., *A Follow-up Study of the Results of Social Casework*.

HUNT, J. MCV., and KOGAN, L. S., *Measuring Results in Social Casework: A Manual of Judging Movement*, New York, 1950.

HUWS JONES, R., 'Evaluation of Social Work', *Social Service Quarterly*, 1962, Vol. XXXV, No. 3.

IRVINE, E. E., 'Transference and Reality in the Casework Relationship', *The British Journal of Psychiatric Social Work*, 1956, Vol. III.

Isa Upanishad, Hindu Scripture, Everyman, 1943.

ISAACS, S., *Social Development of Young Children*, London, 1957.

JANIS, I. L., *Psychological Stress, Psychoanalytic and Behavioral Studies of Surgical Patients*, New York, 1958.

JOHNSTONE, R. L., *Religion and Society in Interaction*, New York, 1975.

JOURARD, S. M., 'I-Thou Relationship Versus Manipulation in Counselling and Psychotherapy', *Journal of Individual Psychology*, 1959, Vol. XV.

JUNG, C. G., *The Collected Works*, Vol. XI and XVI, 1958.

KIERKEGAARD, S., *Fear and Trembling*, Princeton, 1945.

KLEIN, M., HEIMANN, P., and MONEY-KYRLE, R. (Eds.), *New Directions in Psychoanalysis*, New York, 1955.

KNIGHT, EVERETT, *The Objective Society*, London, 1959.

KORZYBSKI, A., *Science and Sanity*, Lakeville, 1948.

KRAEMER, W. P., 'Transference and Countertransference', *The British Journal of Medical Psychology*, 1957, Vol. XXX.

KUBIE, L. S., *Practical and Theoretical Aspects of Psychoanalysis*, New York, 1950.

LAING, R. D., *The Self and Others*, London, 1961.

LAING, R. D., 'Psychotherapy: The Search for a New Theory', *New Society*, October 1964.

LANGER, S., *Philosophical Sketches*, London, 1962.

LAPIERE, R. T., *The Freudian Ethic*, London, 1960.

LAYARD, J., 'The Meaning of Medicine', *The British Journal of Homoeopathic Medicine*, Vol. II.

LAWRENCE, D. H., and FESTINGER, L., *Deterrents and Reinforcement*, London, 1962.

LAZARUS, A. A., 'The Elimination of Children's Phobias by Deconditioning', in *Behaviour Therapy and the Neuroses*, (Ed.) H. J. Eysenck, London, 1960.

LENNARD, H. L., and BERNSTEIN, A., *The Anatomy of Psychotherapy*, New York, 1960.

LEVINE, S., 'Stimulation in Infancy', *Scientific American*, May 1960.

LINDNER, R., *Prescription for Rebellion*, London, 1953.

LIPSET, S. M., *Political Man*, London, 1960.

LITTLE, M., ' "R"—The Analyst's Total Response to His Patient's Needs', *The International Journal of Psychoanalysis*, 1957, Vol. XXXIII, Parts III–IV.

LLOYD, K., 'Helping a Child Adapt to Stress, The Use of Ego Psychology in Casework', *The Social Service Review*, 1957, Vol. XXXI, No. 1.

LOEWALD, H. W., 'On the Therapeutic Action of Psychoanalysis', *The International Journal of Psychoanalysis*, 1960, Vol. XLI, Part I.

MACINTYRE, A. C., *The Unconscious*, London, 1958.

MACKENZIE, N., *Conviction*, London, 1958.

MCLAUGHLIN, F., 'Some Considerations for the Further Development of Psychoanalysis', *The International Journal of Psychoanalysis*, 1963, Vol. XLIV, Part 4.

MANNHEIM, K., *Ideology and Utopia*, London, 1946.

MAO TSE-TUNG, *On Contradiction*, Peking, 1958.

MASLOW, A. H., 'Alfred Korzybski Memorial Lecture', *General Semantics Bulletin*, 1957, Nos. 20–21.

MASLOW, A. H., 'Are our Publications and Conventions Suitable for the Personal Psychologies?', *Report No. 8*, Western Behavioral Sciences Institute, 1961.

MASLOW, A. H., 'Some Frontier Problems in Psychological Health, in *Personality Theory and Counselling Practice*, Ed. by A. Gombs, Florida, 1961.

MASLOW, A. H., 'Fusion of Facts and Values', 11th Annual Karen Horney Lecture, New York, 1963.

MASSERMAN, J. (Ed.), *Psycho-analysis and Human Values*, New York, 1960.

MENG, H., and FREUD, E. L., *Psychoanalysis and Faith, The Letters of Sigmund Freud and Oscar Pfister*, London, 1963.

MENNINGER, K., *Theory of Psychoanalytical Technique*, New York, 1958.

MERTON, R. K., READER, G. G., and KENDALL, P. L., *The Student Physician*, Harvard, 1957.

MEYER, V., 'The Treatment of Two Phobic Patients on the Basis of Learning Principles', in *Behaviour Therapy and the Neuroses*, (Ed.) H. J. Eysenck, London, 1960.

MOWRER, O. H., *Psychotherapy, Theory and Research*, New York, 1953.

MOWRER, O. H., *The Crisis in Psychiatry and Religion*, New York, 1961.

MURRAY, E. J., 'Learning Theory and Psychotherapy : Biotropic versus Sociotropic Approaches', *Journal of Counselling Psychology*, 1963, Vol. X, No. 3.

NACHT, S., 'The Non-verbal Relationship in Psychoanalytical Treatment', *The International Journal of Psychoanalysis*, July 1963, Vol. XLIV, Part 3.

NACHT, S., LEBOVICI, S., and DIATKINE, R., 'Training for Psycho-analysis', *The International Journal of Psychoanalysis*, 1961, Vol. XLII.

NACHT, S., and VIDERMAN, S., 'The Pre-Object Universe in the Transference Situation', *The International Journal of Psychoanalysis*, 1960, Vol. XLI, Parts IV–V.

NEILSEN, N., 'Value Judgments in Psychoanalysis', *The International Journal of Psychoanalysis*, 1960, Vol. XLI, Parts IV–V.

NUNBERG, H., *Practice and Theory of Psychoanalysis*, New York, 1948.

OBERNDORF, C. P., 'The Unsatisfactory Results of Psychoanalytic Therapy', *The Psychoanalytic Quarterly*, 1950, Vol. XIX.

PARSONS, TALCOTT, *The Social System*, London, 1952.

PERLMAN, H. H., 'Are We Creating Dependency?', *Social Service Review*, 1960, Vol. XXXIV.

PINCUS, L. (Ed.), *Marriage: Studies in Emotional Conflict and Growth*, London, 1960.

POPPER, K. R., *The Open Society and Its Enemies*, London, 1957.

POTTER, D., *The Glittering Coffin*, London, 1960.

PRIMROSE, E. J. R., *Psychological Illness, A Community Study*, London, 1962.

QUINE, W. V., 'Paradox', *Scientific American*, April 1962.

RACHMAN, S., 'Learning Theory and Child Psychology: Therapeutic Possibilities', *Journal of Child Psychology and Psychiatry*, 1962, Vol. III, No. 3–4.

RACKER, H., 'Psychoanalytic Technique and the Analyst's Unconscious Masochism', *The Psychoanalytic Quarterly*, 1958, Vol. XXVII.

RANK, O., *Beyond Psychology*, New York, 1958.

RATCLIFFE, T. A., 'Relationship Therapy and Casework', *The British Journal of Psychiatric Social Work*, 1959, Vol. V, No. 1.

READ, HERBERT, 'Psychoanalysis and the Problem of Aesthetic Value', *The International Journal of Psychoanalysis*, 1951, Vol. XXXII, Part II.

REICH, A., 'On Counter-Transference', *The International Journal of Psychoanalysis*, 1951, Vol. XXXII, Part I.

REICH, A., 'Further Remarks on Counter-Transference', *The International Journal of Psychoanalysis*, 1960, Vol. XLI, Parts IV–V.

RIEFF, P., *Freud, the Mind of the Moralist*, London, 1959.

RIEFF, P., 'The Analytic Attitude', *Encounter*, 1962, 105.

RIEFF, P., 'C. G. Jung's Confession', *Encounter*, 1964.

RIESSMAN, F., and MILLER, S. M., 'Social Change Versus the "Psychiatric World View"', *American Journal of Ortho-Psychiatry*, January 1964, Vol. XXXIV, No. 1, pp. 29–38.

ROBERTS, D. E., *Psychotherapy and a Christian View of Man*, New York, 1950.

ROBINSON, V. P., *Jessie Taft, Therapist and Social Work Educator*, Philadelphia, 1962.

THE FAITH OF THE COUNSELLORS

RODGERS, B. N., and DIXON, J., *Portrait of Social Work*, Oxford, 1960.

ROGERS, C. R., *On Becoming a Person*, London, 1961.

ROLO, C. (Ed.), *Psychiatry in American Life*, Boston, 1963.

ROSE, G., 'Assessing the Results of Social Work', *The Sociological Review*, 1957, Vol. V, No. 2.

ROUBICZEK, P., *Existentialism, For and Against*, Cambridge, 1964.

SALTER, A., *The Case Against Psychoanalysis*, New York, 1953.

SARBIN, T. R., 'Role Theoretical Interpretation of Psychological Change', in *Personality Change*, (Eds.) P. Worchel and D. Byrne.

SARNOFF, J., *Personality Dynamics and Development*, New York, 1962.

SAUL, L. J., *Technique and Practice of Psychoanalysis*, Philadelphia, 1958.

SCHAFER, R., 'Generative Empathy in the Treatment Situation', *The Psychoanalytic Quarterly*, 1959, Vol. XXVII.

SCHOECK, H., and WIGGINS, J. W. (Eds.), *Psychiatry and Responsibility*, New York, 1962.

SCHOFIELD, W., *Psychotherapy, The Purchase of Friendship*, New Jersey, 1964.

SEARLES, H. F., 'The Place of Neutral Therapist Responses in Psychotherapy with the Schizophrenic Patient', *International Journal of Psychoanalysis*, January 1963, Vol. XLIV, Part 1, pp. 42–56.

SELBY, L. G., 'Supportive Treatment: The Development of a Concept and a Helping Method', *The Social Service Review*, 1956, Vol. XXX, No. 4.

SHARPE, E. F., *Collected Papers on Psychoanalysis*, London, 1950.

SHEPPARD, M. L., 'Casework as Friendship: A Long Term Contact with a Paranoid Lady', *The British Journal of Psychiatric Social Work*, 1964, Vol. VII, No. 4, pp. 173–182.

SHOBEN, E. J., Jr., 'The Therapeutic Object: Man or Machine?' *Journal of Counselling Psychology*, Vol X, No. 3, 1963.

SHOBEN, E. J., Jr., 'Guidance: Remedial Function or Social Reconstruction?', *Harvard Educational Review*, 1962, Vol. XXXII, No. 4.

SHOR, J., 'The Ethic of Freud's Psychoanalysis', *The International Journal of Psychoanalysis*, 1961, Vol. XLII, Parts I–II.

SODDY, K. (Ed.), *Identity—Mental Health and Value Systems*, London, 1961.

SPACKMAN, I. and POWER, M., 'The Casework', *The Canford Families, The Sociological Review Monograph*, December 1962, No. 6.

STANISLAVSKY, C., *Creating a Role*, London, 1963.

STANISLAVSKY, C., *An Actor Prepares*, London, 1959.

STEVENSON, O., 'The Understanding Caseworker', *New Society*, August 1963.

STEWART PRINCE, G., 'Medical Psychology', *British Journal of Medical Psychology*, 1963, Vol. XXXVI, Part 4.

STONE, L., *The Psychoanalytic Situation*, New York, 1961.

STRAUSS, R., 'Counter-Transference', *The British Journal of Medical Psychology*, 1960, Vol. XXXIII, Part 1.

SUNDBERG, N. D. and TYLER, L. E., *Clinical Psychology*, London, 1963.

SUTTIE, I. D., *The Origins of Love and Hate*, London, 1936.

SZASZ, T. S., and HOLLENDER, M. H., 'A Contribution to the Philosophy of Medicine', *A.M.A. Archives of Internal Medicine*, 1956, Vol. XCVII.

SZASZ, T., 'On the Theory of Psychoanalytic Treatment', *The International Journal of Psychoanalysis*, 1957, Vol. XXXVIII, Parts III–IV.

SZASZ, T., *The Myth of Mental Illness*, London, 1962.

THOMPSON, E. P., *Out of Apathy*, London, 1960.

TILLICH, P., 'The Philosophy of Social Work', *The Social Service Review*, 1962, Vol. XXXVI, No. 1.

TIMMS, N., *Social Casework*, London, 1964.

TINGSTEN, H., 'Stability and Vitality in Swedish Democracy', *Political Quarterly*, 1955, Vol. XXVI, No. 2.

TITMUSS, R. M., *The Irresponsible Society*, London, 1960.

TOWER, L. E., 'Countertransference', *Journal of the American Psychoanalytical Association*, 1956, Vol. IV.

TOWLE, C., *The Learner in Education for the Professions*, Chicago, 1954.

TRIST, E. L., and SOFER, C., *Exploration in Group Relations*, Leicester, 1959.

TRUAX, C. B., 'Effective Ingredients in Psychotherapy: An Approach to Unravelling the Patient-Therapist Interaction', *Journal of Counselling Psychology*, 1963, Vol. X, No. 3.

TYLER, L. E., *The Work of the Counselor*, New York, 1961.

VANCE, F. L., and VOLSKY, T. C., 'Counseling and Psychotherapy : Split Personality or Siamese Twins?' *American Psychologist*, 1962, Vol. XVII, pp. 565–570.

WALDRON, F. E., 'The Choice of Goals in Casework Treatment : a case study', *The British Journal of Psychiatric Social Work*, 1961, Vol. VI, No. 2.

WALKER, N., *Short History of Psychotherapy*, London, 1957.

WALLIS, J. A., *Counselling and Social Welfare*, London, 1960.

WATTS, A. W., *Psychotherapy, East and West*, New York, 1961.

WEIGERT, E., 'Contribution to the Problem of Terminating Psychoanalysis', *The Psychoanalytic Quarterly*, 1952, Vol. XXI.

WEIL, SIMONE, *Gravity and Grace*, London, 1952.

WEIL, SIMONE, *Letter to a Priest*, London, 1953.

WHEELIS, A., *The Quest for Identity*, London, 1959.

WHITAKER, C. (Ed.), *Psychotherapy of Chronic Schizophrenic Patients*, London, 1956.

WICKHAM, E. R., *Church and People in an Industrial City*, London, 1957.

WILSON, A. T. M., 'A Note on the Social Sanctions of Social Research', *The Sociological Review*, 1955, Vol. III.

WILSON, R., 'Unconformity in the Affluent Society', *The Sociological Review*, 1960, Vol. VIII, No. 1.

WIMPERIS, W., *The Unmarried Mother and her Child*, London, 1960.

WINN, R. (Ed.), *Psychotherapy in the Soviet Union*, London, 1962.

WINNICOTT, CLARE, 'Casework and Agency Function', *Case Çonference*, 1962, Vol. VIII, No. 7.

WINNICOTT, D. W., *Collected Papers: Through Paediatrics to Psychoanalysis*, London, 1958.

WINNICOTT, D. W., 'Counter-Transference', *The British Journal of Medical Psychology*, 1960, Vol. XXXIII.

WOLPE, J., 'Reciprocal Inhibition as the Main Basis of Psychotherapeutic Effects', in *Behaviour Therapy and the Neuroses*, H. J. Eysenck (Ed.), London, 1960.

WOLPE, J., 'Isolation of a Conditioning Procedure as the Crucial Psychotherapeutic Factor : A Case Study', *The Journal of Nervous and Mental Disease*, 1962, Vol. CXXXIV, No. 4.

WOOTTON, B., *Social Science and Social Pathology*, London, 1958.

WRENN, C. G., *The World of the Contemporary Counsellors*, Boston, 1973.

INDEX